"Stacey Rawson is a leader in the area of trauma-sensitive practices. Her interest in and passion for helping students who have experienced trauma in their lives is inspiring. *Applying Trauma-Sensitive Practices in School Counseling* is an excellent resource for helping counselors, teachers, administrators and parents understand how trauma affects children's stress response and behavior. She teaches the reader how to meet students where they are at emotionally and provides realistic coping strategies that work."

—*Edward Gigliotti, University of San Diego, USA*

"Trauma-informed practices has resulted in a major shift in how we support the academic, behavioral, social, and emotional needs of students. I have been continually impressed with Stacey Rawson's ability to not only implement these practices in Santee School District but also in her leadership and teaching of others in these practices. This resource guide will allow school professionals to implement current best practices in trauma-informed care of all students."

—*Dr. Kristin Baranski, Superintendent, Santee School District, USA*

"This is the 'go-to' book for school counselors and school counselors-in-training to understand and respond to the impact of trauma on children and adolescents in schools. It is designed to engage learning and to be utilized as a guide to developing a comprehensive trauma-sensitive school counseling practice. This book provides school counseling specific strategies to developing tiered interventions and school-wide programming to further support students impacted by trauma and crises. It's a great contribution to the field!"

—*Erika Cameron, PhD, University of San Diego, USA*

Applying Trauma-Sensitive Practices in School Counseling

Applying Trauma-Sensitive Practices in School Counseling is an essential text for school counselors who need the research, knowledge, and skills to intervene and positively impact the educational outcomes for students with trauma.

This practice-based guide begins with Adverse Childhood Experiences (ACEs). Through case studies and current research, school counselors will learn how trauma effects brain development, social-emotional development, behavior, and academic learning for children and adolescents. The research in the first section leads to a variety of trauma-sensitive strategies for school counselors in the second section. Included are trauma-sensitive programs that school counselors can implement school-wide, along with tools and strategies school counselors can apply in personal practice. Case studies of students with ACEs who improved behaviorally or academically due to school counseling interventions demonstrate the effectiveness of the tools offered in the text.

With up-to-date information about chronic stress in childhood and practical strategies that can be adapted and implemented, this guidebook is crucial for school counselors, especially those who support students with ACEs.

Stacey Rawson, MA, is a practicing school counselor in eastern Washington and an adjunct instructor at Gonzaga University and Eastern Washington University. She has nearly a decade of experience in counseling students with trauma and implementing tiered-intervention counseling programs. Stacey holds an MA in counseling from the University of San Diego and is a credentialed school counselor in both California and Washington.

Applying Trauma-Sensitive Practices in School Counseling

Interventions for Achieving Change

Authored by Stacey Rawson

NEW YORK AND LONDON

First published 2021
by Routledge
52 Vanderbilt Avenue, New York, NY 10017

and by Routledge
2 Park Square, Milton Park, Abingdon, Oxon, OX14 4RN

Routledge is an imprint of the Taylor & Francis Group, an informa business

© 2021 Taylor & Francis

The right of Stacey Rawson to be identified as author of this work has been asserted by her in accordance with sections 77 and 78 of the Copyright, Designs and Patents Act 1988.

All rights reserved. No part of this book may be reprinted or reproduced or utilised in any form or by any electronic, mechanical, or other means, now known or hereafter invented, including photocopying and recording, or in any information storage or retrieval system, without permission in writing from the publishers.

Trademark notice: Product or corporate names may be trademarks or registered trademarks, and are used only for identification and explanation without intent to infringe.

Library of Congress Cataloging-in-Publication Data
A catalog record for this title has been requested

ISBN: 978-0-367-23726-4 (hbk)
ISBN: 978-0-367-23723-3 (pbk)
ISBN: 978-0-429-28140-2 (ebk)

Typeset in Goudy
by codeMantra

This book is dedicated to:
Children.

> To all children and especially those children who experience childhood adversity: you learn in our schools, live in our homes, and leave a mark on our hearts. May this book improve our work as counselors so that we can serve you well.

Contents

Acknowledgments	xi
List of Abbreviations	xii
1 Introduction	1

STEP 1
Understand the Impact of Childhood Trauma on Student Learning and Child Development — 5

2 The ACEs Study: Lasting Effects from Childhood Trauma	7
3 Neurobiology and Learning: How Trauma Changes the Developing Brain	17
4 Mental Health: What's Beneath the Symptoms	33
5 The Role of a Trauma-Sensitive School [NRI] Counselor	48

STEP 2
Develop Trauma-Sensitivity Schoolwide: Support ALL Students to Reach Those with ACEs — 59

6 Trauma-Sensitive Schools: Reframing the "Why" Not the "How"	61
7 Schoolwide Programs that Align with a Trauma-Sensitive Philosophy	77

x   *Contents*

STEP 3
Implement School Counseling Strategies to Support
Students with ACEs: The TSC Model   103

  8 Developing TSC   105

  9 Tiered Interventions: Putting It All Together   135

10 Self-Regulation: Developing Strategies through Skill-
     Building Lessons   157

11 Creating Connectedness: Caring Matters   181

12 Conclusion: Next Steps for Counselor Leaders   204

    Appendix A: Finding your ACE Score   211
    Appendix B: PBIS Matrix Example   213
    Appendix C: Trauma-Sensitive School Counseling Interventions 214
    Appendix D: The ASCA Mindsets & Behaviors for Student
              Success   216
    Index   217

Acknowledgments

Thanks to God for granting me the opportunity to write this book. Trauma-sensitive counseling is a passion of mine, and the opportunity to share my resources and knowledge with others overwhelms me with gratitude. May the information shared in this book improve the lives of all children, each one of whom is created and loved by You.

Thank you my husband Nick for your constant support and love. You believe in me even when I don't see my own potential and you help me persevere when I want to give up. Thank you for doing all our chores for an entire year so that I could have sacred time to write. I love you and I am so grateful for you every day.

Thanks to my two children – Clark and Mae for going to bed on time so that I could write this book after you were asleep. One day, I hope you read it, and that it spurs you toward compassion for others.

Thanks to Ed, Tracie, Mia, Meredith, and Erika for giving me valuable feedback, and making this book something I am proud to share with the world.

Thanks to the school counselors, principals, vice principals, education specialists, and teachers who contributed to this book through your stories, examples, interviews, and resources. I will not name each contributor to protect the privacy of the stories they shared.

Thanks to the Santee School District, Dr. Kristin Baranski, Meredith Riffel, and our Santee School District Counseling Team. Your support of trauma-sensitive counseling, comprehensive counseling programs, and my personal counseling practice made this book possible.

Thanks to the students who I work with each day as a school counselor. You inspire me through your resilience and compassion. I love what I do each day and it is because I work for you.

And finally, thanks to anyone who is doing the work of trauma-sensitive care. Whether you are a parent or a postal worker, a counselor or a chef, we all have a role to play. Treat others with empathy and kindness. Be aware of the culture you create. Thank you for your trauma-sensitive practices, both big and small that make each community a better place to live.

Abbreviations

ACEs	Adverse Childhood Experiences (www.ACEStooHigh.com)
ADHD	Attention Deficit Hyperactivity Disorder
ARC	A 3-pronged approach to trauma-sensitive mental health therapy. Stands for Attachment, Regulation, Competency (Kinniburgh, Blaustein, & Spinazzola, 2005).
ASCA	American School Counseling Association (www.schoolcounselor.org)
CBT	Cognitive Behavioral Therapy
CBITS	Cognitive Behavioral Intervention for Trauma in Schools
FF	Flexible Framework (www.traumasensitiveschools.org)
MTMDSS	Multi-tiered, Multi-domain System of Support (www.hatchingresults.com)
MTSS	Multi-tiered System of Support
PBIS	Positive Behavior Interventions and Supports (www.pbisworld.org)
PTSD	Post-traumatic Stress Disorder
RJ	Restorative Justice (www.iirp.edu)
RP	Restorative Practices (www.iirp.edu)
RTI	Response to Intervention (www.rti.org)
SEL	Social Emotional Learning (www.casel.org)
TSC	A 3-pronged approach to trauma-sensitive school counseling. Stands for Tiered Interventions, Self-Regulation, Connectedness. Also stands for Trauma-Sensitive School Counseling.

1 Introduction

When I pull into the parking lot of my school each morning, my mind begins to whirl. Thoughts race in about to-do lists, student check-ins, administrative meetings, small group curriculum, parent follow-up, classroom lessons to plan, and how I might fit lunch in between recess duty and an IEP meeting. If you are a school counselor too, you know these thoughts all too well. The common push and pull between large caseloads and profound need. We get swept up in the crisis of the day and forget the bigger picture of my comprehensive counseling program. Between a panic attack in math class, bullying behaviors at recess, and the student who eloped from English class, we are triaging symptoms and not truly solving problems.

Our students need more than the occasional check-in, or quick solution to a peer conflict. Often, the roots of these momentary crises lie deeper than a hard math test, an insulting phrase, or forgotten English homework. When 64% of children suffer at least one Adverse Childhood Experience (ACE) before their 18th birthday, and one in five is diagnosed with a mental, emotional, or behavioral health disorder, we know that we must keep digging for answers below the surface-level behaviors (Centers for Disease Control and Prevention, 2019; Felitti et al., 1998). If we aren't merely reacting to crisis after crisis, what else can we do? Where do we start? How do we help? And most pressing on our minds – how do we fit it all into our school day?

My hope is that this book illuminates a path for you. A path toward trauma-sensitivity. A path toward strategic planning. A path toward collaborative care. A path toward increasing our awareness of childhood trauma and developing caring schools where our students who have experienced trauma thrive alongside peers.

We start by looking deeper and asking ourselves "Why?"

Once we know the "why" behind the behaviors and emotions of our students, when can we begin the process of "what now?" In this book, we will answer both "why" and "what now." Through knowledge about ACEs and the effects of childhood trauma, coupled with the application of evidenced-based school counseling interventions, we can journey ahead with our students toward a healthy future.

2 Introduction

Structure of the Book

This book comprises 12 chapters divided into three "steps." It is intended to be read at least once all the way through to understand what trauma is, how it affects students, and what can be done to improve its adverse effects. Each "Step" is a crucial part of the journey toward becoming a trauma-sensitive school counselor, beginning with awareness and ending with implementation of trauma-sensitive interventions. After reading the book once through, Step 3 (Chapters 9–11) can serve as a reference it itself. School counselors can use Step 3 to research a variety of trauma-sensitive, school counseling interventions, or to choose specific strategies from the bank of interventions provided.

Step 1: *Understand the Impact of Childhood Trauma on Student Learning and Child Development* lays the foundation for the book by describing ACEs and the development of the ACEs concept. After describing ACEs and the original ACE research study in Chapter 2, Step 1 goes on to describe how ACEs affect the students we work with each day. Chapter 3 navigates through the structures of the brain and portrays how each structure impacts learning and school success. Chapter 4 describes common symptoms of ACE exposure and their commonalities with mental illnesses and behavioral diagnoses. Chapter 5 introduces the role of school counselors in raising awareness about ACEs and childhood trauma at our schools.

Step 2: *Develop Trauma-Sensitivity Schoolwide: Support ALL Students to Reach those with ACEs* explains the philosophy of trauma-sensitivity and identifies schoolwide practices that support this philosophy. Using research, theory, and examples, Chapter 6 illustrates a framework for trauma-sensitive schools, and Chapter 7 brings it to life through schoolwide programs, including Social-Emotional Learning, Positive Behavior Interventions and Supports, Restorative Practices, and Response to Intervention.

Finally, in Step 3, *Implement School Counseling Strategies to Support Students with ACEs: The TSC Model*, the science of Step 1 and theory of Step 2 are brought together into strategies for practice. The TSC model is a three-part practice model for school counselors who are committed to trauma-sensitivity in their daily work. The three practice areas – Tiered Interventions, Self-Regulation, and Connecting to School (TSC) – comprise 52 different trauma-sensitive interventions. The interventions can be used individually or collectively to benefit traumatized students. Chapter 8 shares the research informing the TSC model, while Chapters 9–11 highlight the resource bank of interventions.

Case Studies from the Field

Throughout this book, there are more than 40 "case studies" of children who have experienced ACEs. These stories were collected from educators across the country. As I compiled these stories of children, their families, and their educators, I became even more aware of the universal nature of trauma. The common themes of adversity and subsequent educational challenges are present, no matter the school, neighborhood, city, or state where a student grows up. ACEs are everywhere. Dr. Nadine Burke Harris, a leading researcher and California state Surgeon General, commonly refers to ACEs as a public health epidemic. I couldn't agree more. This epidemic affects almost 2/3 of American adults and its negative effects on the next generation are felt every day in our schools (Harris, 2018).

The case studies help bring this book to life. By incorporating the research with real-life examples, I hope it is clear how ACEs and the biological under-pinnings of adversity affect the lives of students on a daily basis. This book is not simply theory, research, or wishful thinking. It is grounded in both science and practice, in what can work and what has worked. It gives YOU – the school counselor – strategies, knowledge, and examples to use on your path toward trauma-sensitivity.

While the stories included are all true stories collected from counselors, teachers, and administrators, all names and identifying details have been changed to protect the privacy of the children and families discussed in the story. I would like to thank the real-life students, families, and educators por-trayed in this book for allowing me to use these stories. Your stories bring heightened awareness to the universality of ACEs. Thank you for allowing me to share your examples to help other students, families, and educators just like you. I recognize that many of the personal life experiences described in this book are different than my own. My goal is to treat each story with the dignity, empathy, and kindness it deserves. Ultimately, sharing these stories, along with theory and interventions, will increase trauma-sensitive school counseling practices in schools across the country.

References

Centers for Disease Control and Prevention. (2019, July 19). *Improving Access to Children's Mental Healthcare*. Retrieved from Centers for Disease Control and Prevention: www.cdc.gov/childrensmentalhealth/access.html

Felitti, V., Anda, R., Nordenberg, D., Williamson, D., Spitz, A., Edwards, V., … Marks, J. (1998). Relationship of Childhood Abuse and Household Dysfunction to Many of the Leading Causes of Death in Adults: The Adverse Childhood Experience (ACE) Study. *American Journal of Preventative Medicine, 14*(4), 245–258. Retrieved from www.ajpmonline.org/article/S0749-3797(98)00017-8/pdf

Harris, N. B. (2018). *The Deepest Well: Healing the Long-Term Effects of Childhood Adversity*. New York, NY: Houghton Mifflin Harcourt.

Step 1

Understand the Impact of Childhood Trauma on Student Learning and Child Development

2 The ACEs Study
Lasting Effects from Childhood Trauma

Learning from the Past: What Are ACEs?

It was 1985. In San Diego, California, Dr. Vincent Felitti studied obesity at Kaiser Permanente. Patient after patient successfully lost weight through his research program, and a few never found success. Neither of these outcomes surprised Dr. Fetitti. Occasionally though, a surprising patient did come along. These surprising patients *did* find success with weight-loss, but then oddly reversed course. These were the patients who peaked Dr. Felitti's interest. Why, at the very moment someone overcame a life-long struggle with their weight, would they reverse course and gain it all back – plus more? Through his patient interviews, he found an important connection from one "surprising patient" to another. Seemingly unrelated to obesity, yet strangely connected from patient to patient, was a history of childhood adversity – abuse, neglect, and household dysfunction (Harris, 2018).

In 1990, Dr. Felitti met a physician epidemiologist from the Centers for Disease Control and Prevention (CDC), Dr. Robert Anda. Together, they embarked on the largest and most comprehensive study ever done about the connection between childhood adversity, adult health-risk behavior (such as smoking, binge drinking, unprotected sexual encounters, and drug use), and chronic disease. Between 1995 and 1997, a staggering 17,421 Kaiser patients participated in this study, where they completed a questionnaire about childhood abuse and exposure to household dysfunction. Additionally, questions were asked about their current health and health-risk behaviors in order to draw connections.

After compiling and analyzing the data, Dr. Felitti and Dr. Anda termed the stressful or traumatic events that people experience early in life as Adverse Childhood Experiences (ACEs) (Felitti et al., 1998). One aim of the study was to determine each patient's level of exposure to ACEs, later called the ACE score, by the age of 18 (Harris, 2018). Through analyzing the research, ten categories of ACEs emerged. These ten categories became their scoring method. An ACE score can be as low as 0, meaning no adversity was experienced in childhood, and as high as 10 – meaning a child experienced all ten of the ACE categories before age 18. To learn your own ACE score, a 10-question quiz, called the ACE Questionnaire, is available in Appendix A (ACEs too High, 2012) (Figure 2.1).

8 *Understand the Impact of Childhood Trauma*

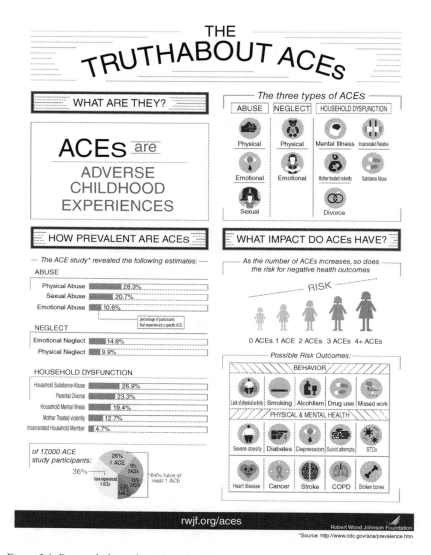

Figure 2.1 Research from the original ACE study was groundbreaking, yet ignored for many years (Robert Wood Johnson Foundation, 2013).

The ten ACE categories are now defined by the CDC. They are defined as follows:

1 *Psychological (Emotional) Abuse*: A parent/guardian living in the home put the child down, insulted them, swore at them, or made them fearful that they may be hurt.

The ACEs Study 9

2 *Physical Abuse*: A parent/guardian living in the home threw something at the child, hit them leaving marks, slapped, pushed, or grabbed them hard enough to injure them.

3 *Sexual Abuse*: Any adult or person at least five years older than the child touched the child's body in a sexual way, make the child touch their body in a sexual way, or attempted to have any type of sexual intercourse with the child.

4 *Substance Abuse in the Household*: An adult living in the same home had problematic drinking, including alcoholism or used recreational drugs.

5 *Mental Illness in the Household*: An adult living in the same home was mentally ill, including depression, or attempted suicide.

6 *Mother Treated Violently*: A mother or maternal figure who lived in the child's home was slapped, hit with a fist or hard object, kicked, bitten, grabbed, pushed, repeatedly hit, or threatened with a knife or gun by someone who was the child's father, father figure, or mother's boyfriend.

7 *Incarcerated Family Member*: A person living in the same home as the child went to prison.

8 *Emotional Neglect*: No one in their family helped the child to feel important, loved, or special. Family members didn't look out for each other or lean on each other for strength or support.

9 *Physical Neglect*: No one in their family protected the child, took care of the child's medical needs, made sure they had enough to eat and clean clothes to wear, or supervised the child.

10 *Parental Separation or Divorce*: Parents of the child were ever divorced or separated (both of them not living in the same house with the child) (Centers for Disease Control and Prevention, 2019b).

Once Dr. Felitti and Dr. Anda's research and analysis was complete, the results amazed them. In their sample of middle class, 70% Caucasian, 70% college-educated, adults from San Diego, more than 63% had experienced at least one ACE. Furthermore, 12.6% were exposed to more than four types of ACEs (Felitti et al., 1998).

In addition to the commonality of ACE exposure, Dr. Felitti and Dr. Anda uncovered a dose-response relationship between ACE exposure and medical diseases, and a dose-response relationship between ACE exposure and high-risk behaviors. This meant that the more categories of ACEs a person was exposed to before the age of 18, the *more likely* they were to develop heart disease, cancer, emphysema. They were also more likely to smoke, binge drink, use recreational drugs, attempt suicide, and have unprotected sex (Harris, 2018).

For example, if I have three ACEs, I am 1.4 times more likely to have heart disease than someone with zero ACEs. But if I have four or more ACEs, I am 2.2 times more likely to contract the same deadly disease. If I have one ACE, I am 1.6 times more likely to be diagnosed with emphysema than someone with zero ACEs. And it goes up from there: 2.2 times more likely to have emphysema with three ACEs and 3.9 times more likely with four or more (Felitti et al., 1998).

10 Understand the Impact of Childhood Trauma

Further ACEs Research

Since the original ACE study, hundreds of studies have confirmed correlations between ACEs and other chronic diseases, including asthma, depression, liver disease, and frequent headaches (Centers for Disease Control and Prevention, 2019a). But the research was slow to catch on. More than a decade after the ACE study, the concept was rarely discussed in medical circles, let alone in other industries. According to Dr. Nadine Burke Harris, in her book *The Deepest Well* (2018), there are three reasons why no one was talking about ACEs (yet):

1   There is a popular belief that poor health outcomes are connected to adversity only through poor health choices. The popular thinking goes that people who have difficult childhoods will inevitably cope with these difficulties in unhealthy ways such as through binge drinking or heavy smoking. The belief continues that smoking and drinking are the only things damaging to their health later in life. This line of thinking allows doctors and researchers to distance themselves from the real issue that exposure to adversity can lead to poor health. The smart, strong, wise, or "better" people can't avoid poor health outcomes solely through their own choices to not smoke or drink. Thankfully, research has proven that this line of thinking is incorrect. Health-risk behaviors like smoking or drinking only account for 50% of the increased likelihood for disease (Dong et al., 2004).
2   Trauma is scary to talk about. Doctors, educators, scientists, and especially family members don't want to talk about the bad things that happened in the past. Doctors think it's the job of psychologists to talk about trauma, educators think it's the job of doctors, parents think it's the job of educators, and the list goes on. It is hard to desire the responsibility of diving into such an emotionally charged subject that for 67% of us, hits very close to home.
3   While Dr. Felitti and Dr. Anda's ACE study explained *what* was affecting adult health negatively, the scientific community in 1998 couldn't yet explain the gaps that explained *how* ACEs affect health outcomes. Thankfully, in the last 20 years, that research gap has been slowly filling in.

As the scientific gaps began filling in, and additional studies provided outcomes consistent with the original ACEs study, the popular interest in ACEs grew. This led to more research on how and why ACEs lead to poor health, and what we can do to reduce the impact.

Here are some examples of additional findings within the ACEs body of research:

- By 2019, 36 states and the District of Columbia had conducted their own ACE studies and produced similar results to the original (ACES too High, 2019).
- Thirty-three percent of children under the age of 5 have already experienced at least one ACE. However, among children with disabilities, 55% will have one ACE by age 5 (Zeng & Hu, 2018).

The ACEs Study 11

- In addition to ACEs, other forms of child victimization are even more common. In any given year, more than 53% of children aged 2–17 will experience at least one physical assault. One in four children will experience a property offense such as robbery, vandalism, or theft (Finkelhor, Ormrod, Storr, Lucia, & Anthony, 2005).
- ACEs are more prevalent in adults who identify their race as black (average ACE score 1.69), Hispanic (average ACE score 1.80), and multi-racial (average ACE score 2.52) as compared to those who identify their race as white (average ACE score 1.52) (Merrick, Ford, Ports, & Guinn, 2018).
- Adults identifying as gay/lesbian or bisexual have higher average ACE scores than adults identifying as heterosexual (Merrick et al., 2018).
- The average ACE score for adults living in households where the combined income is less than $15,000 per year is greater than the average ACE score at any other income bracket level (Merrick et al., 2018).

Implications of ACEs Research on Education

The original ACE study solidly confirmed two significant connections:

1 A connection between trauma in childhood and health-risk behaviors in adults.
2 A connection between trauma and disease.

Spring boarding off those connections, the research inspired by the original study confirms one clear fact:

> Exposure to ACEs is a risk factor for the most common and deadly diseases in the United States, regardless of race, income, educational attainment or neighborhood.

But what does all of this have to do with education and counselors? We are school counselors, not doctors after all! We can't prevent cancer, heart disease, and adult obesity…. Or can we? Many strategies employed by school counselors, teachers, and caring adults CAN alter the outcomes for children experiencing ACEs.

Understanding the link between ACEs, risk-taking behaviors, and disease gives school counselors a unique perspective on their students. This link, and the research that supports it, helps us understand how a student's brain is impacted by ACEs. After we understand how the brain is impacted, we can begin to see the symptoms playing out in our schools. That same impacted brain must learn math. That same impacted brain pays attention – or doesn't pay attention – in class. That same impacted brain tries to make new friends.

> **ACEs EXPLAIN *many behaviors and poor educational outcomes we see in our students.***

12 Understand the Impact of Childhood Trauma

When Alicia was 4, she wasn't a child; she was a parent. As the primary caretaker for her 1-year-old brother, Alicia regularly had to search in her neighbor's garbage cans for food. She changed her brother's diapers, soothed him when he cried, and supervised him while her mother was gone in search of her next high. Parental substance abuse, physical and emotional neglect left Alicia with an ACE score of 3 before she ever entered kindergarten. Once kindergarten began, Alicia was in foster care and the abuse was over, but the trauma didn't just disappear. ACEs affect child development, mental and physical health long after the abuse ends.

Alicia struggled in school. Due to her past physical neglect, Alicia frequently stole food from the cafeteria, teacher, or other students. She ate items that were inedible such as crayons, art supplies, and rocks. She bit her nails severely as she worried about her brother at home, and she struggled to let anyone care for her. Teachers complained that she was defiant, anxious, socially awkward, and lacking self-control. "Doesn't she know stealing is wrong?" they wondered. "Why can't she just let me help her with her coat? She just throws a fit and kicks," they mused to each other. Still, what her teachers didn't know was the WHY. Behavior doesn't exist in isolation. The reasons for the behavior are more important than behavior itself. Through trauma-sensitivity, behavioral symptoms from ACEs can be curbed, but it takes time, effort, and love.

The Five Domains of Stress

The school environment is stressful for all children, even those with no ACEs. There are five domains that can cause potential stress for students at school: Biological, emotional, social, cognitive, and prosocial. These five domains give educators an organizational structure for determining what is the root cause of a student's stress in the classroom and what strategy may be most effective in regulation (Shanker & Hopkins, 2017). Although these five categories are distinct, they are also interactional. Stress in one category is very likely to cause stress in another category and multiply the stressful effects as frustration and anxiety build. Many times, we don't notice the initial stressor. What we see is the larger behavioral result of the built-up stress from multiple domains (Shanker & Hopkins, 2017).

Biological

Biological stress is caused by a student's over- or under-sensitivity to sensory stimulation and/or their ability to get their basic physical needs met. Students may be sensitive visually (through what they see), auditorily (through what they hear), kinesthetically (through touch), or through other senses. Too much sensory input can lead to students feeling overwhelmed and unable to concentrate. If a student's basic physical needs are not met, such as they are not getting enough sleep, enough vitamins, enough exercise, or taking care of their personal hygiene, this can cause underlying biological stress. A good example of this is when a student arrives at school without eating breakfast, or after a late night of studying. Generally, this hungry or tired student is also grouchy, short-fused, and sensitive – for a short time. But when the hunger, lack of sleep, or lack of exercise goes on for years, this biological stress isn't something one quick nap will fix.

Emotional

Both high and low energy states of mind can cause emotional stress for students. Having too much high energy at school can lead to high tension in the form of frustration, anger, overexcitement, and hypervigilance or fear. Having too little energy can cause low-tension stress through sadness, boredom, sluggishness, or feeling sick (Shanker & Hopkins, 2017). These strong emotions lead to both externalizing and internalizing behaviors depending on the student.

Students must understand how these variety of emotions and states of stress feel within their own body. Recognizing the emotional feeling in themselves is the first step toward regulating their emotions and returning to a calm state. All humans fluctuate between many emotions throughout the course of each day. From being frustrated in traffic to happy about a kind text from a friend to worried about a work assignment, emotions come and go rather quickly. But for students with ACEs, emotions like worry, fear, anger, or sadness may feel more permanent, underlying all other emotions of the day with a constant hum of tension.

Cognitive

Cognitive stress at school closely resembles a common teacher complaint: Lack of effort. Students' stress overload can cause a lack of attention, increased distractibility, low problem-solving skills, and difficulty with organization. These attention, organization, and planning skills are referred to as "executive functions" and can be significantly impaired by ACEs (Harris, 2018). When students struggle with executive functioning, memory, and attention, it takes an incredible amount of energy to sustain concentration. Expending this much energy simply to concentrate can detract from other functioning such as social skills, decision making, and cognitive processing (Shanker & Hopkins, 2017).

Using preventative strategies to address low executive functioning skills can decrease students' cognitive stress, allow them to engage with the material and LEARN. Students with cognitive stress and executive functioning challenges may struggle to sustain attention, quickly switch attention from one task to another, remember new material, think abstractly, notice patterns like cause and effect, and ignore distractions. Diagnoses like learning disabilities, ADHD, and speech and language disorders may also increase students' cognitive stress.

Social

Social skills groups and social skills training are common techniques used by school counselors to address limited social functioning. But social stress goes deeper. We must begin before the concrete skills and first address where the stress is coming from. Social stress generally stems from students' difficulties in

14   *Understand the Impact of Childhood Trauma*

perspective taking or perspective sharing (Shanker & Hopkins, 2017). One effect of ACEs in children is a hypervigilance and fear response to even neutral stimuli. Getting bumped in the hallway, looked at, pointed at, or overhearing even a benign comment can put students who are already on high alert into a stress response (Rude, Wenglaff, Gibbs, Vane, & Whitney, 2002).

Social perspective taking is a complex process which includes subconsciously reading non-verbal cues, adapting to cultural differences in socialization, receiving and processing language at a rapid rate, and remembering socially important facts like names, interests, and social groups. Students with ACEs may struggle to remember all the social nuances and process social situations as rapidly as necessary. When a student's stress response is elevated in social situations due to memory challenges or processing delays, this can cause social challenges which then lead to more social stress. We must break the cycle by helping students reduce their social stress instead of just teaching the social rules.

Prosocial

The prosocial stress domain focuses on students' stress that is displayed through cruel or selfish behavior. Teachers and school counselors are uniquely challenged when working with a student who is intentionally mean to other students. It is easy to dismiss them as lacking character, but it is challenging to enter into a safe space with them and allow them process their ACEs or self-regulate. Holding empathy for this student may cause us a great deal of social stress in the process. In the same way, students find it very stressful to navigate social situations with other students who are in distress. Many students who display antisocial behavior are trying to "discharge their chronic [stress] on someone else" which can create a cycle of antisocial behavior (Shanker & Hopkins, 2017, p. 52). My stress is stressing you out. So you are mean to me which causes me stress. Then, I am mean back to you, which causes you more stress. And around and around we go.

Understanding the underlying stressors at school is a necessary step toward developing empathy for students. Before students can become cognitively engaged in academic lessons, they must have their "learning brain" on and their stress level low. Prevention in all school environments can go a long way toward decreasing baseline stress for students and increasing their ability to engage academically and socially at school.

According to the National Child Traumatic Stress Network, observable symptoms of current or past exposure to ACEs in the classroom include:

- Clinginess to teacher or parent
- Worry about safety or self or others
- Irritability
- Increase/decrease in activity level
- Decrease in attention
- Increase in absenteeism

The ACEs Study   15

- Anger outbursts/aggression
- Somatic complaints (frequent headaches, stomachaches, or asking to go to the nurse)
- Decrease in academic performance
- Tendency to be easily startled
- Difficulty with authority, redirection, or criticism
- Inability to interpret social cues or respond appropriately to social situations involving children and adults (National Child Traumatic Stress Network, 2008).

The symptoms of ACEs are visible in classrooms every day.

Understanding ACEs, school stressors, and the observable symptoms of childhood trauma helps school counselors to think about difficult behaviors differently.

Instead of thinking "Why is Johnny always yelling and pushing other kids?" we could ask ourselves "What happened to Johnny that makes him think yelling and pushing is the normal way to interact with others?" Instead of "Why does Kiley never do her homework?" ask "What is making it hard for Kiley to complete her homework each night?"

Aha! Now we have questions we can answer.

Could it be that Johnny saw his mother yelled at and pushed by her boyfriend last week? Does Johnny's high-school-aged brother yell at him and push him around when their parents are too high to notice?

And what about Kiley's homework? Was Kiley's mother working two jobs to support the family since Kiley's dad went to jail last year? She has little time to help her daughter with homework. Or does Kiley need a backpack, school supplies, and a quiet environment to do her homework at home? Aggressive, antisocial, or disengaged behavior doesn't prove the existence of ACEs in a child's life, but it raises a red flag that exposure to ACEs should be further explored.

Compared to children with no ACEs, children with two or more ACEs are 2.67 times more likely to be retained a grade in school and 2.59 times less likely to be engaged in school (Bethell, Newacheck, Hawes, & Halfon, 2014). With statistics like those, it is essential that social-emotional wellbeing and ACEs exposure are part of the conversations with parents and teachers, and ultimately part of administrative decisions about student behavior, academics, and intervention.

References

ACEs too High. (2012). *Got Your ACE score?* Retrieved from ACEs too High: https://acestoohigh.com/got-your-ace-score/

ACES too High. (2019). *ACEs Science 101.* Retrieved from ACEs too High: https://acestoohigh.com/aces-101/

16 Understand the Impact of Childhood Trauma

Bethell, C. D., Newacheck, P., Hawes, E., & Halfon, N. (2014). Adverse Childhood Experiences: Assessing the Impact on Health and School Engagement at the Mitigating Role of Resilience. *Health Affairs, 33*(12), 2106–2115. Retrieved from www.healthaffairs.org/doi/pdf/10.1377/hlthaff.2014.0914

Centers for Disease Control and Prevention. (2019a, April 2). *About the CDC-Kaiser ACE Study*. Retrieved from Center for Disease Control: www.cdc.gov/violenceprevention/childabuseandneglect/acestudy/about.html

Centers for Disease Control and Prevention. (2019b, April 15). *Adverse Childhood Experiences Journal Articles by Topic Area*. Retrieved from Center for Disease Control: www.cdc.gov/violenceprevention/childabuseandneglect/acestudy/journal.html

Dong, M., Giles, W. H., Felitti, V. J., Dube, S. R., Williams, J. E., Chapman, D. P., & Anda, R. F. (2004). Insights Into Causal Pathways for Ischemic Heart Disease. *Circulation, 110*, 1761–1766.

Felitti, V., Anda, R., Nordenberg, D., Williamson, D., Spitz, A., Edwards, V., … Marks, J. (1998). Relationship of Childhood Abuse and Household Dysfunction to Many of the Leading Causes of Death in Adults: The Adverse Childhood Experience (ACE) Study. *American Journal of Preventative Medicine, 14*(4), 245–258. Retrieved from www.ajpmonline.org/article/S0749-3797(98)00017-8/pdf

Finkelhor, D., Ormrod, R., Storr, C., Lucia, V., & Anthony, J. (2005). The Victimization of Children and Youth: A Comprehensive National Survey. *Child Maltreatment, 10*, 5–25. Retrieved from www.unh.edu/ccrc/pdf/jvq/publication_CV73.pdf

Harris, N. B. (2018). *The Deepest Well: Healing the Long-Term Effects of Childhood Adversity*. New York, NY: Houghton Mifflin Harcourt.

Merrick, M., Ford, D., Ports, K., & Guinn, A. S. (2018). Prevalence of Adverse Childhood Experiences from the 2011–2014 Behavioral Risk Factor Surveillance System in 23 States. *JAMA Pediatrics, 172*(11), 1038–1044. doi:10.1001/jamapediatrics.2018.2537

National Child Traumatic Stress Network. (2008). *Child Trauma Toolkit for Educators*. Retrieved from National Child Raumatic Stress Network: www.nctsn.org/sites/default/files/resources//child_trauma_toolkit_educators.pdf

Robert Wood Johnson Foundation. (2013, May). *The Truth about ACEs Inforaphic*. Retrieved from Robert Wood Johnson Foundation: www.rwjf.org/en/library/infographics/the-truth-about-aces.html#/download

Rude, S., Wenglaff, R., Gibbs, B., Vane, J., & Whitney, T. (2002). Negativity Biases Predict Subsequent Depressive Symptoms. *Cognition and Emotion, 16*(3), 423–440.

Shanker, S., & Hopkins, S. (2017). On Becoming a Self-Reg Haven. In W. Steele (Ed.), *Optimizing Learning Outcomes: Proven Brain-Centric Trauma-Sensitive Practices*. New York, NY: Routledge.

Zeng, S., & Hu, X. (2018). Parents Reporting Adverse Childhood Experiences among Young Children with Disabilities: Informing Systems Transformation. *Topics in Early Childhood Special Education, 38*(3), 162–173.

3 Neurobiology and Learning
How Trauma Changes the Developing Brain

Stress

We know it when we feel it. Good, bad, or ugly – stress is a part of our everyday human existence. For children, stress is also a normal part of life. There are three types of stress: Positive, tolerable, and toxic (Figure 3.1).

Positive Stress: Through experiences like learning to share, following rules at school, making a new friend, or solving a challenging math problem, children experience mild to moderate levels of *positive stress*. Their blood starts

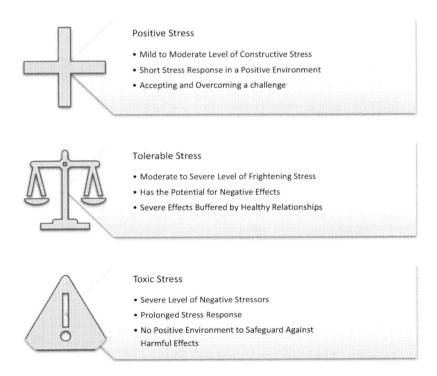

Figure 3.1 There are three types of stress – positive, tolerable, and toxic (Rawson, 2019).

18   *Understand the Impact of Childhood Trauma*

pumping, their heart rate elevates, and their bodies release the stress hormones cortisol and adrenaline in reaction to the stressor. When a young child's stress response system is activated in this way, for a short time and with the guidance and support of trusted adults, the outcome is constructive (National Scientific Council on the Developing Child, 2005/2014). Experiencing positive stress allows children's stress response system to develop in a healthy way. As the stress response system continues to develop, children can more confidently address larger stressors independently and seek help when necessary. They are able to assess a situation, determine the threat level, and react appropriately and automatically within milliseconds (National Scientific Council on the Developing Child, 2005/2014).

Tolerable Stress: As the stressors get larger – such as the death of a loved one or a frightening car accident – children cope well in the context of supportive relationships. This is called *tolerable stress* (National Scientific Council on the Developing Child, 2005/2014). Tolerable stress has the potential for negative effects. In the example of a serious car accident, the child's stress response is activated and their life may well have been in danger. However, because of the acute nature of the trauma (it was only a few minutes in the car and a few hours before everyone was back home safely), the child usually returns to normal functioning rather quickly. In the example of the death of a loved one, the supportive buffer of other caring adult relationships helps the child's brain recover from the experience, even if stress persists for a while.

Toxic Stress: But what about when the stressor is too large or goes on for too long? Or the caregiver is not supportive? This is called *toxic stress.* Toxic stress is defined as "strong, frequent or prolonged activation of the body's stress management system" (National Scientific Council on the Developing Child, 2005/2014, p. 2). ACEs fall into the category of toxic stress. They are chronic, stressful situations that occur within a child's immediate family. ACEs generally involve the primary caregiver, leaving the child without the positive adult buffer needed to turn toxic stress into tolerable stress. When a child experiences the toxic stress of ACEs, it sets off a chain reaction of negative impacts on their developing brain. In severe cases, a child's brain architecture is so severely changed by this stress that it is visible on an MRI (Harris, 2018). In this section, I will discuss various ways that the toxic stress caused by ACEs negatively alters a child's brain development and how those developments impact their learning.

Scientists are still working to solidify the research on neuroscience as it relates to ACEs, but so far this is clear:

1   Almost two-thirds of children experience ACEs (Felitti et al., 1998).
2   ACEs are forms of toxic stress. They are prolonged threats to natural desire to survive (Harris, 2018; National Scientific Council on the Developing Child, 2005/2014).
3   Due to its chronic and severe nature, toxic stress creates dysfunction in the body through the over- and underproduction of the stress hormone cortisol (Johnson, Riley, Granger, & Riis, 2013).

4   Over- and underproduction of cortisol change the developing brain's architecture (National Scientific Council on the Developing Child, 2005/2014).

5   These changes to brain architecture lead to physical and psychological disorders and increase the likelihood for risk-taking behaviors, difficulties with academics, and impaired social functioning (Ayoub et al., 2006; Cole, O'Brien, Gadd, Wallace, & Gregory, 2005; De Bellis, 2005).

The Role of Stress Hormones

After reading this information, you may be thinking to yourself, "Ok, I understand that toxic stress is bad, but why? What happens to our brain when it's so stressed?" I'm glad you asked. It all begins with the role of cortisol.

During childhood, the neural pathways in the brain are incredibly "plastic." They grow, deteriorate, change, and develop at faster rates than any other time during our lives. In fact, more than one million neural connections are formed *per second* in the early years of life (Center on the Developing Child, 2009). This rapid neural development allows children to quickly learn important life skills such as walking, talking, and forming relationships. But it also leaves children very susceptible to the harmful effects of the ACEs. When life is difficult, toxic stress interrupts the normally fast-paced neural development. Neural connections are never formed, formed incorrectly or lost. This leads to life-long problems with the stress response system (National Scientific Council on the Developing Child, 2005/2014).

Two systems that are involved in our stress response are the Sympathetic-Adrenomedullary (SAM) system which produces adrenaline and the hypothalamic-pituitary-adrenocortical (HPA) system which produces cortisol (National Scientific Council on the Developing Child, 2005/2014). Adrenaline is responsible for our body's response to acute stress, such as mobilizing energy, increasing heart rate, and dilating pupils when we are in a "fight-or-flight" mode. Adrenaline is necessary for our survival and is used in very short-term stress situations. Cortisol, however, is released to help the brain and body cope with stress. After the initial adrenaline rush, cortisol mobilizes additional energy, enhances memory, and activates an immune response to heal from the stressor.

After a stressor, cortisol must be "turned off" by our body when we return to a normal balance. This feedback loop of stress, adrenaline release, cortisol release, and calming is natural and useful. But while coping with the constant threat of a physically abusive parent, neglect, or other household dysfunction, our stress response system doesn't know how to respond to a stressor that never stops. The cortisol doesn't get the correct feedback to turn off, in even worse cases, cortisol is so desensitized to stress it never activates at all (National Scientific Council on the Developing Child, 2005/2014).When cortisol levels remain too elevated or too low, the effects are tragic (Figure 3.2).

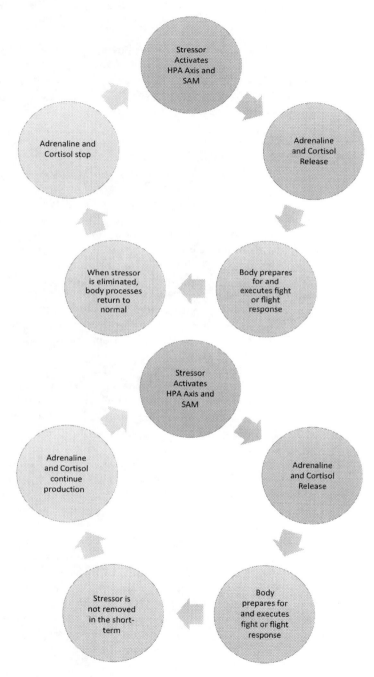

Figure 3.2 (a) Healthy stress cycle (Rawson, 2019). (b) Toxic stress cycle (Rawson, 2019). (c) Dysregulated stress cycle (Rawson, 2019).

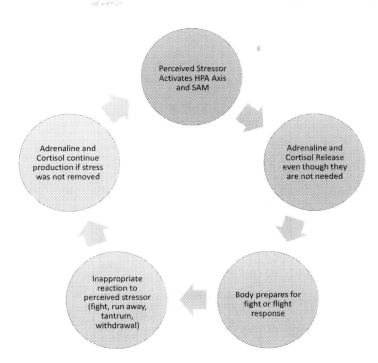

Figure 3.2 (Continued).

Stress Hormones and Learning

> Most ACEs happen at home, but every day students bring the symptoms of these ACEs with them to school.

A lunchbox full of junk food doesn't set children up for success. And neither does a brain full of cortisol. Children with ACEs are unfortunately poised for difficulties at school. Ever wonder why some students struggle to remember their homework? Why some students can't focus? Or why some students overreact to small problems? All of these common behaviors could be due to dysregulated cortisol (Harris, 2018).

The dysregulation of cortisol damages the amygdala, hippocampus, pre-frontal cortex, and many other brain structures. The damage it causes to these brain structures leads to behavioral, emotional, and academic concerns. It suppresses the immune response, impairs memory and learning, dysregulates growth hormones, sex hormones, and insulin production, and increases the likelihood for a variety of physical health conditions (Harris, 2018).

22 Understand the Impact of Childhood Trauma

Ever wondered why some students visit the school nurse more frequently than others? This could also be due to cortisol. Too much or too little cortisol in the brain leads the immune system to turn on or off at the wrong times. Too much cortisol leads to an exaggerated immune response, or feelings of sickness when you aren't sick. Too little cortisol shuts down the immune response prematurely leading to an increased risk for infection (Johnson, Riley, Granger, & Riis, 2013). Feelings of sickness and infectious diseases both lead to trouble focusing and absence from class, ultimately hindering educational success.

In the following sections, we will discuss the impact of ACEs and dysregulated cortisol on specific brain features, including the amygdala, hippocampus, pre-frontal cortex, and others. By the end of this chapter, I hope you see a clear connection between ACEs, cortisol, and nearly every behavioral difficulty in your classroom (Figure 3.3).

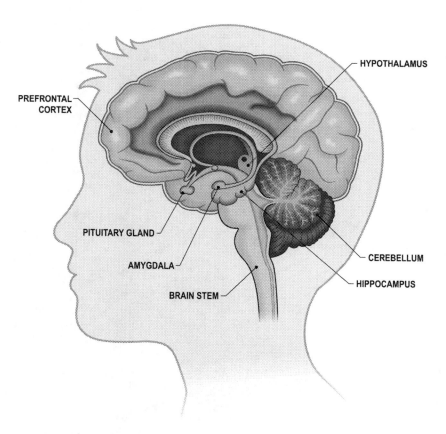

Figure 3.3 The limbic system controls emotional functioning and memory (Kopp, 2014).

Fight or Flight: The Amygdala's Over-Responsiveness

Ever come across a bear in the woods? Or more likely, have you ever had to stop fast on the freeway? Then, you know the feeling. Some call it butterflies in the stomach or an adrenaline rush, but whatever it's called, the feeling happens automatically in the face of danger. When our eyes see the threat of the bear's sharp teeth – or the oncoming car in our lane – they send a signal to the brain, putting it on high alert and preparing our body for some serious stress. The emotional part of our brain will later register this stress response as fear. But before that even happens, the body automatically switches into survival mode. Led by the amygdala – the brain's hub for the fear response – this automatic survival response is an evolutionary necessity. Located near the brain's midline, the amygdala sends signals throughout the body to shut down non-essential functions. It tells the brain to divert resources to the areas of our body that will impact our immediate ability to survive.

Do we need to run from this bear? Blood pumps to our extremities and tenses muscles to prepare for running. We start to sweat. Our heart rate elevates. We are ready to go.

Do we need to avoid the car accident? Our pupils dilate to take in more visual information. Our attention is laser focused on the cars, forgetting about the running to-do list in our heads or the conversation going on in the backseat.

This ability to home in on a life-or-death situation and automatically switch on "survival mode" allowed humans to survive for thousands of years. The amygdala can detect a threat and initiate the fight-or-flight response automatically and with great accuracy, in most cases. If a healthy stress response system was developed in early childhood, the body learns how to turn this response on and off accurately. It can also quickly recover to a calm state after the rush of hormones and physical changes associated with the stress response are over. The stress response is rarely required, and it is meant to be used in very short increments.

Running from a bear or stopping fast in traffic only requires the amygdala's activation for a few seconds. It was never meant to be "on" all the time. When a child experiences the toxic and constant stress of ACEs, it is understandable that the amygdala and surrounding limbic system – the brain structure responsible for emotion and memory – are most impacted. Abuse by nature evokes a strong, fear-based emotional response and creates negative memories.

In a 1997 study on the impact of stress in juvenile rats, the amount of support and care that the baby rats received from their mothers in the first ten days of life impacted their ability to develop a healthy stress response system as far as 24–26 months later. The rat mother's natural "mothering," including grooming and licking behaviors calmed the infant rats after a tolerable stressor of being handed by human researchers. The more the infant rats were licked and groomed when they returned to their mothers, the better they were able to handle stressors in their future (Liu et al., 1997). Their amygdala developed

24 *Understand the Impact of Childhood Trauma*

the ability, in the context of a supportive adult environment, to learn how to assess a threat, respond appropriately, and cope.

> Positive and tolerable stress that is mitigated by supportive adults develops the amygdala into a well-tuned, short-term machine.

But in the case of ACEs, absence of the supportive buffer, and the short-term time period, the amygdala develops in an unhealthy way. Poor care-giving and early life toxic stress can have a profoundly negative impact on emotional regulation. After studying children internationally adopted from orphanages, researchers found a correlation between time spent in the orphanage, larger than normal amygdala volumes, and higher than normal levels of anxiety. These children's brain architectures were different due to their toxic stress from living in an orphanage. The increases in amygdala volume and emotional regulation difficulties were the underlying cause for the children's social-emotional difficulties even once placed with a loving family and adopted (Tottenham et al., 2010). Children who do not develop a regulated stress response system struggle to differentiate between true and perceived stress, and overrespond to minimally stressful events.

At school, 6th grader Nadia was popular. Beautiful, blonde with a big smile, and a bubbly personality. If you weren't her friend, you wished you were. With three younger sisters, all with matching blonde braids, to idolize her, Nadia was the leader of the pack. A "mini-mom" at home and Queen Bee at school. When she came back to school after summer for 7th grade year, something was different. Instead of honor roll, Nadia barely kept Cs and Ds. Instead of perfect braids, she looked like she just woke up, barely taking time to care for herself. Her bubbly personality turned aggressive. Anyone who crossed her got an earful of hurtful insults, including teachers and staff. For what seemed like "no reason," she would run from the classroom crying at any insinuation of criticism or negative feedback.

At first, teachers dismissed her behavior as a "typical middle schooler," moody, lazy, and more concerned about socializing than school. One teacher, however, wasn't so sure. She referred Nadia to school counseling. After many sessions of relative silence, the truth came out. Her ACE score was higher than anyone knew. Her parents were divorced, on the verge of homelessness and living in a one-bedroom apartment with five children. Her mom's addiction to prescription pain killers escalated to a heroin addiction causing her to steal from the family, leave home for weeks at a time, and even kidnap her own daughter, Nadia's 3-year-old sister, to gain sympathy. Nadia couldn't sleep out of fear for the safety of her sisters and her mom. Coming to school was nearly impossible. Nadia struggled to focus, many times falling asleep in class or spending her day in the counseling office sobbing. Her amygdala was on high alert. Subconsciously, she was expecting peers and teachers to abandon her the same way her mom did. She worried about her sisters, resorting to aggression to protect them. She didn't know where her next meal may come from. For Nadia, she was in survival mode, all day, every day. The bear she was running from lived at home.

The Amygdala and Learning

When the amygdala is overused and overstimulated as it is by ACEs, it can lead to a state of hyperarousal. According to Dr. Bruce Perry, "children who have experienced trauma will be in a persistent state of alarm and less capable of concentrating when they enter classrooms" (2016, p. 28). Teachers, counselors, and school staff may notice these children immediately. They have high levels of externalizing behaviors and may already be labeled a "problem kid." These students are living in a constant state of "fight-or-flight." They may feel like everyone is a threat to their safety due to their past abusive experiences with adults. Or, they may be unsure of how to read social cues or the behavioral patterns of others due to the mental illness or erratic behaviors of a parent. The National Child Traumatic Stress Network (2008) provides the following observations about students with toxic stress.

Students with toxic stress may display:

- Anxiety, worry, and fear especially about their own safety
- Fear and anxiety about the safety of others (more clingy with teachers and/or parents)
- Whiny, irritable, or moody temperament
- An increased activity level ("hyper")
- Anger outbursts and aggression
- Decreased concentration
- An inability to interpret and respond appropriately to social cues
- A tendency to be easily startled
- Difficulty with authority or criticism
- An inability to calm down.

When a student's amygdala puts them on high alert, it becomes more difficult for them to build healthy relationships. A child who comes to school expecting to be hurt by someone may play rougher, overreact to the small mistakes of others (pushing in line, bumping in the hallway), and/or inadvertently provoke others. These mistakes in perception may lead to aggressive responses from others and further the child's own narrative that "everyone is out to get me." This narrative sets in motion a familiar cycle of fear and harm (Perkins & Graham-Berrman, 2012).

Losing Trust: The Role of the Hippocampus

When children experience toxic stress, it negatively affects the development of another limbic system structure, the hippocampus. The hippocampus is

26   Understand the Impact of Childhood Trauma

responsible for developing and maintaining short-term and long-term memories, including declarative, episodic, spatial, and contextual memories.

- *Declarative Memories*: the remembrance of facts and figures. My birthday is June 1. My brother is two years old. My bike is red.
- *Episodic Memories*: the remembrance of autobiographical events from the past – a birthday party, meeting a new baby brother, learning to ride a bike, etc.
- *Spatial Memories*: the remembrance of one's environment, including time and place orientation – how big the cake looked at your birthday party, what the hospital smelled like when you met your baby brother, how the pavement felt when you hit it after falling off your bike.
- *Contextual Memories*: the remembrance of associations between objects, people, or landmarks and their environmental framework. Birthday parties always have cake. Doctors and nurses are nice. Hospitals are fun places with babies. The speed at which you must ride your bike to make it home from Johnny's by dinner time.

The hippocampus' memory bank and its ability to encode and retrieve memories make it heavily involved in learning. The hippocampus allows us to store multiplication facts in long-term memory, retrieve them at a moment's notice, and apply them to a unique context. We can remember the fact itself (declarative memory), our 3rd-grade teacher who taught us the multiplication facts (episodic memory), what it feels like to take a college math exam in a lecture hall (spatial memory), and how to use multiplication facts in long division (contextual memory). Because the hippocampus is constantly filtering new information, storing and retrieving memories multiple times per minute, it has a high degree of neuroplasticity. Neuroplasticity is the ability to change, grow, deteriorate, and/or reorganize based on usage or non-usage (Kandola, Hendrikse, Lucassen, & Yücel, 2016).

When children experience the toxic stress of ACEs, the amygdala jumps into flight-or-fight mode immediately. It produces adrenaline and cortisol for survival and shuts down non-essential body functions. The hippocampus is shut down. Memory making slows or ceases because it is non-essential to survival. This is why when asked directly about a traumatic experience, many people cannot recall simple details such as date, time, or who was present (Harris, 2018).

The Hippocampus and Learning

In the classroom, our students with toxic stress are in a constant state of hyperarousal. They scan for threats and feel on edge. They are unable to focus on learning and unable to use their hippocampus for memory encoding and retrieval. Toxic stress and ACEs may result in forgetfulness, learning problems, challenges in retaining new academic material, and ultimately decreases the physical size and capabilities of the hippocampus (Wolpow, Johnson, Hertel, & Kincaid, 2009). ACEs also affect the hippocampus by contextualizing more memories as negative instead of neutral or positive. The hippocampus contextualizes memories based on associations it develops through past events. Maltreated children view the world through a more negative context than non-maltreated children. "Maltreated children, through their focus on negativity, as an adaptive response to the perception of increased threat, appear to divert their attention from material that is positive and benign" (Ayoub et al., 2006, p. 701). In other words, if adults are abusive and unpredictable in the home environment, children are more likely to remember mean or unpredictable people in other contexts. By remembering the negative, they dismiss the positive or neutral people, even within fictional stories (Ayoub et al., 2006).

As the hippocampus is developed in childhood, it creates and houses the child's own representational maps. A representational map is a tool for contextualizing memories, sorting and splitting events and people into categories. Maltreated children tend to categorize themselves as bad/mean and see the world through this lens. They are less able to attend to positive/nice interactions within the classroom context since they view themselves as outside of the positive/nice category. Maltreated children concentrate less on neutral stimuli such as class rules and routines which are outside of the context from which they view the world (Ayoub et al., 2006).

In addition to contextual map-making, preschoolers and early learners are just beginning to develop their sequential memory, moving episodes into time frames. This joint effort between the hippocampus and the pre-frontal cortex to create sequential memories is most easily developed in an environment that is familiar, consistent, predictable, and with a reliable caregiver (Cole et al., 2005). Children who have sequential memory delays have difficulty processing the content of academic lessons, retrieving the knowledge from stored memory, and applying it to later contexts (Cole et al., 2005).

Thinking Like There's No Tomorrow: The Pre-frontal Cortex of Students with ACEs

Landon was the funniest kid in class. He loved to tell jokes, play pranks, egg on his friends, and belly laugh. His smile lit up the room, and he loved one-on-one attention. But he had trouble distinguishing between the time for jokes and the time to be serious. He was frequently in trouble for interrupting, making inappropriate noises, disrupting the learning environment, and disrespecting the teacher. The life of the party just couldn't stop himself. Despite many attempts at reward charts, positive praise, detention, and suspensions, nothing seemed to motivate Landon to stop his class clown behaviors. Many teachers would sigh and express the same sentiment, "Why doesn't he care? Why doesn't he just stop?" It seemed so simple. If he could stop blurting out jokes during math, he would get to go to recess. If he could stop rolling his eyes at the teacher, he would earn "class cash." If he could...

28 Understand the Impact of Childhood Trauma

Landon's ACE score was high. Both his elder brother and elder sister were expelled from school. Landon's parents were divorced, and his Dad was formerly incarcerated. In 4th grade, his 17-year-old sister was incarcerated too. At home, attention was limited, and stress was elevated. Landon was in fight-or-flight mode every day.

Landon couldn't remember the consequences for talking in class. Instead, he thought constantly about the police's visit to his house – the night his brother assaulted their mom. When the teacher asked about math homework, Landon thought about his sister in juvenile hall. She used to help him with homework. Landon's mind was full. There was no place for critical thinking and logical reasoning in survival mode.

The most evolved and complex area of the human brain, the pre-frontal cortex, is sometimes called the "thinking brain," and generally recognized as where learning takes place. The pre-frontal cortex is responsible for all our higher-order and critical thinking. If you are an educator, the pre-frontal cortex is where all your magic happens. It influences our abilities to take each other's perspectives, regulate emotions, control impulses, think abstractly, develop language, make decisions, think about cause-and-effect relationships, and pay attention.

Children raised in unpredictable environments have trouble understanding patterns. Due to the inconsistency of the home environment, and the erratic behavior of parents with mental illness or substance abuse disorders, children with ACEs have a limited understanding of cause-and-effect relationships. In home environments that are unpredictable, children cannot make sense of what is happening. They do not see logical causes for their parents' behavior nor do they see reasonable consequences for their own. Children with ACEs do not grasp their internal locus of control. The internal locus is the belief that one has the ability to make things happen or not happen (Cole et al., 2005). This sense of helplessness and lack of control leaves children fearful of the future, unable to make forward thinking plans, and with difficulty connecting actions and consequences.

In addition to rational decision making, the pre-frontal cortex is responsible for empathy development and perspective taking. Both functions can be impaired by ACEs. Shortfalls in this area of interpersonal communication make it challenging for students to interact in pro-social ways. Children with ACEs find it hard to solve social conflicts, work in groups, take another's point of view, make inferences, participate in dynamic conversations, articulate personal preferences, and accept the differing preferences of others (Cole et al., 2005).

Lastly, the pre-frontal cortex helps us to differentiate between relevant and irrelevant information. This allows us to focus, think critically, organize information, and pay attention. Instead of learning social studies, children with ACEs may be focused on their own thoughts. Thinking about the potential threats in the classroom, the teacher's mood, fear about another person's safety, or sensory overstimulation may look a lot like distraction and lack of focus.

Disassociation from the learning environment due to stress looks similar to boredom, inattention, and daydreaming (Cole et al., 2005).

Most symptoms of toxic stress look similar to the symptoms of Attention Deficit Hyperactivity Disorder (ADHD) due to pre-frontal cortex challenges.

The Pre-frontal Cortex and Learning

Together, all these pre-frontal cortex abnormalities linked to ACEs and the dysregulated stress response can lead to a host of long-term consequences for our students. According to the National Child Traumatic Stress Network (2008), toxic stress and trauma are linked to:

- Lower GPA
- Higher rates of school absences
- Increased dropout
- More suspensions and expulsions
- Decreased reading ability.

One of the most significant roles of the pre-frontal cortex, for students, is its role in managing our executive functioning skills. These are the skills that help any student to be a successful student. These include setting goals, developing a plan, anticipating consequences, and reflecting on past processes. When we think about what prevents students from having low GPAs, suspensions, and dropping out, we think about these skills. The ability to reflect on mistakes will prevent a student from a repeat suspension. The ability to anticipate consequences will encourage students to stay in school instead of dropping out. And the ability to make a plan and follow through on it paves the way for a high GPA.

There are significant deficits in executive functioning skills among maltreated children with post-traumatic stress disorder (PTSD) as compared to their sociodemographic counterparts without PTSD (De Bellis, 2005). These deficits in executive functioning lead to "inattentiveness, inability to focus and poor academic achievement" (De Bellis, 2005, p. 160). When a traumatized student is acting out in class – distracted, withdrawn, or impulsive – they are not just "not thinking" or "trying to get attention." They are unable to access the part of their brain that learns and makes rational decisions. Boys with ACEs have more difficulty than other students with tasks that require them to stop their behaviors to avoid negative consequences (Cole et al., 2005). In the case of Landon, his ACEs diminished the functioning of his pre-frontal cortex. He couldn't think rationally, stop blurting out, and control the class clown behaviors, even when he knew that negative consequences were coming.

Even into adulthood, the negative effects of ACEs on decision making and risk-taking behaviors are clear. Young adults with a history of ACEs are more

30 Understand the Impact of Childhood Trauma

likely to be verbally aggressive toward intimate partners, friends, and strangers (Mumford, Taylor, Berg, & WeiWei Liu, 2019). Physically abused children are more likely to be fired from a job, become a teen parent, or impregnate someone/get pregnant while unmarried (Lansford et al., 2007). Adults with four or more ACEs are 12.2 times more likely to attempt suicide than adults with no ACEs (Felitti et al., 1998).

Other Brain Functions

Here are a few other brain functions worth noting when it comes to their connection to ACEs:

- *Cerebellar vermis*: Formerly thought to only control gross motor movement, the cerebellum's role in regulating emotional and attentional stability has recently been confirmed by science (Teicher, 2000). Research suggests that the cerebellar vermis has a high density of stress hormone receptors, making it highly vulnerable to the effects of cortisol overload associated with ACEs. Abnormalities to the vermis are associated with psychiatric, mental health, and developmental disorders, including autism, ADHD, depression, and schizophrenia (Teicher, 2000).
- *Hypothalamus and Ventral Tegmental Area (VTA)*: Responsible for the reason no one can eat just one Oreo, the hypothalamus is the pleasure center of the brain. Connected to the VTA, the hypothalamus is responsible for motivation, rewards, and addiction. These structures rely on dopamine, the "feel-good neurotransmitter," to function. They translate the dopamine into pleasurable sensations (Harris, 2018, p. 69). When there is too much cortisol in the body (meaning the body is in a state of toxic stress), it decreases the VTA's dopamine receptors. This leads the hypothalamus to require even *more* Oreos to feel satisfied. Or more sex, or more marijuana, or more of anything that makes someone feel good. According to the original ACE study, there is a dose-response relationship between ACE exposure and activities, generally considered the "risk-taking" behaviors that satisfy the VTA. With four or more ACEs, a person is 5.5 times more likely to become addicted to alcohol, 2.5 times more likely to smoke tobacco, and ten times more likely to use intravenous drugs than a person with zero ACEs (Felitti et al., 1998).
- *Locus Coeruleus*: This part of the brain, closely associated with the prefrontal cortex, leads our aggressive behaviors and regulates impulse control. A dysfunctional locus coeruleus can be due to toxic stress, ACEs, and the addition of too much noradrenaline (a secondary stress *hormone*) in the brain. This results in increased aggression, stimulation, and fear. It can also cause sleep problems due to hypervigilance (Harris, 2018). Sleep troubles and insomnia are more common for children with ACEs than those without ACEs and especially common for girls and those from racial/ethnic minority groups who have ACEs (Wang, Raffeld, Slopen, Hale, & Dunn, 2016).

References

Ayoub, C. C., O'Connor, E., Rappolt-Schlichtmann, G., Fischer, K. W., Rogosch, F. A., Toth, S. L., & Cicchetti, D. (2006). Cognitive and Emotional Differences in Young Maltreated Children: A Translational Application of Dyamic Skill Theory. *Development and Psychopathology, 18*(3), 679–706.

Center on the Developing Child. (2009). *Five Numbers to Remember about Early Childhood Development.* Retrieved from Center on the Developing Child: www.developingchild. harvard.edu

Cole, S., O'Brien, J., Gadd, M. R., Wallace, D., & Gregory, M. (2005). *Helping Traumatized Children Learn: Supportive School Environments for Children Traumatized by Family Violence.* Boston, MA: Massachusetts Advocates for Children and Harvard Law School, Trauma and Learning Policy Initiative.

De Bellis, M. D. (2005). The Psychobiology of Neglect. *Child Maltreatment, 10*(2), 150–172.

Felitti, V., Anda, R., Nordenberg, D., Williamson, D., Spitz, A., Edwards, V., … Marks, J. (1998). Relationship of Childhood Abuse and Household Dysfunction to Many of the Leading Causes of Death in Adults: The Adverse Childhood Experience (ACE) Study. *American Journal of Preventative Medicine, 14*(4), 245–258. Retrieved from www.ajpmonline.org/article/S0749-3797(98)00017-8/pdf

Harris, N. B. (2018). *The Deepest Well: Healing the Long-Term Effects of Childhood Adversity.* New York, NY: Houghton Mifflin Harcourt.

Johnson, S., Riley, A., Granger, D., & Riis, J. (2013). The Science of Early Life Toxic Stress for Pediatric Practice and Advocacy. *Pediatrics, 131*(2), 319–327.

Kandola, A., Hendrikse, J., Lucassen, P. J., & Yücel, M. (2016). Aerobic Exercise as a Tool to Improve Hippocampal Plasticity and Function in Humans: Practical Implications for Mental Health Treatment. *Frontiers in Human Neuroscience, 10*, 179–188. Retrieved from www.frontiersin.org/articles/10.3389/fnhum.2016.00373/full

Kopp, J. (2014). *Brain Cross-Section with Labels Stock Illustration.* iStock. Retrieved from www.istockphoto.com/vector/brain-cross-section-with-labels-gm502041209-43608806

Lansford, J., Miller-Johnson, S., Berlin, L., Dodge, K., Bates, J., & Pettit, G. (2007). Early Physical Abuse and Later Violent Delinquency: A Prospective Longitudinal Study. *Child Maltreatment, 12*(3), 233–245.

Liu, D., Diorio, J., Tannenbaum, B., Caldji, C., Francis, D., Freedman, A., … Meaney, M. J. (1997). Maternal Care, Hippocampal Glucocorticoid Receptors and Hypothalamic-Pituitary-Adrenal Responses to Stress. *Science, 277*(5332), 1659–1662. Retrieved from https://pdfs.semanticscholar.org/7621/0205c43518042a41e6430dd2b83dc90447e6.pdf

Mumford, E., Taylor, B., Berg, M., & WeiWei Liu, N. M. (2019). The Social Anatomy of Adverse Childhood Experiences and Agression in a Representative Sample of Young Adults in the U.S. *Child Abuse and Neglect, 88*, 15–27.

National Child Traumatic Stress Network. (2008). *Child Trauma Toolkit for Educators.* Retrieved from National Child Raumatic Stress Network: www.nctsn.org/sites/default/files/resources//child_trauma_toolkit_educators.pdf

National Scientific Council on the Developing Child. (2005/2014). *Excessive Stress Disrupts the Architecture of the Developing Brain: Working Paper No. 3 Updagted Edition.* Retrieved from https://developingchild.harvard.edu/wp-content/uploads/2005/05/Stress_Disrupts_Architecture_Developing_Brain-1.pdf

Perkins, S., & Graham-Berrman, S. (2012). Violence Exposure and the Development of School Related Functioning: Mental-Health, Neurocognition and Learning. *Aggression and Violent Behavior, 17*(1), 89–98.

32 Understand the Impact of Childhood Trauma

Perry, B. (2016, December 13). The Brain Science behind Student Trauma. *Education Week*, p. 28.

Teicher, M. (2000, October 1). *Wounds that Time Won't Heal: The Neurobiology of Child Abuse*. Retrieved from Cerebrum: www.dana.org/Cerebrum/2000/Wounds_That_Time_Won%E2%80%99t_Heal__The_Neurobiology_of_Child_Abuse/

Tottenham, N., Hare, T., Quinn, B., McCarry, T., Nurse, M., Gilhooly, T., … Davidson, M. (2010). Prolonged Institutional Rearing is Associated with Atypically Large Amgdala Volume and Difficulties in Emotional Regulation. *Developmental Science*, 13(1), 46–61. Retrieved from www.ncbi.nlm.nih.gov/pmc/articles/PMC2817950/pdf/nihms105649.pdf

Wang, Y., Raffeld, M. R., Slopen, N., Hale, L., & Dunn, E. C. (2016). Childhood Adversity and Insomnia in Adolescence. *Sleep Medicine*, 21, 12–18. Retrieved from www.ncbi.nlm.nih.gov/pmc/articles/PMC4964593/

Wolpow, R., Johnson, M., Hertel, R., & Kincaid, S. (2009). *The Heart of Learning: Compassion, Resiliency, and Academic Success*. Retrieved from Compassionate Schools Initiative at the Office of Public Instruction: www.k12.wa.us/CompassionateSchools/HeartofLearning.aspx

4 Mental Health
What's Beneath the Symptoms

Inattention. Lack of interest in school. Withdrawal. Aggression. Hyperactivity. Social Problems. Irrational worry. Lack of perspective taking. Children with ACEs commonly display symptoms that look and sound like familiar mental health diagnoses. From PTSD to Autism, and Generalized Anxiety to ADHD, children with ACEs develop mental health disorders more frequently than children without ACEs (Ackerman, Newton, McPherson, Jones, & Dykman, 1998). The most common mental health diagnoses for abused children (in order of frequency) are as follows:

1 Separation Anxiety Disorder
2 Oppositional Defiant Disorder
3 Phobic Disorders (anxiety)
4 Post-Traumatic Stress Disorder (PTSD)
5 Attention Deficit Hyperactive Disorder (ADHD)

(Ackerman et al., 1998)

As school counselors, we work with students daily who meet the criteria for one or many of these diagnoses. Having more than one diagnosis at a time is referred to as having comorbid diagnoses. Due to developmental delays caused by ACEs, comorbidity is common for traumatized children (van der Kolk, Roth, Pelcovitz, Sunday, & Spinazzola, 2005). In this section, we will cover some of the most common mental health diagnoses for children with ACEs, including attachment disorders, depression, anxiety, ADHD, Post-Traumatic Stress Disorder, and Learning Disabilities.

Attachment Theory

Central to a broad understanding of child development is an understanding of attachment. According to the landmark research study referred to as the "Strange Situation Test," there are three types of primary attachments among humans – secure, insecure resistant, and insecure avoidant (Ainsworth & Bell, 1970). To come to this conclusion, Ainsworth researched their attachments between mother and baby while they were together, while they were apart, and while they were in the presence of "strangers" (Figure 4.1).

Secure Attachment
- Distressed when separated from their mother
- Avoidant of strangers unless mother is present. When mother is present, friendly toward strangers.
- Happy to see their mother when she returns.
- Child plays and explores confidently when their mother is present

Insecure Avoidant Attachment
- Unphased when separated from their mother
- Infant is ok with strangers, plays and interacts with strangers regardless of mother's presence
- Seems uninterested when their mother returns.
- Both mother and stranger can soothe the child equally well.

Insecure Resistant Attachment
- Intensely distressed when separated from their mother
- Fearful of strangers
- Seems angry toward their mother when she returns, may even hit or push her.
- Cries more than other 2 attachment types

Figure 4.1 Children form one of three attachment styles with their primary caregiver (Rawson, 2019).

Infants who had a *secure attachment* to their mother were happy to be with her, would explore the play area freely and confidently, and would seem distressed when she left. The securely attached mothers were able to soothe the infant in a way that a stranger could not. Insecurely attached infants did not find the same comfort in their mother. They either seemed indifferent toward her or soothed by anyone. They did not seem to care about her presence (*insecure avoidant*) or they were hostile toward her (*insecure resistant*). Insecure resistant children avoided the mother's efforts to soothe them and seemed unusually fearful of strangers (Ainsworth & Bell, 1970).

This study formed the basis for an entire body of research about secure attachments during childhood. It is generally concluded that forming secure attachments to caregivers during infancy allows children to develop trust in themselves and others. Through these early secure attachments, they learn healthy communication and socialization skills, including how to rely on others for help. Developing these skills at an early age positively impacts the child's relationships both in youth and throughout their adult life (van der Kolk, 2005).

For children with ACEs, secure attachments between infants and caregivers do not form easily. When the caregivers are a direct source of stress (in the case of physical, emotional, or sexual abuse) or unavailable to soothe the infant's distress (due to addiction, mental illness, or neglect), this causes a breakdown of the secure attachment.

The infant cannot regulate their own emotions yet. And unfortunately for infants with ACEs, there may be no one to soothe them back to regulation.

When a caregiver is abusive one day while drunk, and kind and loving the next day, their children cannot comprehend what is happening or develop the logical sense of cause and effect. This inability to detect patterns in others' behavior creates a sense of helplessness and an inability to rely on others. Foster care or kinship care can also lead to poor attachment, specifically when a child is moved to multiple placements and lacks stability of environment (D'Andrea, Ford, Stolbach, Spinazzola, & van der Kolk, 2012). Due to their inability to rely on adults for emotion management, children with ACEs may become hyperaroused – constantly feeling threatened or on edge – or disassociated – not engaged in reality. They have difficulty "learning from experience" since their past experiences did not easily make patterns or sequences (van der Kolk, 2005).

By not forming a secure infancy attachment, many children with ACEs carry attachment difficulties with them to school, to work, and into their own adult relationships. Insecurely attached children with ACEs perceive threats where none exist and struggle to effectively regulate their emotions. They are also prone to social difficulties (D'Andrea et al., 2012). Social difficulties for children with ACEs include poor perspective taking, expectations of harm from others, inability to understand social norms, and poor boundaries.

Before their fourth birthday, Aiden and Evan had lived in four homes. After their mom was incarcerated, they lived with their dad, until he too was incarcerated. Grandma took the boys in until her home was deemed unacceptable due to a leaking roof, mold damage, and unsanitary conditions. When they arrived in foster care, their fourth placement in three years, the boys were hyperaroused. Living in fear of another transition, they were irritable, prone to tantrums, and struggled to be soothed.

Used by their biological parents as entertainment, the boys were frequently given alcohol and forced to fight with each other. As their parents and other adults watched and bet on the outcome of the fight, the boys experienced physical and emotional abuse. They had insecure resistant attachments to parents and to each other, cuddling together at night for safety and fighting each other during the day. Upon entering school, the boys were labeled aggressive, defiant, and manipulative. They had no basis for a secure attachment with their teacher and often cursed, screamed, and threw objects at her. When the boys used these same violent tactics on the playground, students were scared of them and their unpredictability. They struggled to make friends. The boys' resistant attachment and aggressive behavior was a stark contrast to most students' secure attachment and caring demeanor.

36 *Understand the Impact of Childhood Trauma*

These difficulties and feelings of isolation from peers may lead to further attachment and behavior difficulties at school. Lack of perspective taking is a common cause of playground conflicts and increased aggression. Behaving outside of social norms can lead to social rejection, avoidance, or withdrawal from friendships. Unfortunately, children with insecure attachments are often labeled as antisocial, withdrawn, manipulative, rebellious, oppositional, unmotivated, or lazy (van der Kolk, 2005).

Anxiety and Depression in Children with ACEs

Anxiety and depression are two of the most common mental illnesses among teens. According to the National Institute for Mental Health, 31.9% of adolescents aged 12–17 had an anxiety disorder, with 8.3% of these falling in the clinically significant range (National Institute of Mental Health, 2019). In 2017, 13.3% of the U.S. adolescent population had at least one major depressive episode, defined as a period lasting at least two weeks where a person exhibits the symptoms of major depressive disorder (National Institute of Mental Health, 2019). With statistics like these, school counselors must have a broad understanding of these mood disorders, how they are related to ACEs, and how to work with students who are experiencing symptoms (Figure 4.2).

Exposure to ACEs puts children and teens at-risk for major depressive disorder and/or generalized anxiety disorder (Avanci et al., 2012; Balistreri & Alvira-Hammond, 2016; Barber, Kohl, Kassam-Adams, & Gold, 2014). Among children aged 6–10 who had been exposed to family dysfunction and trauma, more than 10% had clinical depression, compared to less than 6% of the general population (Avanci et al., 2012). Teens who reported higher levels of ACEs were 9% more likely to report poor health and 32% more likely to report poor emotional health than their counterparts with no ACEs (Balistreri & Alvira-Hammond, 2016).

Erika lived with her mom in Indianapolis for most of her childhood. Growing up was not easy. Her mom struggled with drug abuse and was frequently neglectful. But at age 10, it got worse. Erika's mom began sending her to an uncle's house many nights each week while she got high. Erika's uncle sold her body to visitors each night. Man after man paid to have sex with her and Erika had no escape. Finally, after reporting what was happening to a teacher at school, Erika was removed from her uncle's care and placed in foster care. But her trauma wasn't over. She was diagnosed with clinical depression due to the sexual and emotional abuse. At school, Erika struggled to be a "normal teenager." She was highly defensive, distrusting of all adults, and struggled in social situations. She had anger outburst and was anxious around strangers. Erika developed a learning disability, lacked focus at school, and became addicted to drugs herself. Positive attachments in foster care, therapy, and medication are helping Erika cope with her depression and her past, but her road to recovery is long.

Mental Health   37

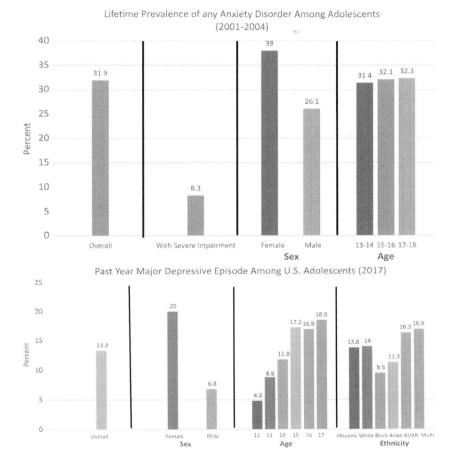

Figure 4.2 (a) 31.9% of adolescents aged 12–17 had an anxiety disorder (National Institute of Mental Health, 2019). (b) Depressive episode (National Institute of Mental Health, 2019).

In children, many symptoms of major depressive disorder are similar to symptoms of toxic stress. Symptoms that overlap include:

- Anger outbursts, irritability, and/or frustration over seemingly insignificant things.
- Withdrawal or loss of interest in previously pleasurable activities or hobbies.
- Sleep disturbances, including insomnia (hyperarousal) or sleeping too much.
- Anxiety, agitation, worry, or fear.

38   *Understand the Impact of Childhood Trauma*

- Slowed thinking and/or difficulty attending and concentrating in school.
- Feelings of worthlessness, fixating on past traumas/experiences.
- Frequent or recurrent thoughts of death, suicidal thoughts, suicide attempts, or suicide.
- Unexplained physical problems, such as stomachaches or headaches (somatization).

(Mayo Clinic, 2019a; National Child Traumatic
Stress Network, 2008)

Similarly, the symptoms of generalized anxiety disorder and toxic stress that overlap include:

- Disproportionate and persistent worrying or anxiety about events or people, including over-reactions to seemingly insignificant events (bells, alarms, physical touch, sudden movement, etc.).
- Overthinking plans and solutions, focusing on "worst-case" scenarios or details of past events.
- Perceiving situations, events, and/or people as threatening, even when they aren't.
- Inability to let go of a worry or thought.
- Restlessness, increase in physical activity level.
- Difficulty concentrating and paying attention, possibly leading to decreased academic performance and attendance issues.

(Mayo Clinic, 2019b; National Child Traumatic
Stress Network, 2008)

Child and adolescent anxiety and depression are also associated with lower academic performance. High levels of anxiety and depression increase students' worry about both home and school-related concerns, leading to lack of concentration and difficulty test-taking (Owens, Stevenson, Hadwin, & Norgate, 2012). Excessive worry from depression and anxiety decreases working memory, causing difficulties in learning, retaining, and recalling information when needed (Owens et al., 2012).

One of the most severe symptoms of anxiety, depression, and ACE exposure is suicidality and suicidal thoughts. In the original 1998 ACE study, exposure to ACEs was linked to an increased risk for suicide attempts. Exposure to two or more ACEs puts someone at three times the risk for a suicide attempt than someone with no ACEs and exposure to more than four ACEs increases the risk 12 times as much as no exposure (Felitti et al., 1998). Currently, suicide is the second leading cause of death for children, teens, and young adults aged 10–24 in the U.S. (National Institute of Mental Health, 2019). There is no data available from NIMH about suicidal thoughts of teens, but suicidal thoughts are higher for young adults aged 18–24 than any other adult age group. 10.8% of young adults aged 18–24 have thought about suicide within the last year (National Institute of Mental Health, 2019).

Mental Health   39

While these statistics are both shocking and tragic, it comes as no surprise to us counselors. Within schools, counselors are on the front lines of suicidal crises. We regularly work with students who are at-risk for a suicide attempt and who disclose suicidal ideation. Thankfully, many evidence-based strategies exist to help students find healthier coping skills and diminish suicidal thoughts. Later in the book, we will discuss preventative work to reduce the likelihood of suicide attempts among teens.

Post-traumatic Stress Disorder

The disorder having the most overlapping symptoms with toxic stress is Post-traumatic Stress Disorder (PTSD) (D'Andrea et al., 2012). The overlap includes:

Intrusive Memories

- Recurrent, unwanted, or disturbing memories, dreams and thoughts of the traumatic event.
- Severe emotional distress or physical reactions to something that reminds you of the traumatic event, including specific people, places, objects, and sounds (slamming doors, sirens, etc.).

Avoidance

- Trying to avoid thinking or talking about the traumatic event, seeming to be "emotionally numb" to the event.
- Avoiding places, activities, or people that remind you of the traumatic event.

Negative Changes in Thinking and Mood

- Negative thoughts about yourself, other people or the world, including wanting revenge, difficulty with authority or redirection, and distrust of others.
- Memory problems, including not remembering important aspects of the traumatic event.
- Difficulty maintaining relationships, withdrawal from family and friends.
- Lack of interest in activities and hobbies you once enjoyed, changes in academic performance.
- Difficulty experiencing positive emotions, tendency toward hopelessness, anger and irritability.

Changes in Physical and Emotional Reactions

- Being easily startled or frightened.
- Worried about the recurrence of trauma (hyperarousal).
- Self-destructive behavior, such as substance abuse, cutting and/or suicidal ideation.

40 *Understand the Impact of Childhood Trauma*

- Trouble sleeping.
- Trouble concentrating.
- Irritability, angry outbursts, or aggressive behavior.
- Overwhelming guilt or shame.

(Mayo Clinic, 2019c; National Child Traumatic
Stress Network, 2008)

Due to their symptom similarities, researchers, including Bessel van der Kolk, sought to answer the question "Do all children with toxic stress from ACEs have PTSD? Or are there differences between PTSD and the post-ACE experience?" (van der Kolk et al., 2005).

Many psychiatrists argue that PTSD is a diagnosis appropriate for any survivor of trauma who experiences psychological distress following the trauma, whether the trauma is one-time or continuous (as is the case for ACEs). In his book *The Body Keeps the Score,* van der Kolk suggests that PTSD is not a developmentally accurate diagnosis for children with ACEs because it does not describe the ways in which ACEs affect the developing brain. He believes that PTSD only accurately describes the way trauma affects a fully developed adult brain (van der Kolk, 2005).

A diagnosis of PTSD due to ACEs does not take into consideration disrupted attachment patterns, loss of ambition and independent motivation, psychosomatic concerns (increased stomachaches, headaches, etc.), lack of awareness of danger and feelings of self-blame. Additionally, many ACEs do not fit the official definition of "trauma" required for a PTSD diagnosis, which includes "actual or threatened death or serious injury, or a threat to the physical integrity of the self or others" (van der Kolk, 2005, p. 6). Students who experience the toxic stress of ACEs may not always have their life in danger, but they are affected by trauma nonetheless.

In schools, PTSD is not commonly addressed. PTSD symptoms are often exhibited outside of the school environment. Some students with PTSD can regulate more normally at school than at home (Perkins & Graham-Berrman, 2012). Other diagnoses such as emotional disturbance are more commonly associated with ACEs and child abuse in the school environment (Perkins & Graham-Berrman, 2012).

Fortunately, due to the large number of overlapping symptoms, the interventions for children with PTSD (or emotional disturbance) are generally effective for children exposed to ACEs (van der Kolk et al., 2005). Interventions focused on resolving attachment disruptions, teaching self-regulation skills, and addressing emotional dysregulation due to trauma can be beneficial for children exposed to ACEs regardless if they have a PTSD diagnosis or not (van der Kolk, 2005).

ADHD and Other Behavioral Concerns

In 2016, 9.4% of the U.S. children had a diagnosis of Attention Deficit Hyperactive Disorder (ADHD). This represents 6.1 million children aged 2–17 (Centers for Disease Control and Prevention, 2019). ADHD is the most

Mental Health   41

diagnosed childhood neurodevelopmental disorder. It is generally diagnosed for children during elementary school. Two-thirds of the time it is diagnosed comorbidly with another emotional, psychological, or behavioral disorder (Centers for Disease Control and Prevention, 2019). ADHD is a chronic disorder characterized by a person's inability to focus and concentrate on tasks due to impulsivity, hyperactivity, or distractibility.

Educators know that ADHD is a frequent topic of lunchroom conversation. Whether its complaining about a parent's denial of their child's symptoms, discussing which prescription ADHD medication is best, or generally labeling students as "so ADHD," the nonchalance with which ADHD is discussed can be disturbing. This dismissiveness about ADHD as a serious medical diagnosis has led to a disturbingly high rate of overdiagnosis especially among children with ACEs (D'Andrea et al., 2012; Elder, 2010). According to Elder (2010), nearly 20% of all ADHD diagnosis may be incorrect, due to subjective factors such as teacher's perception of immaturity of the student due to relative age within the class.

ADHD is commonly diagnosed for children with ACEs due to its symptoms, many of which deal with pre-frontal cortex limitations (Jimenez, Wade Jr., Schwartz-Soicher, Lin, & Reichman, 2017). In their study of 1,572 urban children, Jimenez et al. found ACE exposure before the age of 5 and between the ages of 5 and 9 to be highly associated with an ADHD diagnosis at age 9. Both children with ADHD and children with ACEs may present with disrupted executive functions, difficulty planning ahead, an inability to concentrate, memory disturbance, and hyperactivity (D'Andrea et al., 2012).

Children with ACEs may be unable to focus in class due to fears about their own safety, recurring thoughts of trauma, or anxiety about the wellbeing of others. They also commonly disassociate from their immediate environment if they find it emotionally overwhelming. This can look very similar to ADHD inattentive type due to the distractibility, inability to complete tasks, and difficulty processing information presented by the teacher (Cole, O'Brien, Gadd, Wallace, & Gregory, 2005). Even though students who disassociate due to trauma may not upset the classroom environment the way a more hyperactive or aggressive student does, they are likely not engaged in the learning and therefore will struggle more academically (Steele, 2017). Here are a few studies that have corroborated this evidence that ACEs lead to difficulty with concentration and learning:

- Abused children demonstrated poorer executive functioning skills compared to non-abused children even in emotionally neutral environments and tasks (Reider & Cicchetti, 1989).
- Executive functioning diminished among maltreated children when they were primed for aggression prior to a task (Reider & Cicchetti, 1989).
- Abused children perform worse on neuropsychological tests of attention and concentration (Porter, Lawson, & Bigler, 2005).
- Physical abuse is associated with diverting attention from seemingly threatening stimuli in neutral contexts (e.g. students disengage in academically challenging classes even when abuse happened at home) (Pine et al., 2005).

42 *Understand the Impact of Childhood Trauma*

- Compared to a control group, abused and neglected children showed weaker auditory attention and visual motor integration (Nolin & Ethier, 2007).
- Maltreated children are less able to problem solve than their non-maltreated peers (Ayoub et al., 2006).

In addition to poor concentration and focus, ADHD is typically characterized by impulsivity and over-reactivity. Both ACEs and ADHD impair areas of the pre-frontal cortex, which manages self-regulation. Traumatized children often overreact when they are reminded of the trauma in some way, even through seemingly minor situations or remarks (Cole et al., 2005). In the classroom, this may look like a "0 to 60" kid who has explosive behaviors such as flipping desks, screaming, hitting, or eloping.

Darrian was one of the youngest kindergarteners in his class. He never went preschool. The first day of kindergarten was so overwhelming to him; he ran from the playground out the school gate – headed straight for home. Darrian was afraid of school. Daily, he went into fight-or-flight mode by engaging in explosive verbal and physical outbursts.

Before kindergarten, Darrian's father was arrested and sent to jail for domestic violence toward Darrian's mother. Darrian saw it all. Darrian's mother was dealing with her own mental health struggles due to the violence, so Darrian lived with his grandmother. Darrian was quickly diagnosed with ADHD and PTSD due to his past trauma, impulsivity, hyperarousal, and distrust of others.

Currently, the best practice for diagnosing ADHD is to use symptom checklists and behavioral observations. There is no discussion of underlying biology or trauma exposure (Harris, 2018). Using this system of observations, children with four or more ACEs are 32.6 times more likely to be diagnosed with a learning or behavior problem (most commonly ADHD) than children with 0 ACEs (Harris, 2018). Dr. Nadine Burke Harris is currently the Surgeon General of California and a huge advocate for universal pediatric medical screenings for ACEs. According to Dr. Harris, knowing the ACE score of her patients makes her a better doctor as she considers more than just "run-of-the-mill ADHD" as the cause for her patients' difficulties in school (Harris, 2018, p. 61).

Does Darrian truly have ADHD? Until policies change and doctors are required to search for causes deeper than observable symptoms, we may never know. So how does the ADHD diagnosis serve Darrian? This question will be answered with time. For some students, a diagnosis may open doors for additional interventions that lead to positive outcomes. For others, inappropriately prescribed medications can lead to worsening symptoms and frustration for children and caregivers.

No matter the diagnosis, we must look deeper. What is beneath the behavior?

How we address the root of the problem is more important than how we minimize the symptoms.

SPED Eligibility: Learning Disabilities, Language Deficits, and Cognitive Delays

Jackson loved football. He loved to run, climb, play, kick, throw – basically anything active and outdoors. He was the tetherball champion at recess and frequently beat much older students at the game. On the playground, he was king, but in the classroom, he was not. In 3rd grade, he was reading at a 1st-grade level, not even high enough to be grouped with the lowest readers in his grade. He couldn't sit still. Constantly bouncing, moving, tapping, and fidgeting, he disrupted class constantly. His social awareness was lacking and he was often sent to the principal's office for bullying, fighting, and insulting other students. Due to his office visits, he missed valuable class time and opportunities for positive socialization. Many teachers dismissed his symptoms as "so ADHD" and told him "you just need to learn to behave." But what was causing these academic and behavioral challenges? It was ACEs.

Jackson's mother abandoned him at a young age. He was raised by his dad who suffered a traumatic work accident leaving him injured and less able to care for Jackson. Jackson's stepmom was trying her best to work, go to college, and raise Jackson, while also taking care of Jackson's injured father. Home was not a warm and caring place. His father was dismissive of his learning needs, emotionally abusive and neglectful. He frequently came to school dirty and without needed supplies.

Jackson qualified for special education due to his ADHD diagnosis and a specific learning disability in 3rd grade. Since getting the academic and behavioral help he needed, his behavior, mood, and peer relationships have all improved.

One fundamental question about ACEs and disabilities is which causes which. Are disabled children more likely to experience ACEs, or do ACEs lead to disabilities? We may never be able to fully answer this question, but one thing is certain: Maltreatment and intellectual disabilities are linked. Thirty-one percent of students receiving special education (SPED) services are maltreated compared to less than 10% of students without SPED services (Sullivan & Knutson, 2000). Specific disabilities are even more positively associated with ACEs:

- Students with intellectual disabilities (formerly called mental retardation) are four times more likely to be a victim of abuse or neglect.
- Students with behavior disorders (referred to in SPED as emotionally disturbed) are seven times more likely to have experienced neglect or abuse.
- And students with a speech and language impairment have five times the risk for neglect and abuse as compared to their nondisabled peers.

(Sullivan & Knutson, 2000)

According to a 2004 study of 7,940 low-income children in the St. Louis area, while controlling for socioeconomic and medical factors, child maltreatment

44 Understand the Impact of Childhood Trauma

predicted eligibility for SPED services (Jonson-Reid, Drake, Kim, Porterfield, & Han, 2004). In the same study, Johnson-Reid et al. (2004) found that chronic abuse and neglect had a dose-response relationship to the risk of entry into SPED services. This means that for every report of maltreatment, the risk increased. In their study, the risk of entry into special education increased 7% for every reported instance of maltreatment prior to age 8.

Students with ACEs also commonly develop language impairments or delays due to dysfunctional home environments where expressive and receptive language is not learned at an early age (Perkins & Graham-Berrman, 2012). Language-impaired children may also exhibit symptoms that look like ADHD or Autism Spectrum Disorder due to the following common symptoms:

- Difficulties understanding emotions and social situations
- Aggression and frustration from an inability to communicate
- Withdrawal and low-self-esteem
- Hyperactivity and inattention
- Reading disabilities

(Perkins & Graham-Berrman, 2012)

While trauma is not a criterion for eligibility into special education, many of the symptoms of ACEs are criteria for eligibility. Difficulties with visual or auditory processing, academic performance significantly below the grade level, diagnosed mental illness or behavioral conditions and language impairments are all commonly associated with ACEs and would be considered eligible criteria for SPED services (Jonson-Reid et al., 2004).

Alex met the school counselor the third day of first grade. When he told his teacher "My dad spit on my mom last night. I couldn't sleep because she was crying," the teacher immediately called for help. CPS reports were filed, counseling services were put in place, but Alex's struggles were just beginning. Months went by, his reports of domestic violence grew more frequent and by mid-fall, even daily visits to the counselor's office couldn't turn off his "fight-or-flight" mode. Alex struggled academically and socially. He would frequntly elope from class, throw items off his desk, yell, kick, hit other students, and sob uncontrollably. He was more than a year behind his peers in reading and his attention span was minimal.

The school counselor didn't know if Alex fit the criteria for special education. What she did know was that in the general education classroom, Alex was not learning, not making friends and not comfortable. After collaborating with his classroom teacher, parent, and the school's resource specialist, Alex was referred for a psychoeducational evaluation.

Through the assessment, it was determined that Alex exhibited symptoms of ADHD and Emotional Disturbance that impeded his learning. His ACEs contributed to his developmental and mental health disorders. After the evaluation, Alex was placed more appropriately in a smaller, special education class where he recieved the individualized attention, theraputic services, and behavior modifications he needed for success.

Mental Health   45

Low academic achievement is frequently associated with ACEs and child maltreatment. According to McLean, Taylor, and O'Donnell (2016), 27.8% of children in their study who were involved with child protection services had low reading achievement. This was more than three times the low reading achievement of their non-maltreated peers. Even more significant, specific types of maltreatment, including sexual abuse and neglect, led to 50% increased risk of low reading achievement (McLean, Taylor, & O'Donnell, 2016). A history of maltreatment and adversity is also associated with lower standardized test scores and overall IQ scores (Cook, Blaustein, Spinazzola, & van der Kolk, 2003).

This low academic achievement in the early years is linked to poor educational outcomes in the long term. High school students with ACEs and behavioral challenges at school are 2.5 times more likely to drop out of high school than their peers without ACEs (Porche, Fortuna, Lin, & Alegria, 2011). Detention and suspension further the likelihood of dropout from school. Behaviors such as aggression, hyperactivity, distrust of authority, and disengagement can lead to exclusion from the learning environment.

Students of color with both trauma exposure and a diagnosable mental illness are at an even higher risk for dropout. African American students with conduct disorders and Afro-Caribbean students with depressive disorders are more likely to drop out than their non-Latino White peers with similar adversity and mental illnesses. Latino students with anxiety disorders are also more likely to drop out than non-Latino whites with a similar history (Porche, Fortuna, Lin, & Alegria, 2011).

> Unfortunately, many educators are not well versed on psychological conditions. They may interpret symptoms of anxiety, depression or conduct disorders as laziness, disrespect or lack of interest in school.

When symptoms are assumed to be based on student choices, educators may not refer the students to special education, counseling, or other necessary services which aim to prevent further academic declines and dropout (Porche, Fortuna, Lin, & Alegria, 2011).

References

Ackerman, P., Newton, J., McPherson, W., Jones, J., & Dykman, R. (1998). Prevalence of Post-traumatic Stress Disorder and Other Psychiaric Diagnoses in Three Groups of Abused Children (Sexual, Physical and Both). *Child Abuse, 22*(8), 759–774.

Ainsworth, M. D., & Bell, S. (1970). Attachment, Exploration, and Separation: Illustrated by the Behavior of One-Year-Olds in a Strange Situation. *Child Development, 41*(1), 49–67. doi:10.2307/1127388

Avanci, J., Assis, S., Oliveira, R., & Pires, T. (2012). Childhood Depression: Exploring the Association between Family Violence and Other Psychosocial Factors in Low-Income Brazilian Schoolchildren. *Child and Adolescent Psychiatry and Mental Health, 6*(26), 26. Retrieved from https://capmh.biomedcentral.com/articles/10.1186/1753-2000-6-26

46 Understand the Impact of Childhood Trauma

Ayoub, C. C., O'Connor, E., Rappolt-Schlichtmann, G., Fischer, K. W., Rogosch, F. A., Toth, S. L., & Cicchetti, D. (2006). Cognitive and Emotional Differences in Young Maltreated Children: A Translational Application of Dyamic Skill Theory. *Development and Psychopathology, 18*(3), 679–706.

Balistreri, K., & Alvira-Hammond, M. (2016). Adverse Childhood Experiences: Family Functioning and Adolescent Health and Emotional Well-Being. *Public Health, 132*, 72–78. doi:10.1016/j.puhe.2015.10.034

Barber, B. A., Kohl, K. L., Kassam-Adams, N., & Gold, J. I. (2014). Acute Stress, Depression, and Anxiety Symptoms among English and Spanish Speaking Children with Recent Trauma Exposure. *Journal of Clinical Psychology in Medical Settings, 21*(1), 66–71. doi:10.1007/s10880-013-9382-z

Centers for Disease Control and Prevention. (2019). *Data and Statistics about ADHD.* Retrieved from Centers for Disease Control and Prevention: www.cdc.gov/ncbddd/adhd/data.html

Cole, S., O'Brien, J., Gadd, M. R., Wallace, D., & Gregory, M. (2005). *Helping Traumatized Children Learn: Supportive School Environments for Children Traumatized by Family Violence.* Boston, MA: Massachusetts Advocates for Children and Harvard Law School, Trauma and Learning Policy Initiative.

Cook, A., Blaustein, M., Spinazzola, J., & van der Kolk, B. (2003). *Complex Trauma in Children and Adolescents.* Retrieved from National Child Traumatic Stress Network: www.nctsn.org/sites/default/files/resources//complex_trauma_in_children_and_adolescents.pdf

D'Andrea, W., Ford, J., Stolbach, B., Spinazzola, J., & van der Kolk, B. (2012). Understanding Interpersonal Trauma in Children: Why We Need a Developmentally Appropriate Trauma Diagnosis. *Journal of Orthopsychiatry, 82*(2), 187–200.

Elder, T. (2010). The Importance of Relative Standards in ADHD Diagnoses: Evidence Based on Exact Birthdates. *Journal of Health Economics, 29*, 641–656.

Felitti, V., Anda, R., Nordenberg, D., Williamson, D., Spitz, A., Edwards, V., … Marks, J. (1998). Relationship of Childhood Abuse and Household Dysfunction to Many of the Leading Causes of Death in Adults: The Adverse Childhood Experience (ACE) Study. *American Journal of Preventative Medicine, 14*(4), 245–258. Retrieved from www.ajpmonline.org/article/S0749-3797(98)00017-8/pdf

Harris, N. B. (2018). *The Deepest Well: Healing the Long-Term Effects of Childhood Adversity.* New York, NY: Houghton Mifflin Harcourt.

Jimenez, M. E., Wade Jr., R., Schwartz-Soicher, O., Lin, Y., & Reichman, N. (2017). Adverse Childhood Experiences and ADHD Diagnosis at Age 9 Years in a National Urban Sample. *American Pediatrics, 17*(4), 356–361.

Jonson-Reid, M., Drake, B., Kim, J., Porterfield, S., & Han, L. (2004). A Prospective Analysis of the Relationship between Maltreatment and Special Education Eligibility among Poor Children. *Child Maltreatment, 9*(4), 382–394.

Mayo Clinic. (2019a). *Depression (Major Depressive Disorder).* Retrieved from Mayo Clinic: www.mayoclinic.org/diseases-conditions/depression/symptoms-causes/syc-20356007

Mayo Clinic. (2019b). *Generalized Anxiety Disorder.* Retrieved from Mayo Clinic: www.mayoclinic.org/diseases-conditions/generalized-anxiety-disorder/symptoms-causes/syc-20360803

Mayo Clinic. (2019c). *Post-traumatic Stress Disorder.* Retrieved from Mayo CLinic: www.mayoclinic.org/diseases-conditions/post-traumatic-stress-disorder/symptoms-causes/syc-20355967

McLean, M., Taylor, C., & O'Donnell, M. (2016). Pre-existing Adversity, Level of Child Protection Involvement, and School Attendance Predict Educational Outcomes in a Longitudinal Study. *Child Abuse and Neglect, 51*, 120–131.

National Child Traumatic Stress Network. (2008). *Child Trauma Toolkit for Educators*. Retrieved from National Child Raumatic Stress Network: www.nctsn.org/sites/default/files/resources//child_trauma_toolkit_educators.pdf

National Institute of Mental Health. (2019). *National Institute of Mental Health Statistics*. Retrieved from National Institute of Mental Health: www.nimh.nih.gov/health/statistics/index.shtml

Nolin, P., & Ethier, L. (2007). Using Neuropsychological Profiles to Classify Neglected Children with or without Physical Abuse. *Child Abuse and Neglect, 31*, 631–643.

Owens, M., Stevenson, J., Hadwin, J., & Norgate, R. (2012). Anxiety and Depression in Academic Performance: An Exploration of the Mediating Factors of Worry and Working Memory. *School Psychology International, 33*, 433–449. doi:10.1177/0143034311427433.

Perkins, S., & Graham-Berrman, S. (2012). Violence Exposure and the Development of School Related Functioning: Mental-Health, Neurocognition and Learning. *Agression and Violent Behavior, 17*(1), 89–98.

Pine, D., Mogg, K., Bradley, B., Montgomery, L., Monk, C., McClure, E., … Kaufman, J. (2005). Attention Bias to Threat in Maltreated Children: Implications for Vulnerability to Stress-Related Psychopathology. *American Journal of Psychiatry, 162*, 291–296.

Porche, M., Fortuna, L., Lin, J., & Alegria, M. (2011). Childhood Trauma and Psychiatric Disorders as Correlates of School Dropout in a National Sample of Young Adults. *Child Development, 82*(3), 982–998.

Porter, C., Lawson, J., & Bigler, E. (2005). Neurobehavioral Sequelae of Child Sexual Abuse. *Child Neuropsychology, 11*, 203–220.

Reider, C., & Cicchetti, D. (1989). Organizational Perspective on Cognitive Control Functioning and Cognitive-Affective Balance in Maltreated Children. *Developmental Psychology, 25*, 382–393.

Steele, W. (2017). *Optimizing Learning Outcomes: Proven Brain-Centric Trauma-Sensitive Practices*. New York, NY: Routledge.

Sullivan, P., & Knutson, J. (2000). Maltreatment and Disabilities: A Population-Based Epidemiological Study. *Child Abuse and Neglect, 24*(10), 1257–1273.

van der Kolk, B. (2005). Developmental Trauma Disorder. *Psychiatric Annals, 35*, 401–408. Retrieved from Traumatic Stress Institute: https://traumaticstressinstitute.org/wp-content/files_mf/1276541701VanderKolkDvptTraumaDis.pdf

van der Kolk, B., Roth, S., Pelcovitz, D., Sunday, S., & Spinazzola, J. (2005). Disorders of Extreme Stress: The Empirical Foundation of a Complex Adaptation to Trauma. *Journal of Traumatic Stress, 18*, 389–399. Retrieved from www.traumacenter.org/products/pdf_files/specialissuecomplextraumaoct2006jts3.pdf

5   The Role of a Trauma-Sensitive School [NRI] Counselor

From 2010 to 2020, the healthcare field took an increasingly larger role in raising awareness about ACEs and their impact on physical health and mental well-being. Organizations like the CDC, Center for Youth Wellness, and the American Association of Pediatrics are championing the cause of preventing ACEs and reducing the impact of trauma. More recently joined by big names in the education field like the National Education Association and the U.S. Department of Education – Office of Safe and Healthy Students, the movement is growing. But this broad policy push doesn't always look like the reality in the local doctor's office or neighborhood elementary school.

School counselors along with teachers, nurses, pediatricians, and childcare providers must work daily to bring well-intentioned policies to life. Through our unique role in the education system, school counselors have a broad impact on bringing ACE awareness to schools. As bridge-builders between mental health/community services and education, we bring knowledge about ACEs to our work and improve collaboration. As student advocates, we use our voice, influence, and collaborative support to improve outcomes for our traumatized students. And as staff trainers, school counselors educate others about ACEs and their impact on students. Broad awareness, advocacy, and collaborative efforts create a meaningful and lasting change.

School Counselors Are Bridge-Builders

Many doctors are still diagnosing Attention Deficit Hyperactive Disorder (ADHD) and other behavioral conditions based on symptoms checklists without ever discussing trauma history or doing a physical check-up (Harris, 2018). The disconnect between ACEs as the potential cause of behavior problems and the challenging behavioral symptoms that ensue only grows when a misdiagnosis enters the mix.

In schools, there is often no direct connection to the healthcare field. Many schools have only one school nurse *per district*. This person typically oversees LPNs or CNAs at the school sites who serve as health clerks. These health clerks are inundated with the day-to-day needs of sick children and can't always collaborate or participate in larger decisions about student's educational needs. Schools rely on the written recommendations of pediatricians, outside

The Role of a Trauma-Sensitive School   49

of the educational sector, when considering educational accommodations and interventions for students. For a diagnosis like anxiety, depression, post-traumatic stress disorder (PTSD), or ADHD, students need someone who can understand both the medical and educational needs of the student.

What if school counselors could bridge this gap? As professional student advocates with an understanding of how biology affects learning, school counselors are well positioned to consider and recommend alterative explanations for students' educational difficulties. What if they aren't lazy, but instead tired because they sleep each night on the floor? What if she isn't defiant, but instead frightened and protecting herself? Without any background knowledge of ACEs and ACE science, teachers and administrators may be reluctant to see the connection between trauma and learning. But with our scientific knowledge, we can explain to our site administration and staff not just *that* ACEs impact students, or *how* ACEs impact students, but WHY.

Having basic knowledge of how trauma biologically predisposes students to difficulty at school puts us in a league of our own. Just like being the only one who knows how the sound system works in the multipurpose room. But better. When student's behavioral concerns can be discussed in a scientifically accurate way, instead of in terms of volition ("he just wants the negative attention!"), we are more likely to make progress toward truly addressing the student's needs. Advocacy for counseling interventions, more brain-based learning strategies, and less suspensions is only possible through an ability to articulate WHY students have challenging behaviors. It is due to their trauma.

The science is irrefutable. No one can say "well I think he was too young to remember what happened. It can't affect him now" or "Well, that happened at home. This is school. She should know she's fine here." Or "They know right from wrong. They just don't want to do the right thing." These statements are not backed by evidence and in fact the research on toxic stress proves the opposite.

- FACT: Even infants are affected by trauma they will never remember (Harris, 2018).
- FACT: What happens at home affects children's ability to function in every other environment (Harris, 2018).
- FACT: Even though students know right from wrong, they can't always apply it when they are in a state of constant stress (Harris, 2018).

Understanding ACE science also allows counselors to make stronger connections with families. Parents or guardians of children with ACEs need to know how their child's brain may be different due to past experiences. Many adults who I have trained during parent workshops or staff development later come to me and say "I never knew why I _____, but now I do." We could fill in the blank with so many things – overeating, smoking, addiction to exercise, quick to anger, struggling reader. Helping adults make connections in their own lives will, in turn, help children.

50 *Understand the Impact of Childhood Trauma*

A Psychologically Healthier Adult Can Be a More Effective Parent or Educator

A background in ACE science allows school counselors to work closely with other health and wellness support staff like school nurses and school psychologists. Collaborating with the school nurse is a great way to get a pulse on which kids may be impacted by trauma. Students who frequently go to the nurse with issues like stomachache or headache may have more psychosomatic concerns than true health conditions. Remember: Dysregulated cortisol can make kids feel sick, even when they aren't (Johnson, Riley, Granger, & Riis, 2013).

Working together with school nurses, counselors can address the possibility of connections between behavior and physical ailments with parents. Could Sara's stomachaches be caused by anxiety? Liam gets sick easily, could he have a suppressed immune system? Alex falls asleep in class, what might be putting him "on high alert" at home? Being able to ask the right questions leads to finding the right answers. It also gives parents ideas and questions to bring to their child's pediatrician, helping the pediatrician think from a trauma-sensitive lens as well.

School Counselors Are Student Advocates

While everyone would agree that the main goal of a school is to academically educate its students, there is a growing consensus that the responsibility of the school is farther reaching than just teaching reading and math. School at its most basic level is a 13-year learning program where students are categorized into peer groups. This is both social and academic in nature. In the past, schools focused much more on the academic aspects of the program than the social. But recently, social and emotional learning (SEL) is growing in popularity. Schools have a responsibility to provide a free and equitable education to all students, and while some come to school ready to learn, many do not. Schools must fill the gap between where students are and where they need to be – using both academic and social/emotional interventions.

School Counselors Must Advocate for Social-Emotional Interventions and Mental Health Services

While the desire to fully integrate academics and social/emotional well-being in schools is shared by many educators, making this desire a reality is a challenge (Atkins, Hoagwood, Kutash, & Seidman, 2010). More than 70% of children who access mental health or behavioral health services do so through their school. Most of these services are "pull-out" services and compete with academic time by removing students from class to meet their emotional needs. This system leaves students potentially more disengaged from their social and academic peer group.

There is limited research to back the effectiveness of pull-out mental health therapy services within the school environment (Atkins et al., 2010). A more

The Role of a Trauma-Sensitive School   51

effective strategy is a comprehensive integration of mental health in schools –
through preventative work like teaching core SEL competencies within the
classroom, enhancing mental health support structures, and building leadership capacity of school counselors and teachers who already work within the
school (Atkins et al., 2010).

As school counselors, we have a graduate-level education on developing and
maintaining comprehensive school counseling programs. Integrated school/
mental health programs like the one developed by Atkins et al. (2010) fit very
well into the ASCA National Model for a school counseling program. Both
programs emphasize teaching a core SEL curriculum to all students. Both
create a system of interventions to address student needs based on data and
evidence (American School Counselor Association, 2019).

Due to the universal nature of ACEs, using trauma-sensitive practices in
conjunction with a comprehensive school counseling program is an essential
to meet the mental health needs of students. Educators mitigate the effects of
trauma by making connections with students, teaching self-regulation, and
using educational best practices within their classrooms and offices.

School Counselors Must Advocate for Students with Disabilities

On a more personal level, school counselors must advocate for students with
ACEs, learning disabilities, and mental illnesses. By challenging a teacher's
punitive discipline philosophy or their assumption about the motives of a student, counselors advocate for the possibility that ACEs are a factor. We advocate for the opportunity to think beyond what is seen on the surface and into
what lies underneath. By asking the right questions at the right time, counselors help teachers think about ACEs role in a student's education. Students
with ACEs can access extra assistance and help schools accommodate for their
students with mental illnesses, learning disabilities, and behavioral challenges.
While school counseling is not a replacement for long-term mental health
therapy, many school counselors directly support students with mental illness
on a short-term basis. In small groups or as an intermediary before long-term
therapy begins, school counselors provide a safe space for these students.

School Counselors Must Advocate for the Connection between
ACEs and Student Behavior

Some days, the job of a school counselor feels like a professional meeting goer.
From IEP meetings to student study teams, intervention planning to 504s, we
are inundated with requests to discuss students and their educational progress. But we are more than meeting goers. We can use these meetings as an
opportunity to connect the dots between ACEs and student learning. What
better way to advocate for students than to reframe the conversations in these
meetings. Is student behavior "their own bad choice?" If so, the logical answer
is "There's nothing we can do to fix it." But what if we presented another

52 *Understand the Impact of Childhood Trauma*

option. "I think the behavior may be outside their control. I know we can help in so many ways." Framing behavior through its basis in trauma can also move discipline from punitive to preventative.

Questions we ask could sound like:

- How will special education testing help Kiara feel welcomed in her classroom?
- Will threatening retention really increase Patrick's motivation in school?
- If Landon loses recess for the rest of this month, in what way will that positively change his playground behavior?
- What impact will isolating Kaliyah's desk in the classroom have on her ability to self-regulate?

Proposed interventions like special education testing, isolation, detention, or retention COULD re-traumatize a student with existing ACEs and make the undesired behavior become more frequent or more intense. The best interests of students are our number one priority in these meetings. As school counselors, we are not bound by parent perceptions, teachers union demands, special education financing, or any other barriers that weigh on administrators.

We can disrupt the status quo and wonder aloud if there might be a better way.

Here are the possibilities we could present instead of the punitive discipline or special education:

- What would it look like to include Kiara in differentiated learning groups inside her classroom?
- How might goal setting increase Patrick's motivation positively instead of the negative motivator of threatening retention?
- What skills is Landon lacking on the playground? How can he be taught these skills and encouraged to implement them while playing?
- What are some of Kaliyah's triggers in the classroom? How can we remove these triggers and increase her perception of safety without removing her?

School Counselors Are Staff Trainers

One way school counselors can bridge the gap between ACEs research and the school is to provide staff development on ACEs. A thorough training should include

1 What are ACEs? How prevalent are they?
2 What is the impact of ACEs on students at school?
3 How and why do ACEs impact learning (impact of ACEs on the developing brain)?
4 What can we as a school staff do to improve outcomes for students with ACEs?

The Role of a Trauma-Sensitive School   53

All of these training components are necessary, but one stands out as a typical "favorite" for teachers. Explaining how ACEs affect the brain and, in turn, affect learning is a lightbulb moment for many educators. It connects the dots between challenging behaviors and students' personal lives. It gives teachers rationale for proposed trauma-sensitive interventions and motivation to attempt them. Equipping teachers with evidence-based interventions is great but explaining why they work – using brain science – is magic. Teachers feel empowered and are more likely to use the strategies when they understand why the strategies work.

- Is a "calm-down corner" just a nice idea, or does it give students extra time to engage their pre-frontal cortex in planning and reflection?
- Are movement breaks just fun or does the sensory input balance out any dysfunction in the cerebellar vermis?

Using brain science gives rationale and purpose to your strategies and your work.

While this book gives basic information about how ACEs affect student learning, training resources are available to school counselors who want to go deeper. One such resource is the Trauma Learning and Policy Initiative (TLPI), www.traumasensitiveschools.org. A collaborative effort between Harvard Law School and Massachusetts Advocates for Children, TLPI's mission is "to ensure that children traumatized by exposure to family violence and other adverse childhood experiences succeed in school" (Trauma Learning and Policy Initiative, n.d.). TLPI provides resources for schools, including *Helping Traumatized Children Learn*, Volumes 1 and 2. These policy reports are also program guides for educators to implement whole-school, trauma-sensitive programs. The inquiry-based process set forth in these reports helps guide schools toward gaining a critical mass of staff support and transforming their culture for the long term (Cole, O'Brien, Gadd, Wallace, & Gregory, 2005). Reading through these TLPI reports and discussing them with administrators provide an excellent foundation for counselor-developed staff training on ACEs. Additionally, the U.S. Department of Education in conjunction with the American Institutes for Research offers a Trauma Sensitive Schools Training Package through the National Center on Safe Supportive Learning Environments, https:// safesupportivelearning.ed.gov/trauma-sensitive-schools-training-package.

School counselors can reach out to other local and state resources like state departments of education and county offices of education for trauma-sensitive trainings in their local area. For example, the San Diego County office of Education provides "Trauma Informed Practices in Schools" Training: www.sdcoe.net/student-services/student-support/Documents/Trauma %20Informed%20Practices%20for%20Schools%20(TIPS)%20training%20information.pdf, and the Office of the Superintendent of Public Instruction (OSPI) in Washington State provides Compassionate Schools Training: www.k12.wa.us/ CompassionateSchools/Resources. Counselors have access to their own training through the American School Counseling Association, with a certificate

54　*Understand the Impact of Childhood Trauma*

program available in Trauma and Crisis Management, www.schoolcounselor.org/school-counselors/professional-development/asca-u-specialist-trainings/trauma-and-crisis-management-specialist.

Once school counselors are adequately trained about the impact of ACEs, they are well positioned to help others. Once staff is trained, counselors' advocacy for the ACEs-to-education connection during intervention meetings, IEP discussions, and administrative briefings may be better received.

School Counselors Are a Safe Space

Students with ACEs need to feel safe at school. Due to their dysregulated stress response system, these students are more likely to feel that school is scary, unwelcoming, or a place they don't fit in. School counselors create a sense of safety and belonging by creating calm environments, modeling emotional support, normalizing the ACE experience, and responding appropriately to mental health emergencies.

A school counselor's office should be an emotionally and physically safe place for students. By providing a quiet, distraction-free, peaceful environment, a school counseling office is a haven for dysregulated students. Counseling offices should have comfortable seating, sensory regulating items like fidgets, stuffed animals, kinetic sand, Play-Doh, and be aesthetically peaceful. Counseling offices are models for other spaces at school. Administrative offices and classrooms can use the same strategies to make their spaces more calming and welcoming for students.

Active listening doesn't come naturally to everyone. As counselors, we often forget that other professional educators do not have the same training and counseling skill set. It is imperative that counselors model emotional safety for both students and adults to see. Here are some tips to create emotional safety when interacting with students:

1　Say hello, shake hands, or in some way greet students when you see them.
2　Start every conversation with something positive.
3　Make eye contact.
4　Put away your phone and computer. Be present in every conversation.
5　Sit side by side instead of across a desk to show support and equality.
6　Nod to show responsiveness and indicate that you are following along with what they are saying.
7　Listen without giving advice.
8　Ask open-ended questions.
9　Keep information confidential.
10　Use positive, strengths-based language.
11　Avoid putting down others in front of a student.

ACEs happen. More than 2/3 of our students will experience one before they are 18. School counselors normalize the ACE experience to provide a sense of safety for students. In high schools, and with some middle school students,

The Role of a Trauma-Sensitive School 55

ACEs can be a part of student conversations. Counselors can give information about the effect of ACEs on learning and the strategies to build resilience and overcome the impact of toxic stress. This psychoeducational work is important for students. Knowledge is power. The more students understand what is happening to them and why, the better prepared and capable they are to make changes in their own life.

Lastly, school counselors create safety by reducing the stigma around mental health by providing mental health education and triage within schools. In order to decrease students' flippant use of "I'm so depressed" or "You are so OCD," we need to educate students on these mental illnesses and teach them appropriate help-seeking behaviors and coping strategies. However, due to the high prevalence of undiagnosed mental health issues among teens, counselors must be vigilant to notice students' risk-factors and symptoms in order to intervene early.

But counselors can't do it alone. In order to effectively address adolescent mental health needs, counselors must educate students and staff to recognize the risk-factors and symptoms of mental illness. Students can be the eyes and ears to spot concerning among in their friends. And teachers have daily opportunities to observe student behavior and detect harmful patterns or sudden changes in mood. When students and teachers can spot these risk-factors and refer students more accurately to school counselors, counselors can then be more effective in their own role to support students directly or refer them to necessary outside-of-school mental health services.

A vital role for any school counselor is also the role of suicidal ideation risk assessor. This is not the role of a teacher or administrator, but a trained mental health professional such as a school counselor, school psychologist, or mental health therapist working on campus. While suicidal ideation risk assessments are part of crisis counseling and a (hopefully) rare occurrence, they do not need to be only reactive in nature. As with other topics of social/emotional relevance, suicide, self-injury, and other unhealthy coping skills should be discussed and presented through prevention programs beginning at the middle school level.

In the state of California, suicide prevention, intervention, and postvention programs are now required by law in any public school serving grades 7–12 (California Department of Education, 2018). Evidence-based suicide prevention programs like Signs of Suicide (SOS) (www.mindwise.org/what-we-offer/suicide-prevention-programs/) train students how to look for warning signs of suicidal ideation, teenage depression, self-injury, and bullying among their peers. SOS developed an acronym to assist students in remembering how to respond to a friend at-risk. ACT stands for Acknowledge, Care, Tell. *Acknowledge* your friend has a serious concern, show the friend you *Care* about them, and *Tell* a trusted adult that your friend needs help.

Resources for School Counselors

In order to do the work of bridge building, advocacy, and creating a safe space, we as counselors must be trained in trauma-sensitivity. We are one of the mental health and social-emotional experts on campus and should be abreast of

56 *Understand the Impact of Childhood Trauma*

the latest news and research about ACEs and their impact on education. Online learning communities are a great place to explore new research, learn about new policy initiatives, and collaborate with other like-minded educators with the same mission – to improve their school's trauma-sensitivity. Here are a few sources to subscribe to today:

- ACES Too High – https://acestoohigh.com/resources/
- ACEs Connection – www.acesconnection.com/
- TLPI Online Learning Community – https://traumasensitiveschools.org/get-involved/creating-trauma-sensitive-schools/
- Center for Youth Wellness – https://centerforyouthwellness.org/building-a-movement/

For more information on neuroscience and ACEs, check out the following resources:

- *The Deepest Well: Healing the Long Term Effects of Childhood Adversity* by Dr. Nadine Burke Harris www.amazon.com/Deepest-Well-Long-Term-Childhood-Adversity/dp/132850266X/
- *The Body Keeps the Score* by Dr. Bessel van der Kolk www.amazon.com/Body-Keeps-Score-Healing-Trauma/dp/0143127748/
- *The Kid's Guide to Staying Awesome and In Control* by Lauren Brukner www.amazon.com/Kids-Guide-Staying-Awesome-Control/dp/1849059977/

For more resources to address student mental health concerns, I recommend the following resources:

- Instant Help Workbooks for Teens: www.newharbinger.com/imprint/instant-help-books
  These books have been my basis for many small groups and individual counseling sessions for students who are diagnosed or symptomatic of mental illnesses. These workbooks provide discussion topics, activities, and resources for middle and high schoolers who are dealing with depression, anxiety, eating disorders, anger, ADHD, OCD, bipolar disorder, and more.
- *The School Counselor and School Social Worker Treatment Planner* and *The School Counselor and School Social Worker Homework Planner* by Sarah Edison Knapp www.amazon.com/dp/1119384761/ref=rdr_ext_sb_ti_sims_1 and www.amazon.com/Counseling-Treatment-Planner-Updates-PracticePlanners/dp/1119063094/
  These two books work in tandem together to give school-based mental health providers goals and session topics for students with a variety of mental health and emotional concerns. The treatment planner provides counselors direction and outlines for short-term therapeutic sessions, and the homework planner gives follow-up student worksheets and activities that coincide with the therapeutic goals.

References

American School Counselor Association. (2019). *ASCA National Model: A Framework for School Counseling Programs* (4th ed.). Alexandria, VA: American School Counselor Association.

Atkins, M. S., Hoagwood, K. E., Kutash, K., & Seidman, E. (2010). Toward the Integration of Education and Mental Health in Schools. *Administration and Policy in Mental Health and Mental Health Services Research, 37*(1–2), 40–47.

California Department of Education. (2018, August 14). *Youth Suicide Prevention.* Retrieved from California Department of Education: www.cde.ca.gov/ls/cg/mh/suicideprevres.asp

Cole, S., O'Brien, J., Gadd, M. R., Wallace, D., & Gregory, M. (2005). *Helping Traumatized Children Learn: Supportive School Environments for Children Traumatized by Family Violence.* Boston, MA: Massachusetts Advocates for Children and Harvard Law School, Trauma and Learning Policy Initiative.

Harris, N. B. (2018). *The Deepest Well: Healing the Long-Term Effects of Childhood Adversity.* New York, NY: Houghton Mifflin Harcourt.

Johnson, S., Riley, A., Granger, D., & Riis, J. (2013). The Science of Early Life Toxic Stress for Pediatric Practice and Advocacy. *Pediatrics, 131*(2), 319–327.

Trauma Learning and Policy Initiative. (n.d.). *History and Background.* Retrieved from Helping Traumatized Children Learn: www.traumasensitiveschools.org/about-tlpi/

Step 2

Develop Trauma-Sensitivity Schoolwide

Support ALL Students to Reach Those with ACEs

6 Trauma-Sensitive Schools
Reframing the "Why" Not the "How"

This chapter explores the characteristics of a trauma-sensitive school, how to create shared vision for trauma-sensitivity, and how to maintain a trauma-sensitive program. It addresses common barriers to implementing this new approach and bolsters school counselor's ability to be a trauma-sensitive leader on campus.

Every fall, millions of children head back to school, ready to begin a new school year. Some are eager. Excited to meet a new teacher and make great friends, they are ready to take on any challenge thrown their way. Some are hesitant. Unsure of what the year may hold and wary to leave the comforts of home, they are concerned about how they may fare. And still others have already given up before it even starts. Expecting yet another hostile teacher, a stream of trips to the principal's office, and academic curriculum that overwhelms them, they think that school will never be a place they fit in.

We know that two-thirds of all students have at least one ACE. And those who have at least four ACEs are 32 times more likely to be labeled a "behavior problem" or be behind academically (Harris, 2018). And what about our kids who give up before school even starts? It is safe to say that a large portion have experienced ACEs. We know their amygdala will overreact when they get in trouble – leading to larger than normal upset reactions. We know their hippocampus is smaller than normal, causing trouble in memory and learning. We know their pre-frontal cortex may be shut down during class due to fear and hyperarousal. With this unbearable mix of biology working against them, is there anything educators can do? What must happen to make THIS year not a repeat of last year?

School counselors have decades of research to draw from and hundreds of ways to help these students. Research shows that educational outcomes for students with ACEs can be improved by:

- Engaging students in school through curriculum and activities.
- Empowering student's voices and choices.
- Enhancing connections with teachers and peers.
- Implementing positive behavior systems and predictable routines.
- Practicing social skills.
- Developing students' ability to self-regulate.

(Cole, O'Brien, Gadd, Wallace, & Gregory, 2005)

But with so much research and so many possible interventions, where should a school counselor start? We start with a big goal.

62 Develop Trauma-Sensitivity Schoolwide

The goal: to create a safe and effective learning.

How will we do this? Through the adoption and implementation of a trauma-sensitive school model. In this chapter, we will explore what characterizes a trauma-sensitive school, how to create shared vision for trauma-sensitivity, and how to maintain a trauma-sensitive program. I will address common barriers to implementing this new approach and bolster school counselor's ability to be a trauma-sensitive leader on campus.

Creating Shared Values

"Positive school climate" is a common education term that refers to a caring and supportive school environment where learning can flourish. Positive school climate leads to a variety of favorable student outcomes, including academic achievement, feelings of connectedness, belonging, and enhanced self-efficacy (Centers for Disease Control and Prevention, 2009). But positive school climates don't just happen. They are the outcome of dedicated efforts to create a system of positive values and norms. The daily implementation of shared values ensures that the desire to create a positive climate becomes a reality. Trauma-sensitivity is a specific type of positive school climate. Without the underlying values of positivity, and shared responsibility, a trauma-sensitive approach will have no legs to stand on.

According to the Trauma and Learning Policy Initiative (TLPI), there are six characteristics of a trauma-sensitive school (Figure 6.1):

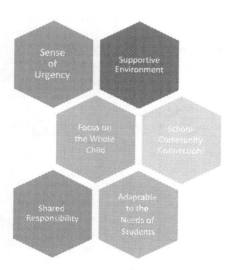

Figure 6.1 Six defining characteristics of a trauma-sensitive school (Rawson, 2019).

Trauma-Sensitive Schools 63

1   *Sense of Urgency*: "A shared understanding among all staff" that ACEs affect the development, behavior, and academic achievement of numerous children in any school. And an agreement that a trauma-sensitive approach is necessary to improve their outcomes.
2   *Supportive Environment*: "The school supports all children to feel safe physically, socially, emotionally, and academically."
3   *Focus on the Whole Child*: "The school addresses students' needs in holistic ways, taking into account their relationships, self-regulation, academic competence, and physical and emotional well-being."
4   *School-Community Connections*: "The school explicitly connects students to the school community and provides multiple opportunities to practice newly developing skills."
5   *Shared Responsibility*: "The school embraces teamwork and staff share responsibility for all students."
6   *Adaptable to Student Needs*: "Leadership and staff anticipate and adapt to the ever-changing needs of students" who have experienced trauma.

(Trauma and Learning Policy Initiative, 2019c)

So how does a staff full of diverse educators with a variety of professional and personal backgrounds come to a common value of trauma-sensitivity? First, educational leaders must help staff bring conscious awareness to the school's culture. School culture is affirmed through traditions, patterns, unspoken expectations, stories, and symbols passed among the staff through social interactions (Craig, 2016). This creates a sense of "how things are done at our school" for any new member to the culture, including students, staff, and parents. School culture can be very difficult to change, especially for someone new and considered "outside" of the culture. Many counselors find immediate push back when they attempt to change an ingrained culture quickly or as a new member to the team. Bringing awareness to the culture before making changes allows staff to reflect on their personal and collective values. It gives time to analyze the culture from various perspectives. It provides space to consider other options before making decisions to change their own school culture.

If a school staff values accountability, they may believe "all students *choose* whether to listen or get distracted," then a system of punitive discipline for not listening – where students lose recess or earn after school detention – makes perfect sense. The logic follows that to encourage listening, the school must create consequences for choosing not to listen. These created consequences are punitive consequences. They create a system where students are powerless and often shamed for their behavior. This value of "Accountability" followed by a value of punitive disciple is common in schools.

However, some students are biologically predisposed to disassociate due to trauma. They struggle with listening, can't control their instinct to withdraw when anxious, and have worse short-term memory than students without ACEs (Harris, 2018). So, what then? Should these students be held to the

64 Develop Trauma-Sensitivity Schoolwide

same accountability standard? The system of accountability and consequences breaks down in this instance. Instead of shame and consequences coercing the student to behave better, our student with ACEs will begin to behavior worse. The shame causes fear and stress, making them feel unsafe and more likely to have a "fight-or-flight" response. Knowledge about trauma's impact on academics can begin to disrupt the shared assumption that "all students choose to listen." But a one-time training may not change everyone's beliefs.

Many teachers and educators' values are not within their conscious awareness. Implicit biases and subconscious assumptions make it challenging for educators to change deeply held assumptions. Many educators may hold subconscious or espoused beliefs that a student was "too young to remember what happened to them," that they "should know the difference between a bad homelife from a good school," or that students have complete control over their behaviors in all circumstances. These assumptions can limit an educator's openness to a trauma-sensitive philosophy. The research about ACEs' effects on children's behavior and academic outcomes is well-documented. The evidence of a need for trauma-sensitive schools is available to any educator who is open to it. But many will not find it for themselves. And many more who see it may not think it would fit with the culture of their schools. School counselors who are aware of ACEs and understand how toxic stress affects the brain can bring this awareness to their staff and begin the slow process to shift the culture.

Within any group of people, there are early adopters of a new philosophy, program, or product. If a school's culture is resistant to information about ACEs, try starting with one early adopter. Is there another counselor who would be on board? A teacher who is already using trauma-sensitive strategies? An administrator who is focused on enhancing school climate? Use allies to change the culture one educator at a time.

> Before a school becomes a trauma-sensitive school, there must be trauma-sensitive educators within it.

When the goal is to create a fully trauma-sensitive school, administrative support and leadership on the issue is imperative. A few early adopters can begin a movement, but they can't make it the law of the land. Administrators must articulate and maintain the vision of the trauma-sensitive philosophy in order to achieve the critical mass necessary to create a system-wide change. The staff will need clear direction, purpose, and motivation to move toward trauma-sensitivity, a monumental mindset shift for some people. One way to increase the likelihood of adoption is to use incentives. Administrators could provide incentives to early adopters to recognize their support and enhance those educator's abilities to be leaders within the movement. For example, principals may use discretionary funds to pay early adopters for coaching other teachers in trauma-sensitivity. They could compensate their school's mental health professionals for training staff on ACEs and toxic stress.

After setting the vision and strategy, administrators must create a partnership between themselves and staff. Trauma-sensitive leaders are collaborative. They should be inclusive of various viewpoints and take staff's contributions seriously, incorporating shared ideas into the trauma-sensitive plan (Craig, 2016). Administrators must also be aware of the increased emotional capacity required by trauma-sensitivity. There are four components of collaborative leadership needed to achieve trauma-sensitivity:

1 *Schedule Common Planning Time*: Schedule common planning time for educators to develop trauma-sensitive approaches that are consistent between classrooms and within all aspects of the school day. These new approaches may include new schoolwide expectations through PBIS, new teaching strategies, or planning enrichment activities to enhance school connectedness.
2 *Create Partnerships*: Create partnerships with community wellness and mental health agencies. These partnerships will ease the burdensome feeling many teachers carry when they know about students' trauma but feel they can't adequately help.
3 *Provide Training*: Provide school staff access to training and coaching for the implementation of trauma-sensitive strategies within the classroom.
4 *Collaborate on Interventions*: Facilitate collaboration and a successful tiered-intervention model by ensuring that teachers have adequate coverage and time to attend team meetings.

(Craig, 2016)

Once the trauma-sensitive vision is established, school leaders may wonder where to go next. With a staff motivated to change, any leader is well positioned. But sustained change requires systematic planning. If trauma-sensitivity is the destination, then the Flexible Framework from the seminal book *Helping Traumatized Children Learn* is the roadmap.

Not "Just Another Program"

In 2004, a group of researchers and professors from Massachusetts Advocates for Children (MAC) and Harvard Law School formalized a partnership to address the growing impact of childhood trauma on learning. They called their partnership the TLPI (Trauma and Learning Policy Initiative, 2019a). Between 2000 and 2005, MAC and grant-funded schools in Massachusetts developed an organizational planning tool for creating trauma-sensitive schools. With money from the Massachusetts legislature through the Safe and Supportive Learning Environment grant program, the Flexible Framework came to life (Trauma and Learning Policy Initiative, 2019b).

The Flexible Framework is not a curriculum or program, but instead is a planning tool. It helps schools develop trauma-sensitivity. Through implementing and evaluating six elements of the school's structure, philosophy, and practices, schools can build on the trauma-sensitive vision they developed. By adding, removing, or tweaking their existing methods, each school creates its own trauma-sensitive program. These individualized programs are responsive to the unique cultural and educational needs of that school and community (Cole et al., 2005).

The Flexible Framework has six elements:

1. Leadership
2. Professional Development
3. Access to Resources and Services
4. Academic and Non-academic Strategies
5. Policies and Protocols
6. Collaboration with Families

(Trauma and Learning Policy Initiative, 2019b)

For a school to become trauma-sensitive, the school's policies and procedures in these six areas must align to a trauma-sensitive vision (Figure 6.2).

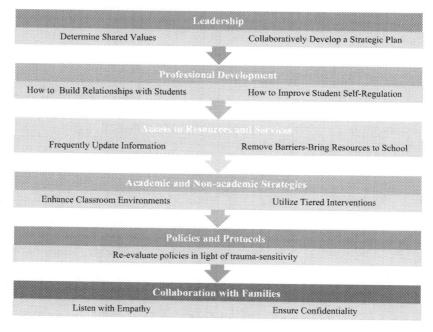

Figure 6.2 The Flexible Framework allows schools to be systematically trauma-sensitive while still responsive to their students' unique needs (Rawson, 2019).

Leadership

Trauma-sensitivity leadership teams develop strategic plans prior to the implementation of any interventions. Strategic planning teams include a variety of stakeholders, including administration, counselors, other mental health staff, teachers, classified staff, parents, and even students when appropriate.

TLPI provides a detailed guide for leadership who are ready to move from a trauma-sensitive vision into action. Helping Traumatized Children Learn, vol. 2 offers a cyclical vision setting, action planning, implementation, and evaluation process for schools.

Professional Development

In addition to raising awareness of ACEs and the impact of trauma on learning, there are other essential topics of professional development for trauma-sensitivity. Trauma-sensitive leaders use information gathered from the value-creation process to identify necessary professional development topics. If school staff are concerned about discipline, a training topic might be restorative practices (RP) or behavior contracts. If staff are worried about sharing resource information with families, administrators could focus on family communication. Trauma-sensitive professional development is based on staff interest, staff concern, or schoolwide data. Here are other topics to consider when developing a trauma-sensitive school:

1. *Relationship Building*: Strengthening teacher-student and other adult-student relationships within the school environment,
2. *Accessing Resources*: Identifying and accessing outside of school resources for children in need of extra support, and
3. *Improving Student Self-Regulation*: Helping traumatized children improve self-regulation, emotion management, social skills, and academic engagement.

(Cole et al., 2005)

In the Santee School District, a suburb of San Diego, many counselors felt the urgency to create trauma-sensitive counseling programs and schools within their district. After the district's counseling/social work team studied the impact of trauma and were trained on ACEs and schoolwide, trauma-sensitive initiatives, they were determined to implement trauma-sensitivity in their schools. Coordinating with district-level leadership, they implemented professional development sessions to boost their schools' awareness of ACEs, relationships with students, and teaching of self-regulation skills. After securing grant funding for trauma-sensitive professional development at one school site, the grassroots efforts of these counselors began to spread. Professional development led to shifts in practice. What was happening at one school gained the

68 Develop Trauma-Sensitivity Schoolwide

attention of administrators and teachers at other schools. Within three years, 2/3 of the schools in the Santee School District had trained their teaching staff about the impact of trauma on learning.

Access to Resources and Services

How many staff members know how to access transportation vouchers for homeless students? Mental health therapy for a child with Medicaid insurance coverage? Housing assistance for victims of domestic violence? Food banks for refugees? While these services exist in almost every local community, many educators don't know how to link the students in their classroom to the services they need.

In many schools, the school counselor may act as the gatekeeper to this information. This puts undue burden on one person (or a few people) to facilitate the process. Part of a school counselor's job may be to develop these partnerships and inform teachers about them, but the counselor can't be the only one who can access them. Many counselors provide information about community resources on their website or in the school's main office where it is directly accessible to parents. Training is provided for current teachers and school front office staff on how to locate community resources. But as time passes, a once great resource system can easily break down. Agency employees leave, funding systems change, and referral processes are updated. To decrease the breakdown of this process, information about resources is shared during new teacher onboarding, and resource lists must be updated continuously.

In one southern California school district, the McKinney Vento Liaison (employee who supports homeless and foster youth) trains school health clerks, bus drivers, and front office secretaries annually to access these resources. In addition to simply the "how" of resource access, they share the "why." Giving these front-line staff members knowledge about ACEs and toxic stress allows them to be more empathetic to the parents they serve every day.

To go beyond simply distributing information, counselors bring resources directly to school. Many community resource providers wish that they had the direct access to students and families that the schools provide. Counselors can work directly with community resource providers to gain access to the school. Another benefit for bringing community partners to the school campus is increased family participation and follow-through on referrals.

Bringing mental health professionals to staff trainings allows staff to hear information from voices outside of their own school walls. Sometimes, a training from an outside provider may impact staff in a different way than listening to the principal or counselor who they hear from often. Often, local university professors are an untapped resource for professional development. They bring a wealth of knowledge and up-to-date research. Hosting a community resource fair or bringing providers to school events like fall carnivals, back-to-school night, new student orientations, or sporting events is another way for the providers to connect directly to families. Families who hesitate to share traumatic information with the classroom teacher may be more likely to access help directly at a school event. For example, a military family may feel more connected and willing to share about family difficulties with a military family/school liaison at the resource fair. This person has firsthand knowledge of military life challenges and can more adequately address this family's needs.

Academic and Non-academic Strategies

Seasoned teachers, counselors, and educators have a wide variety of teaching strategies in their "tool kit." From a favorite classroom management technique, to a unique way of presenting long division, educators have numerous techniques at their disposal. But which of these techniques will work for our students with ACEs? While not all traumatized students act the same, many of them have symptoms that overlap with learning-disabled students, language-impaired students, or students with a mental illness.

The following teaching strategies help to engage traumatized students despite the challenges they may face with classroom engagement, critical thinking, sequential memory, language processing, and emotion management. Many strategies on this list were also identified in the book *Helping Traumatized Children Learn* as best-practices for educating traumatized students. Strategies to use in classrooms that include students with ACEs (aka all classrooms):

- Building on student strength's and interests.
- Creating predictability in scheduling and transitions.
- Enhancing the physical safety of the classroom.
- Using visual schedules.
- Providing access to grade-level curriculum for all students, scaffolding when necessary.
- Implementing Positive behavior supports.
- Setting clear and consistent behavior expectations.
- Presenting academic information in multiple ways (e.g. Academic and auditory).
- Frontloading academic vocabulary.
- Providing graphic organizers.
- Offering physical manipulatives.
- Ensuring appropriate referrals to special education, counseling, or other interventions when necessary (based on student data).
- Developing non-academic relationships with students.
- Supporting student participation in extracurricular activities.
- Fostering a sense of belonging through community-building activities.
- Encouraging student leadership and participation in decision-making processes, giving students voice and choice in their education.
- Allowing students opportunities for reflection on their past successes and failures.

(Cole et al., 2005)

70 *Develop Trauma-Sensitivity Schoolwide*

Policies and Protocols

An essential aspect to consider when developing a trauma-sensitive approach is the role of existing school and district policies. How these policies affect school climate and students' perceptions of safety and belonging at school is vitally important. School and district staff should re-evaluate their current policies regarding discipline, communication, safety planning, and community collaboration in light of their trauma-sensitive vision (Cole et al., 2005).

At a charter school in San Diego, staff noticed a disconnect between the discipline practices of the school and its vision to be whole child focused and sensitive to the needs of its unique community. With a predominately Hispanic and low-income population, ACEs were high and so were discipline referrals. Students who were "high-flyers" to the office could miss as much as 90 minutes of class waiting to speak with an administrator or counselor due to the high volume of others in the same situation. This disruption to instructional time frustrated teachers and was a contributing factor in low student achievement.

When the staff expressed concerns about missed academic time and recidivism, administration took the concerns seriously. Using a collaborative model, the principal and instructional leadership team worked with teachers and support staff to create a new discipline policy. The new policy consistently implemented Positive Behavior Interventions and Supports (PBIS) and RP in all environments across campus. Using these strategies and the progressive, predictable discipline protocol they created, the school saw a dramatic decrease in suspensions and time spend out of class within one year. Suspensions dropped from 84 to 33 and student's missed class time was reduced through new in-class discipline expectations.

Changing policy is hard work. But without the support and documentation of trauma-sensitive policies, the best efforts of individual trauma-sensitive educators will crumble in the unsupportive system. Adopting new trauma-sensitive procedures, including rewriting student and staff codes of conduct, ensures that these policies will be implemented long after the current administration, counselor, or other proponent of trauma-sensitivity has moved on.

Collaboration with Families

Lastly, any school becoming trauma-sensitive will work with families to make this vision a reality. Families are the gatekeepers of a child's ACE information. Whether or not a family trusts the school will ultimately determine whether the crucial ACE information is shared and whether the school can use it to improve the child's learning. Schools must work to understand the student's unique cultural background as well. Culture affects the way a student views school, the way family is structured, and the way information is shared. If the school claims to be trauma-sensitive, and their policies, teaching strategies, or individual attitudes are both trauma- and culturally sensitive, it will worsen tension and distrust between schools and families.

Trauma-Sensitive Schools   71

Counselors encourage their school staff to use active listening and empathy when interacting with families. All educators must remain aware that both students and parents experience ACEs. If 2/3 of the adult U.S. population has at least one ACE, then so do 2/3 of our schools' parent populations. Interactions with parents should be positive, consistent, meaningful, and collaborative, just as interactions with students in the classroom.

Finally, staff must thoughtfully consider the consequences of their actions with families. How staff members handle communication about child abuse reporting, restraining orders, custody documentation, transfer of records, and medical information should be examined to ensure that the families' safety and confidentiality are prioritized.

Reducing Staff Burnout through Meaningful Support

Creating a trauma-sensitive school is a difficult work. While there are great moments and joyous celebrations of progress, there are also deep frustrations and disappointments. Working directly with traumatized students challenges an educator's emotional, physical, and cognitive capacities, and can lead to teacher burnout.

Every year, thousands of teachers across the U.S. pack up their classroom and walk out of a school for the last time. But these teachers aren't retiring. Two-thirds of the 200,000 teachers who leave the profession each year do so for reasons other than retirement (Carver-Thomas & Darling-Hammond, 2017). Teacher turnover is a serious concern, especially in schools that serve low-income populations and large populations of students of color. Teacher turnover rates in Title 1 schools (serving low-income populations) are 50% higher than the rates at more affluent schools. Turnover rates in school serving large populations of students of color are 70% higher than schools with a majority white student population. One of the highest levels of teacher turnover was among special education teachers who left their jobs 80% more often than general education teachers (Carver-Thomas & Darling-Hammond, 2017). Rates of school counselor turnover are similar to teachers' rates, given the similar stressors and work environment. According to one study of 1,280 Florida school counselors, 10.6% were planning to retire or quit their jobs during that school year and another 13% were considering leaving the profession (Baggerly & Osborn, 2006; Craig, 2016).

The list of stressors that cause teachers and counselors to leave the profession is long. Topping the list are:

- Accountability pressure/stress
- Lack of principal/administrative support
- Lack of opportunities for professional growth
- Dissatisfaction with working conditions (which include student behavior, parent support, resources provided, collegiality, interference of non-teaching or non-counseling duties, and decision-making influence and control).
(Carver-Thomas & Darling-Hammond, 2017)

72 Develop Trauma-Sensitivity Schoolwide

While those stressors are common to many careers, educators also have unique stressors not seen elsewhere. Teachers are responsible for creating long-term emotional relationships with children, listening to students' stories of personal adversity, not overreacting in the face of difficult circumstances (don't show the kids you're crying!), managing student misbehavior, and delivering academic content to large groups (Craig, 2016). Just writing this makes me stressed!

Teacher stress is more common when working with students exposed to ACEs. It is hard to create meaningful relationships with 30 1st graders. It is nearly inconceivable when 2/3 of them have trouble with attachment. It is hard to engage students academically; it is grueling when 2/3 of them are dis-associated, hyperaroused, and distracted. It is hard to keep personal emotions under control. It is unimaginable when you listen every day to heartbreaking stories of adversity from students you love.

It's common for teachers, counselors, and other educators to report symp-toms of secondary trauma, also known as compassion fatigue. Secondary trauma occurs naturally as a symptom of hearing about or witnessing some-one else's traumatic experience and feeling helpless to intervene. Symptoms of secondary trauma include many similar symptoms to PTSD. These include avoidance of certain people or events that are reminiscent of the traumatic event, withdrawal, isolation, anger, and impaired work habits (difficulty focus-ing, tardiness, forgetfulness, etc.). Additional symptoms include anger, sadness, grief, mood swings, irritability, headaches, and stomachaches.

Until recently, most of the research around secondary trauma discussed its prevalence among emergency responders, child protection workers, and direct therapeutic providers. Now, researchers recognize that secondary trauma is common among educators. And to make matters worse, educators receive significantly less training than other professions on how to handle its effects (Perry, 2014). There are six reasons why educators and other care providers experience secondary trauma:

1   *Empathy:* Teachers' and counselors' ability to "walk in the shoes" of their stu-dents, seeing things and feeling things from the student's perspective opens them up to internalize the pain and trauma they hear about (Perry, 2014).
2   *Insufficient Recovery Time:* Educators are not given enough time off for self-care after hearing about a traumatic experience, filing a CPS report, testifying in court, or other secondarily traumatizing events. Many teach-ers hear stories in between class periods and must continue teaching as if nothing happened just a few minutes later (Perry, 2014).
3   *Unresolved Personal Trauma:* Since 2/3 of the adult U.S. population has at least 1 ACE in their background, that means so do teachers and school staff. Hearing stories of students' trauma can trigger memories of their own (Perry, 2014).
4   *Children's Vulnerability:* When children are maltreated, it evokes strong moral responses from other members of society who seek to protect these most dependent members of our community (Perry, 2014).

Trauma-Sensitive Schools 73

5 *Isolation within the Workplace*: Teachers typically function in a working model of "independent-delivery," meaning that they are on their own most of the day without any group support. Due to this isolation within their own classroom or office, teachers and counselors are more susceptible to secondary trauma (Perry, 2014).

6 *Lack of Systemic Resources*: Teachers and school staff lack training on effective strategies to help these students or access to resources for them. This leaves educators with a sense of hopelessness and can lead to disassociation and burnout (Perry, 2014).

Secondary trauma is very common and very treatable, but it takes a system to acknowledge it exists, appropriately prevent and address it. Most importantly, the school leader needs to be well-educated about the effects of secondary trauma. That way, they can intervene when there are persisting symptoms among staff. School counselors also help with monitoring staff morale. If counselors or principals notice a staff member acting unusually angry, lacking motivation, or avoidant, they reach out to that person and check in about potential secondary trauma.

Second, trauma-sensitive schools provide training and support to teachers on appropriate strategies for working with traumatized students. Giving tangible classroom management, teaching and relationship building strategies give teachers hope and support while working with challenging students. There is more for teachers to learn than just RTI strategies and pedagogy. Trauma-sensitive schools set aside time for common planning or discussion of challenging student cases. Trauma-sensitive teachers access the school counselor to address deeper student needs and assist in making referrals to outside resources. Teachers cannot address trauma in isolation.

In the Santee School District, schools with high military populations partnered with the University of San Diego's School Counseling Program to provide needed support to teachers. Given the high levels of trauma seen in military populations, these schools knew that they must work collaboratively to support both students and their teachers. Professors from the University of San Diego visit these schools regularly to consult with teachers and administrators about students with ACEs and their challenges in the classroom. Professors do student observations, coach teachers in trauma-sensitive practices, collaboratively plan classroom interventions, and follow up to provide teacher support. This program has allowed teachers to do more than simply "vent" their frustrations. They learn effective strategies to meet student needs, create actionable plans, and are supported in implementing and reflecting on these changes.

Lastly, trauma-sensitive leaders provide training to their staff on the symptoms of secondary trauma and appropriate self-care activities. By training staff to reduce secondary trauma's impact through proper sleep, exercise, nutrition, spending time in healthy community, spiritual practices, and seeking mental health care when needed, they will build an emotionally healthier staff and workplace. Ultimately, that improves the well-being of both teachers and students.

The Role of the School Counselor

The school counselor plays a pivotal role in the development of a trauma-sensitive school. As one of the few, or potentially the only, mental health experts on a school campus, the counselor creates a comprehensive program to enhance school climate, reduce the impact of trauma on learning, and help staff avoid re-traumatizing students and themselves. In Step 3 of this book, the TSC model will be presented. It is a framework for school counselors to organize trauma-sensitive interventions within the context of a comprehensive school counseling program. Specific trauma-sensitive interventions within the TSC model will be discussed in Chapters 9–11.

In this section, the broad workplace functions and duties of the counselor at a trauma-sensitive school will be explored using the outline provided by ASCA (American School Counselor Association, 2016).

Trauma-Sensitive School Counselors...

- "Recognize the signs of trauma in students" (American School Counselor Association, 2016). By using active listening, counselors easily identify potential ACEs during direct services such as individual or group counseling. School counselors notice "red flags" for ACEs as they read student referrals or discuss individual student needs with administrators or teachers. Counselors use this information to direct appropriate services to the student and advocate for their unique needs due to potential trauma.
- "Understand [that] traumas need not predict individual failure if sufficient focus on resilience and strengths is present" (American School Counselor Association, 2016). Counselors believe that students with ACEs are fully capable of realizing life-long academic, career, and personal-social success. The likelihood of these successes is dramatically increased when students have enough caring, adult support. Through this support, students can improve their feeling of self-worth and self-efficacy to build a sense of resiliency.
- "Avoid practices that may re-traumatize students" and "recognize the role technology can play in magnifying trauma incidents for students" (American School Counselor Association, 2016). Practices that may re-traumatize students include punitive discipline models that lead to academic and social isolation, including physical restraints and solitary confinement. Counselors do not force students to discuss traumatic events. They do not pass judgment on students' experiences. Passing judgment can exacerbate guilty and shameful feelings associated with the trauma. Counselors keep student information safe and confidential to allow them to share their own stories. Confidentiality limits the risk of harmful gossip, cyberbullying, and assumptions based on past trauma.
- "Create connected communities and positive school climates that are trauma-sensitive to keep students healthy and in school and involved

in positive social networks" (American School Counselor Association, 2016). Counselors address student needs through a systemic approach to improve the school environment for all students. By focusing their efforts on preventative work to enhance school connectedness, prevent bullying, and build students' social-emotional skills, counselors can impact academic achievement, school engagement, and ensure trauma-sensitivity schoolwide.

- "Implement effective academic and behavioral practices, such as positive behavioral interventions and supports and social and emotional learning" (American School Counselor Association, 2016). Evidence-based schoolwide programs like these can reduce student misbehavior, boost student engagement, and enhance feelings of safety and belonging at school.
- "Promote safe, stable and nurturing relationships" (American School Counselor Association, 2016). They understand the importance of developing healthy attachment relationships between students and adults on campus. School counselors create these relationships between themselves and their students, as well as educate other school staff to build the same meaningful connections. By ensuring that every student is safe, known, cared for, and connected, counselors can help students meet their basic needs. After basic needs are met, students are then ready to engage in academic content, learn, and thrive.
- "Provide community resource information to students and families dealing with trauma" and "collaborate with community resources to provide support for students" (American School Counselor Association, 2016). Counselors are a bridge between the school and the community. By utilizing their time to build relationships with community service providers, educate staff on how to access these services, and bring resources to the school campus, counselors are not just gatekeepers of this information but instead are the distributors.
- "Educate staff on the effects of trauma and how to refer students to the school counselor" (American School Counselor Association, 2016). Counselors cannot be an island to themselves. If we as school counselors are the only one in the building with knowledge of the effects of trauma on learning, we are doing a disservice to our students. Counselors can train staff on ACEs, coach teachers on trauma-sensitive interventions, and reduce the likelihood of "putting out fires" by setting up an accessible referral system. When teachers feel supported through training, coaching, and collaboration, they are less likely to refer low-level needs to reactive counseling. They are more likely to use the counseling referral system for appropriate high-level concerns.

Ultimately, using all of these strategies in combination, school counselors "promote a trauma-sensitive framework for policies, procedures and behaviors to entire staff" (American School Counselor Association, 2016). As student advocates, counselors keep up-to-date with current research on ACEs and the

76 Develop Trauma-Sensitivity Schoolwide

effects of trauma on learning. By doing this, counselors are well poised to address barriers to learning as they arise throughout the year. Counselors who disseminate trauma impact information, advocate to decrease zero-tolerance discipline, increase school connectedness, and ensure equity for all students will be the most successful in creating a trauma-sensitive environment.

References

American School Counselor Association. (2016, August). *The School Counselor and Trauma-Informed Practice.* Retrieved from American School Counselor Association: https://www.schoolcounselor.org/asca/media/asca/PositionStatements/PS_TraumaInformed.pdf

Baggerly, J. N., & Osborn, D. S. (2006). School Counselors Career Satisfaction and Commitment: Correlates and Predictors. *Professional School Counseling, 9,* 197–205. doi:10.5330/prsc.9.3.547188866k76qg76

Carver-Thomas, D., & Darling-Hammond, L. (2017). *Teacher Turnover: Why It Matters and What We Can Do about It.* Palo Alto, CA: Learning Policy Institute.

Centers for Disease Control and Prevention. (2009). *School Connectedness: Strategies for Increasing Protective Factors among Youth.* Atlanta, GA: U.S. Department of Health and Human Services.

Cole, S., O'Brien, J., Gadd, M. R., Wallace, D., & Gregory, M. (2005). *Helping Traumatized Children Learn: Supportive School Environments for Children Traumatized by Family Violence.* Boston, MA: Massachusetts Advocates for Children and Harvard Law School, Trauma and Learning Policy Initiative.

Craig, S. (2016). *Trauma Sensitive Schools: Learning Communities Transforming Children's Lives, K-5.* New York, NY: Teachers College Press.

Harris, N. B. (2018). *The Deepest Well: Healing the Long-Term Effects of Childhood Adversity.* New York, NY: Houghton Mifflin Harcourt.

Perry, B. (2014). *The Cost of Caring: Secondary Traumatic Stress and the Impact of Working with High-Risk Children and Families.* Retrieved from Child Trauma Academy: https://childtrauma.org/wp-content/uploads/2014/01/Cost_of_Caring_Secondary_Traumatic_Stress_Perry_s.pdf

Trauma and Learning Policy Initiative. (2019a). *History and Background.* Retrieved from Trauma and Learning Policy Initiative: https://traumasensitiveschools.org/about-tlpi/

Trauma and Learning Policy Initiative. (2019b). *The Flexible Framework.* Retrieved from Trauma and Learning Policy Initiative: https://traumasensitiveschools.org/trauma-and-learning/the-flexible-framework/

Trauma and Learning Policy Initiative. (2019c). *The Solution: Trauma Sensitive School.* Retrieved from Trauma and Learning Policy Initiative: https://traumasensitiveschools.org/trauma-and-learning/the-solution-trauma-sensitive-schools/

7 Schoolwide Programs that Align with a Trauma-Sensitive Philosophy

If there's one thing the education industry is great at, it's coming up with the "next great thing," always accompanied by a fabulous acronym. And if there's one thing teachers know, it's that the "next great thing" is never the perfect solution it sounds like it will be. Positive Behavior Interventions and Supports (PBIS), Response to Intervention (RTI), Multi-Tiered Systems of Support (MTSS), Restorative Practices (RPs), Social-Emotional Learning (SEL), and the list could go on and on. While all these systems and programs have unique qualities and wonderful student benefits, none of them broadly address issues for the whole educational system. RTI is for academics, PBIS is for behavior, and others are for discipline, emotional intelligence, and special education. As an educational philosophy and not just a program, trauma-sensitivity can encompass the whole system. Instead of simply one intervention or one path, trauma-sensitivity is a broad way of looking at our students. It helps educators to explain student behaviors – social, emotional, and academic behaviors – not excuse them, grade them, or punish them.

> Trauma-sensitivity asks not "what's wrong with them?" but instead, "what happened to them?"

One thing that trauma-sensitivity is NOT is a canned curriculum or a specific set of steps. As described in the previous chapter, the best way to develop this philosophy at a school site is through a framework system, not a pre-determined model. As counselors work with their schools and collaborate with staff, one central question will arise:

> So we have this new trauma-sensitive philosophy. We sense the urgency to address trauma. Now what do we DO?

In this section, we will discuss all those acronym programs, because they are what to *do*. This chapter gives school counselors an overview of four programs and discusses how each program's goals and key elements align with a trauma-sensitive school philosophy. These are examples of programs that could be used but none are required or officially endorsed. No school should expect to implement all these schoolwide programs – nor do they need to!

78 Develop Trauma-Sensitivity Schoolwide

SEL, PBIS, RTI, and RP are all programs with evidence-based success that align with the trauma-sensitive vision to:

- "[Support] all children to feel safe physically, socially, emotionally, and academically."
- "[Address] students' needs in holistic ways, taking into account their relationships, self-regulation, academic competence, and physical and emotional well-being."
- "[Connect] students to the school community and [provide] multiple opportunities to practice newly developing skills."
- "[Embrace] teamwork and share responsibility [among staff] for all students."

(Trauma Learning and Policy Initiative, 2019)

The term MTSS is also used when discussing schoolwide programs and tiered interventions. For consistency in this book, we will refer to RTI as the data-based and tiered intervention system for students' academic needs. We will refer to PBIS as the data-based and tiered intervention system for students' behavioral and social/emotional needs. MTSS will refer to a tiered intervention system that incorporates both RTI and PBIS, thereby meeting students whole-child needs within a school setting (Figure 7.1).

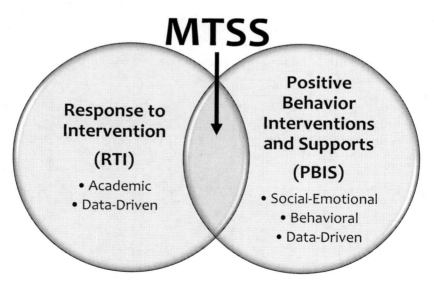

Figure 7.1 MTSS refers to both academic and behavioral/social-emotional tiered intervention systems (Rawson, 2019).

Social-Emotional Learning: Creating Caring and Motivated Students

SEL is not a new idea in education. Teachers have been infusing lessons about kindness, friendship, cooperation, and motivation into their lessons for decades. From character education to drug prevention, and moral development to violence reduction, schools were inundated in the early 90s with great ideas for whole-child education. But there was no way to coordinate or organize these efforts (CASEL, 2019a). Starting in 1994, the Collaborative for Academic, Social and Emotional Learning (CASEL) began the hard work of bringing all positive youth development initiatives under a systematic framework that could be aligned school to school, district to district, and state to state (CASEL, 2019b). Now, schools can operationalize the meaning of SEL, teach SEL standards, and assess students' mastery of SEL competencies.

Social-Emotional Learning is "the process through which children and adults understand and manage emotions, set and achieve positive goals, feel and show empathy for others, establish and maintain positive relationships, and make responsible decisions" (CASEL, 2019c).

CASEL determined five competencies for SEL. Under this umbrella of five topics, all social-emotional skills can be categorized. The five areas are self-awareness, self-management, social awareness, relationship skills, and decision making. Using these five competencies, educators can better coordinate their SEL lessons, policies, and practices to ensure that SEL is not just a monthly lesson, but is embedded throughout every school day.

Why Teach SEL?

SEL is a widely researched topic in education. How SEL makes students feel, how it impacts their perceptions of school, their prosocial behaviors, and their attendance have all been studied with positive outcomes. While these outcomes are great for student well-being, many district and school leaders want to know if this "feel-good initiative" is simply that or something more. A common question about SEL is "Does it impact academic achievement?"

According to a meta-analysis of 213 SEL programs involving 270,034 students, the answer is overwhelmingly YES (Durlak, Weissberg, Dymnicki, Taylor, & Schellinger, 2011). Students with SEL embedded in their schools improved their academic performance by 11 percentage points and made notable gains in positive student attitudes, prosocial behavior, and social-emotional skills. These improvements were significant because they continued for more than six months after the interventions were over (Durlak et al., 2011).

The explicit instruction of the SEL competencies is central to implementation, but the positive impact of SEL on academic achievement is due to both

80 Develop Trauma-Sensitivity Schoolwide

instruction of the SEL skills and many other facets of an SEL program. The change in interpersonal, instructional, and environmental supports that happen while implementing SEL has a significant impact on the school climate and the students (Durlak et al., 2011). SEL programs enhance:

- High expectations for academic success
- Caring adult-student relationships
- School connectedness
- Proactive classroom management
- Group work and cooperative learning
- Safe environments
- Predicable routines

(Durlak et al., 2011)

In 2017, CASEL and some of the same researchers from the 2011 meta-analysis conducted a second meta-analysis of SEL, this time specifically on the effects of SEL after the interventions are long over. Once again, the findings were significant. This study cemented SEL as an integral part of schooling. The impact of SEL on academic achievement is now unquestionable. 3.5 years after SEL interventions, the academic achievement of students exposed to SEL programs was 13 percentile points higher than peers with no SEL exposure. Additionally, at other follow-up periods, between 6 months and 18 years after SEL interventions, conduct problems, emotional distress, and drug use were all significantly lower for students with SEL program exposure during their school years. In addition, positive attitudes toward self, others, and school were higher, and development of social and emotional skills was enhanced (Taylor, Oberle, Durlak, & Weissberg, 2017).

Core Competencies

SEL encompasses a broad variety of topics ranging from acceptance to accountability, and citizenship to consent. In an effort to consolidate and streamline that wide variety of SEL activities into measurable consistent practices, CASEL developed five umbrella core competency areas (see Figure 7.2). These five SEL competencies are based on the idea that SEL should encompass three broad areas: Intrapersonal, interpersonal, and cognitive competence (CASEL, 2019c). The five core competencies are explained below.

1 *Self-awareness*: The ability to accurately perceive your own beliefs, thoughts, and feelings, and recognize how they impact your behaviors. Self-awareness also includes the ability to assess your own strengths and weaknesses, to have a sense of self-confidence, and a positive attitude toward challenges.
2 *Self-management*: The ability to implement self-regulation as it relates to your own thoughts, feelings, and behaviors. This also includes effectively

managing stress and impulsivity. Developing and working toward goals are included under the self-management umbrella.
3 *Responsible Decision Making*: The ability to use ethics, safety concerns, and social norms to guide choices about personal behavior. Responsible decision making also includes a realistic sense of consequences for various behaviors and the ability to be considerate of the needs of others.
4 *Social Awareness*: The ability to empathize with others who come from cultures and backgrounds different than your own. The ability to understand and apply ethical and social norms for behavior, including how to seek help.
5 *Relationship Skills*: The ability to create and maintain healthy relationships with individuals and groups. Relationship skills also include communication, listening, cooperation, respect, negotiation, and self-control.

(CASEL, 2019c)

Figure 7.2 CASEL wheel of competencies: Self-awareness, self-management, social awareness, relationship skills, and decision making (Rawson, 2019).

82 Develop Trauma-Sensitivity Schoolwide

Best Practices for Alignment with Trauma-Sensitivity

SEL and trauma-sensitive schools have many core tenets in common. Both focus on the need for explicitly taught self-regulation skills, the need for more safe, caring environments, and the need to build capacity for critical thinking.

Teaching SEL competencies increases in the application of prosocial skills and decreases problematic behaviors (Taylor et al., 2017). In a trauma-sensitive school, one focus area is teaching skills that didn't fully develop due to ACEs. Children with ACEs have difficulty grasping cause and effect relationships, controlling impulses, and planning ahead due to the effect of the trauma on their pre-frontal cortex (van der Kolk, 2005). The impact of SEL on externalizing behaviors such as impulsivity and lack of emotional regulation is due in part to the enhancement of the executive functions (Greenberg, 2006). Executive functions, a main task of the pre-frontal cortex, include inhibitory control, working memory, and planning. Skills taught during SEL lessons such as emotion identification, problem solving, and communication directly impact the executive functions. Therefore, they decrease the problematic behaviors common among students exposed to ACEs.

For one elementary school in San Diego, teaching SEL skills was a core component of their program. The staff knew that no student was prepared to learn until their basic needs, feelings of safety, and need to belong were fulfilled. When the school's mission called for "whole-child education," the school counselor and principal implemented SEL to meet this goal. The school used the SEL curriculum *Second Step* to teach the prosocial skills of empathy, emotion management, problem solving, and self-management (called Skills for Learning in the curriculum). By teaching the *Second Step* curriculum weekly in every classroom, the school developed common language around SEL, including helpful steps students followed to self-regulate or problem solve. Each year, students deepened their knowledge of prosocial skills by using this consistent curriculum. For example, in kindergarten, students learned how to manage themselves by listening and following directions, while third graders learned about making a plan and communicating assertively. Each year, student antisocial behaviors decreased due to the acquisition of new SEL knowledge and application of SEL skills. The negative impact of ACEs decreased as students learned skills to overcome their behavioral challenges.

Response to Intervention: Raising the Bar for All Students

RTI is a system identifying students' academic concerns, differentiating academic instruction to better address these concerns, and improving academic achievement for students who are struggling within a general education classroom (McInerney & Elledge, 2013). RTI gained immense popularity after the 2002 reauthorization of the Elementary and Secondary Education Act. This reauthorization expanded district-level accountability for the learning outcomes of all students, especially those identified to be struggling with basic skills. Schools and districts needed a framework to address students' academic gaps in a systematic way. They began implementing RTI to meet this need. Today, more than 35 states have officially adopted RTI as a differentiated support system to meet the requirements of this law (McInerney & Elledge, 2013).

According to the National Center on Response to Intervention, there are four essential components to a successful RTI model (Figure 7.3):

1. Schoolwide, multi-tiered instructional system;
2. Universal screening for academic skill;
3. Frequent progress monitoring of students' academic growth; and
4. Data-driven decision making for movement between the tiers of support (National Center for Response to Intervention, 2010).

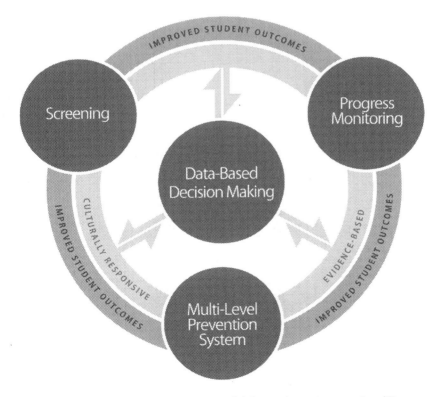

Figure 7.3 Four components of an RTI model for academic intervention (Center on Response to Intervention at American Institutes for Research, 2019).

What Are Tiered Interventions?

"Tiered interventions" is a term commonly used to refer to a system of progressively individualized and focused instruction within a school setting. This system efficiently organizes students to meet their academic needs and close gaps in their learning. Typically, this progressive system is outlined as a three-level pyramid, including a primary, universal level of support for all students, a secondary level of support for 10–15% of students, and a tertiary level of support for 1–5% of students. Within each level, there may be multiple evidence-based instructional practices and interventions to address separate areas of need, but with the same level of intensity (National Center for Response to Intervention, 2010) (Figure 7.4).

These are many common misconceptions about tiered interventions.

1   Myth: An RTI system is a good teaching strategy.

- Fact: The tiered intervention system is not an instructional practice alone. It is a way of organizing various evidence-based instructional practices into a system for rapidly identifying and responding to student needs.

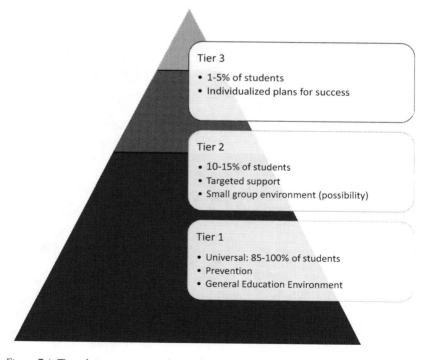

Figure 7.4 Tiered interventions have three levels: Tier 1 – Universal Strategies; Tier 2 – Targeted Support; Tier 3 – Intensive, Individualized Intervention (Rawson, 2019).

Schoolwide Programs   85

2   *Myth: Teachers pick which students get Tier 2 and Tier 3 support.*

- *Fact*: Teachers can't choose which students fit into each tier. In order to quickly identify and respond, schools must use quality universal screening tools and progress monitoring assessments. These assessments identify students with academic concerns and move them into an intervention to appropriately address the concern.

3   *Myth: RTI/Tiered Interventions and Special Education are the same thing.*

- *Fact*: Tiered interventions are not considered Special Education and should, if *implemented* with fidelity, decrease the likelihood that a student needs special education services (National Center for Response to Intervention, 2010).

4   *Myth: Tier 2 and Tier 3 services replace the need for effective Tier 1 strategies.*

- *Fact*: Higher tiered interventions should also not replace lower tiered interventions. For example, a student who needs specialized math instruction should not miss out on the general education math instruction to attend the secondary level support group. Secondary- and tertiary-level intervention should be in addition to evidence-based, high-quality classroom instruction.

Data-Driven Decisions

Implementing an RTI model to improve students' academic achievement requires two types of assessments: Universal screening and progress monitoring. Using these assessments, educators can objectively and accurately identify students in need of academic support and adjust the level (or "tier") and type of support needed throughout the year.

Universal screening is a brief assessment for all students. This screening gives teachers a snapshot of each student's academic levels. Examples of universal academic screening tools include DIBELS, Achieve 3000 level set, and i-Ready Diagnostics. Schools use the assessment results to determine a "cut point." A cut point is a score on the assessment scale that determines whether a student needs additional intervention. Cut points determine moves from both Tier 1 to Tier 2 and Tier 2 to Tier 3. Universal screening is typically conducted at the beginning of a school year, but can be done more than once per year to ensure that no student is falling through the cracks.

The second type of assessment is progress monitoring. Progress monitoring is used to quantify rates of student academic growth, assess academic performance over time, or evaluate the effectiveness of an instructional intervention. Progress monitoring assessments help educators accurately represent changes in students' academic achievement and confirm if that student is making adequate academic progress in their current intervention (National Center for Response to Intervention, 2010). Frequent progress monitoring creates a feedback loop by which educators can pivot their academic instruction quickly in order to better address student needs.

86 Develop Trauma-Sensitivity Schoolwide

Best Practices for Alignment with Trauma-Sensitivity

ACEs affect the ability of students to learn within the classroom by increasing their state of arousal and decreasing their critical thinking and executive functions. RTI is a trauma-sensitive practice because it creates safe environments where traumatized children can access academic learning specialized for their needs. Academic difficulties and academic-related anxiety can lead to low self-confidence and externalizing behaviors as students try to cope with their frustration and uncertainty. In this classroom, this may look like off-task behavior and disengagement. The opportunity to receive small group or individualized instruction can reduce a student's anxiety about classroom learning. Small group intervention allows students to be more engaged in the learning and build self-confidence by closing academic gaps. This, in turn, will lead to better classroom behavior, less fear and hyperarousal, and ultimately improved academic performance.

Students with ACEs may also have difficulty with cognitive processing, cause and effect relationships, interpreting patterns, problem solving, organization, sequencing and encoding and retrieving information from memory. The areas of the brain which are responsible for those activities are negatively affected by toxic stress (Harris, 2018). Difficulties with processing and memory may not be readily apparent within a general education setting as these difficulties look like distractibility and lack of attention. As a data-driven practice, RTI assessments will objectively identify any students who need extra academic assistance, without bias based on behavior.

Universal screening, a key feature of RTI, detects academic concerns early, so schools have time to intervene and address the students' needs. Once teachers know that students scored low in an academic area, they can begin searching for the root cause of the difficulties. After the root cause is determined, teachers can choose a fitting intervention to address the academic gaps. Instead of brushing off the problem because a student "just wasn't paying attention," objective screening tools require that all students be treated equitably. Low achievement is a focus of concern regardless of a student's relationship with the teacher, classroom behavior, skin color, family background, or other factors that reduce equity.

Positive Behavior Interventions and Supports (PBIS): Re-Teaching, Reinforcing and Reintegrating

PBIS is a framework for establishing and implementing preventative behavioral interventions. While PBIS can be applied with a few students, one classroom, or a whole school, we will be focusing on the schoolwide approach. Therefore, it will be referred to from now on as SWPBIS (schoolwide PBIS). SWPBIS is an evidence-based practice that incorporates systems to teach prosocial behaviors. As a part of the system, SWPBIS provides interventions and behavior supports to improve problem behaviors. The goal of SWPBIS is

Schoolwide Programs 87

to develop a positive school climate through consistency of expectation and positive reinforcement in order to improve academic achievement (Horner, Sugai, & Anderson, 2010).

SWPBIS is very similar in nature to RTI and includes a tiered intervention system, universal screening, progress monitoring, and data-driven decision making. The main difference between the two systems is that RTI focuses on students' academic needs and SWPBIS focuses on behavioral and social-emotional gaps.

SWPBIS builds on the theory and practices of applied behavior analysis, including consistent procedures, operationally defined behavior expectations, explicit behavioral instruction, frequent positive reinforcement, and clear consequences. These strategies attempt to minimize the benefit of negative behavior. SWPBIS uses data use to identify gaps in behavior and monitor student progress toward behavior goals (Horner et al., 2010).

Building Schoolwide Consistency

SWPBIS is not a program, but instead a framework for a two-to-three-year plan of developing and implementing effective, preventative schoolwide behavioral expectations. This framework relies heavily on professional development and teacher coaching to ensure that predictable, consistent, positive, and safe behaviors are developed at a whole-school level (Horner et al., 2010).

The first step in SWPBIS is to build staff capacity for leadership in the implementation process. A team of administrators, teachers, counselors, special education staff, classified staff (aides, office staff, kitchen staff, etc.), and parents begins the SWPBIS process. This leadership team attends professional development on PBIS and positive school climate. Once trained, the SWPBIS team selects 3–5 broad behavioral expectations (also known as core values) that all students in the school will follow. These could be written as a phrase (Respect Yourself, Respect Others, and Respect Property) or an acronym (ROAR – Respect, Ownership, Acceptance, Responsibility). After the initial selection process in the SWPBIS committee, all decisions must be accepted by the majority of the staff for schoolwide implementation to be realized (Figure 7.5).

After determining the school's 3–5 values/expectations, the committee and/or staff will create a PBIS matrix. The matrix operationally defines the broad expectations into positively stated, specific expectations based on location within the school. Teams will think about defining what these expectations look like, sound like, or feel like in various areas of the school campus. For an example, see Appendix B: PBIS Matrix Example (Carlton Hills School Staff, 2018).

Once the matrix has been developed and adopted by staff, students must be brought into this new process. One core tenet of SWPBIS is that behavior is taught.

No one expects students to know algebra before its taught. The same goes for behavior.

Figure 7.5 (a) Examples of 3–5 schoolwide values for PBIS – PAWS (Rawson, 2019). (b) Examples of 3–5 schoolwide values for PBIS – ROAR (Rawson, 2019).

If school staff expects students to behave in the ways listed on the matrix, those behaviors must be taught. A great time to do this type of explicit behavioral teaching is at the beginning of the school year or after a long break, like winter break. School staff creates a plan for teaching the expectations to students in all settings.

In one suburban school near San Diego, teachers commit to spending the first 20 days of school teaching their SWPBIS expectations. In this school, the SWPBIS matrix contains 20 squares. Each square represents the expectation for demonstrating one of the four schoolwide values in one of five common areas in the school. School administrators and counselors created a calendar of dates and aligned each date to one matrix square. For 20 days, all teachers would teach the same value and expectations across campus. From kindergarten to 8th grade, every student was learning what respect looked like in the library. The next day, every student learned what responsibility looked like in the hallways. Teachers used their own creativity and best teaching practices to teach these behavior expectations just as they would use best practices to teach math.

Positive Reinforcement: Catching the Good

Central to the name of SWPBIS is the word positive. Expectations are framed in a positive way. Behaviors are taught in a positive manner. Students' positive behaviors are rewarded.

Schools should determine consistent ways to reward and praise students who are adhering to the SWPBIS expectations or making progress toward improved behavior. Positive praise can take on many forms, from small specific verbal praise to large awards assemblies, raffles, and prizes. All adults on campus from cafeteria workers to custodians and principals to parents can positively praise student behavior. When praising students, adults should include the specific behavior they want to reinforce through praise and also the specific core value they noticed. This specificity helps students make connections between the expectations/values they learned and what behavior they are displaying. For example, "Wow Makenzie, I saw you keeping your hands to yourself. That shows a lot of respect to our class, thank you!"

Intervention and Reintegration: When They Don't Know... We Teach

Similar to the RTI framework, SWPBIS relies on universal screening tools and progress monitoring. This focus on student data ensures that students who need extra assistance are receiving support at a "Tier 2" or "Tier 3" level. These tiers take into consideration the intensity of the intervention and the number of students who participate. All students receive Tier 1/universal behavior instruction and positive reinforcement within the classroom and school environment. Data such as office referrals, suspensions, and detentions provide evidence for moving students from Tier 1 only to receiving Tier 2 supports in addition to Tier 1.

Using this data, students are moved to a higher tier when it becomes clear, based on a cut point (e.g. 2–3 office referrals), that the Tier 1 interventions are not enough. These may include common behavioral language, common expectations, explicit behavior instruction in a whole group setting, and positive rewards. Tier 2 services typically include small group interventions such as social skills training groups or brief interventions like Check In/Check Out. The interventions in Tier 2 are targeted and delivered in small groups or individually. Tier 2 interventions should focus on addressing any barriers to positive student behavior.

90 *Develop Trauma-Sensitivity Schoolwide*

A common practice at the Tier 2 level is a Student Study Team, or Student Success Team (SST) meeting. This meeting, which includes parents, classroom teacher, administrator, counselor, and intervention teachers, looks holistically at the student's needs. By gathering information about student strengths, health history, academic background, and present levels, the Student Study Team can make targeted recommendations to help this student progress forward behaviorally or academically. Recommendations may include support such as a rapport building intervention to develop a more positive relationship with the classroom teacher, a personalized behavior management system (sticker charts, self-monitoring, behavior charts, etc.), or changes to the student's school environment such as adding a calm-down area in their classroom or giving them access to breaks throughout the day. Complex data collection through functional behavior assessments (FBAs) and behavior progress reports identify students who need to move from Tier 2 supports into the more intensive Tier 3.

Tier 3 services are individualized behavior interventions for students with severe behavioral needs. In order to properly serve students at the Tier 3 level in SWPBIS, evaluations like a FBA must be done to provide adequate data. An FBA is an in-depth analysis of the causes of student behavior. FBA data is based on expert observations of the students while they are demonstrating their typical behaviors. Behavior specialists who conduct the FBA are looking for patterns and trends in triggers/antecedents to the typical behavior, consequences/benefits of the typical behavior, and times of day or environments where the behaviors occur (McIntyre, 2019).

Using this data, teams can pinpoint the underlying reasons for the behaviors and seek to extinguish them. The plans created using FBA data are called Behavior Support Plans (BSP) and are implemented by classroom teachers, intervention teachers, and counselors. A similar plan called a Behavior Improvement Plan (BIP) is implemented as part of the special education process. The plan creates goals for improved behavior and steps to help the students achieve these goals. Some intervention suggestions for Tier 3 are student-specific, reward-based behavioral management systems; individualized counseling to develop appropriate self-regulation or communication skills; changes to the student's learning environment; and changes to the consequence system for that student (McIntyre, 2019)

Best Practices for Alignment with Trauma-Sensitivity

SWPBIS's system of social-emotional and behavioral prevention and intervention is a near-perfect match with a trauma-sensitive school model. When a trauma-sensitive philosophy on student behavior is coupled with SWPBIS's clear expectations, consistent implementation, and data-informed behavior interventions, great student outcomes are possible. However, without a trauma-sensitive philosophy, SWPBIS can become another source of students' trauma. Students who experienced ACEs often display

Schoolwide Programs 91

challenging behaviors such as verbal or physical aggression. When we simply label these behaviors as "good" or "bad" and reinforce them accordingly, we miss the opportunity to dive deeper into the "why." Many of the challenging behaviors that traumatized students exhibit at school are behaviors that helped them survive at home with an abusive or neglectful parent (Dunning, 2019). Labeling those protective factors as "bad" can be confusing for students and detrimental.

When SWPBIS and trauma-sensitivity are aligned well, behavior management is based on self-regulation rather than compliance. For example, students are taught through Tier 1 interventions how to calm themselves down when they are feeling scared, worried, or angry. Students can only use critical thinking skills from their pre-frontal cortex when they are in a non-aroused state. If a student feels unsafe or out of control, they can't analyze pros-and-cons, try out calm-down strategies, or think about consequences before they act. Threats, negotiations, and bribes will not serve to improve student's behavior or ensure compliance. In fact, they could make it worse.

Behavior is the main language of trauma.

(Dunning, 2019)

When students have ACEs, they may lack the appropriate skills or social-emotional development to communicate their emotions and need for support. When these skills are missing, the common way to communicate is by lashing out. This may include yelling, kicking, throwing objects, sobbing, or other "temper tantrum" behaviors.

Tiered Interventions that Align PBIS and Trauma-Sensitive Schools

Tier 1 (Universal)	Tier 2 (Small Group/ At-Risk)	Tier 3 (Individual/ High-Risk)
• Social Emotional Wellness is a school priority • Every classroom is a safe and caring learning environment • SEL Curriculum • Direct Instruction of Self-Regulation • Staff model appropriate behaviors • School rules are clear, positive and consistent • Explicit behavioral instruction of what appropriate behavior looks like and sounds like across school environments • School policies and culture are trauma-sensitive	• Students move into Tier 2 interventions based on referral, suspension or other behavior data. • Social-emotional skill building groups focus on gaps in student behavior. • Student Study Team conducts holistic team meetings to address student behavior from a trauma-sensitive perspective • Check and Connect • Check-in/ Check-out • Daily behavior progress reports • Student Think Time/ Reflection • Sensory Regulation	• Referrals to mental health services (on or off campus) • Functional Behavior Assessment • Creation of individual Behavior Support Plan • Intensive Progress Monitoring

Figure 7.6 Tiered interventions that align PBIS and trauma-sensitivity (Rawson, 2019).

92 *Develop Trauma-Sensitivity Schoolwide*

The student is not attempting to manipulate the situation, escalating themselves on purpose, getting attention or any other unhelpful hypothesis. The student is out of control of their own behavior and instinctively returning to their fight-or-flight response (Figure 7.6).

By making safety, consistency, and caring among our top priorities, we can reduce the instances of the fight-or-flight response and, in turn, reduce these challenging behaviors.

Restorative Practices: Building Trusted Communities of Support

One of the most common "buzz words" in education during the 2010s was RPs. Vaguely defined and generally misunderstood, RPs both gained and lost popularity all over the country. Schools nationwide were being held accountable for high suspension rates and racial disparities within their suspended populations. A new approach was needed. Touted as an innovative way to reduce discipline referrals and suspensions, administrators flocked to participate in RP. Since traditional detentions, suspensions, and punishments weren't effective, everyone was looking for something else that would curb misbehavior.

But just as quickly as it was implemented, RP was rejected by many teachers and parents, claiming that its approach to achieve discipline through a social and cooperative process was too lenient, took too much time, and was ineffective (Brodsky, 2016). As I write this book, the data is still not clear as to the academic or long-term outcomes of RP. Regardless of academic outcomes, RP is a powerful social tool when used correctly. Counselors who are trained for RP dispel myths and show its effectiveness when implemented appropriately.

The Rise and Fall of Zero-Tolerance Discipline

Since the mid-1980s when the U.S. government began its "War on Drugs" campaign, the idea of zero-tolerance discipline has been a theme in education. A no-nonsense approach, zero-tolerance meant that students would be suspended or expelled for a broad range of offenses regardless of context, individual stories, or previous (or lack thereof) disciplinary actions (Skiba, 2004). You do the crime; you do the time. No questions asked.

The zero-tolerance theory assumes that potential troublemaking students will watch other students face severe consequences and that observation alone will discourage the potential troublemaker from causing a problem. The problem with this theory is that there is no evidence to back it up. Despite having clear, firm consequences, and removing troublemaking students from campus, zero-tolerance discipline does not improve school climate or academic achievement (Skiba, 2004). In fact, studies show that zero-tolerance discipline can make these worse. Between 30% and 50% of suspensions are for repeat offenders and students' reputation on campus, skin color, and income level are all more likely predictors of student suspension than the misbehavior. This unequal treatment leads to lower student perceptions of safety and equity on school campuses (Skiba, 2004).

As the data against zero-tolerance grew, so did the desire to find alternative, more effective forms of school discipline. In the early 2000s, studies by the CDC, the U.S. Surgeon General, and the U.S. Department of Education all searched for the most effective forms of youth violence prevention. None of these studies indicated zero-tolerance as an effective method. Other methods identified as promising included bullying prevention, conflict resolution, professional development to improve classroom management, parent involvement, and wraparound services using community agencies (Skiba, 2004). RP and trauma-sensitivity incorporate all of these.

Restorative Practices at Work in Schools

RP is "a social science that studies how to build social capital and achieve social discipline through participatory learning and decision making" (Wachtel, 2016). In other words, RP relies on communities of people to manage each other's behaviors by cooperating to prevent or fix problems. Sociologists and criminologists studied RPs, specifically one practice called restorative justice, as an alternative method of discipline for community and juvenile crime. These studies had promising results. Restorative justice reduced crime, violence, and bullying, restored relationships, strengthened communication and civility, and repaired harm (Wachtel, 2016).

The underlying theory in RP is called the social discipline window. The social discipline window (see Figure 7.7) describes four straightforward approaches to maintaining "social norms and behavioral boundaries," one of which is encapsulated in RP (Wachtel, 2016).

1   TO: This punitive style of limit setting relies on high power and control from one party (school staff) in order to force another party (students) into submission. This method has little support, compassion, or flexibility. It can seem arbitrary and abusive. It may remind traumatized students of the vast power differential at home between themselves and an abusive parent. It has a high likelihood of re-traumatizing students when used in schools. Zero-tolerance discipline is an example of TO.
2   NOT: This irresponsible and neglectful form of discipline ignores problems and provides no support. It pretends that problems do not exist, leading to an insecure environment where students feel unsafe and uncared for. This method may lead to a large increase in student misbehavior since unsafe environments frequently trigger stress in students with ACEs.
3   FOR: This permissive form of discipline says "anything goes!" It provides support and care, but no limit setting or appropriate social boundaries. This is the teacher who is friends with the students, allowing them to

94 *Develop Trauma-Sensitivity Schoolwide*

break rules and create chaotic environments. Because this adult wants to be the "nice one," they do not institute restrictions. While this type of discipline provides love and support, it leads to feelings of uncertainty and misunderstanding, and can create unsafe situations that trigger stress in students with ACEs.

4 WITH: This restorative style of discipline is characterized by both high levels of support and strong, consistent boundaries. Limits are set *with* the students through group expectation setting, and community circles and restorative conferences help the students and staff hold each other accountable for behaving outside of the boundaries. While there is flexibility in the types of consequences in the restorative style, there is no lack of accountability.

(Watchel, 1999)

RPs in schools include many processes to develop this "WITH" form of social discipline. Networks of strong relationships, community trust, mutual understanding, and a positive school climate create the social capital necessary for RP to be successful. Within these broad categories of positive social systems, four specific RPs exist to create a powerful and equitable discipline system (see Figure 7.8). These processes in order from least formal/most preventative to most formal/most reactive are as follows:

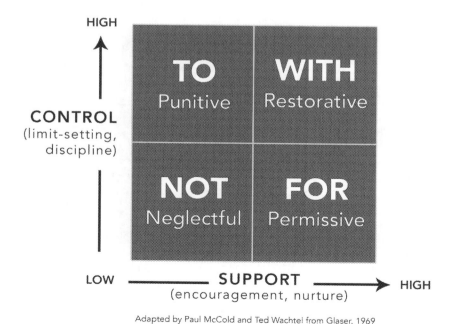

Figure 7.7 Social discipline window (Watchel, 1999).

Restorative Practices Continuum

informal   **formal**

| affective statements | affective questions | small impromptu conversations | circle | formal conference |

Figure 7.8 Continuum of restorative practices from least formal to most formal (Watchel, 1999).

1   Affective statements and questioning
2   Community circles
3   Restorative circles
4   Restorative justice conferences.

(Wachtel, 2016)

Through these four practices, schools can give students the opportunity to share feelings, beliefs, and opinions. After sharing, students can build relationships, solve problems, and participate in "righting the wrongs" within the community.

Affective statements are informal RPs that communicate feelings and allow for behavioral reflection as a part of everyday conversation between teachers and students. For example, when a student misbehaves and a teacher responds with "When you shouted out, I felt shocked" or "When you hit me, I felt confused." That allows the student to learn about how their actions affected someone else and to hear directly from the victim, not the principal or another intermediary. Affective questions are similar in that they help the student reflect on how their behavior affected others.

These small changes to communication can have large impacts in the way students and teachers talk to one another by increasing the reciprocal respect. Also, using these questions and statements can reduce the need for more formal RPs, which can be time-consuming.

Community circles are another preventative, restorative practice. In education, these circles have many names: Class meeting, morning meeting, circle time, etc. The premise of the circles is that in order to encourage empathy and kindness between peers, the peers must first know each other and trust each other. Circles allow all students within a class to both talk and listen in a safe, equitable environment. Circles allow students to share their perspectives and opinions, offer support, exchange information, and resolve conflict (Wachtel, 2016).

Circles can be sequential. Sequential circles allow each student in order around the circle, to share an opinion or thought on a particular topic posed by

96　Develop Trauma-Sensitivity Schoolwide

the "circle keeper" (facilitator). This sequence ensures that all voices are heard and respected in the classroom. Circles can also be non-sequential, where conversation moves more freely, but still with decorum. This allows students to choose when and if they want to speak. Non-sequential circles allow for depth in the conversation while providing a safety net of "passing" to those who are not yet willing to be vulnerable.

Restorative circles are formalized, reactive circles. These circles allow for students to solve a community problem together in a civilized way. For example, students and their teacher might discuss how to keep their classroom cleaner, what types of activities to have during "free time," or how a student disruption can be avoided in the future. A script of affective questions can be used to help the group or offending students understand how their actions created a problem for others.

Being a substitute teacher is a tough job. But being a middle school substitute teacher is in a league of its own. As a long-term substitute for an 8th-grade classroom, Ms. Wilson quickly found out that middle school students don't easily trust newcomers. As soon as she arrived, the anxiety was evident. Students were on edge, verbally and physically aggressive, testing boundaries and creating chaos. After many weeks of increasingly hostile behavior, she felt that there was no hope for her to gain control of the classroom environment and change student behavior. The school's vice principal suggested restorative circles as a strategy to regain trust, boost student empathy, and enhance feelings of safety and belonging for both the students and Ms. Wilson. Working together, Ms. Wilson and the school's vice principal held a series of restorative circles to discuss the recent teacher change, student behavior, and chaotic classroom environment. Within one week, office referrals had decreased, students' mood improved, and their feelings of understanding and empathy for their teacher increased.

Lastly, the restorative conference is the most formal and most reactive of the RPs. This conference is a "structured meeting between offenders, victims [and potentially family members or supporting friends] in which they deal with the consequences of the crime or wrongdoing and decide how best to repair the harm" (Wachtel, 2016). It is different than a counseling session or a conflict mediation because the power to solve the problem lies solely with the two involved parties. Within schools, these conferences are facilitated by the vice principal, school counselor, teacher, or other trained adult. Conferences provide victims with a chance to express their feelings, confront their offender, ask questions, and have a voice in the outcome. Many times, in schools, victims are not given this opportunity. If a student hits another student, the offending student may get a trip to the office and detention but never returns to the victim to "right the wrong." The process of restorative conferences allows for closure for both victim and offender. Offenders are held accountable for their actions but also provided an opportunity to be reintegrated into their class and community as someone who made amends for their actions and repaired the harm (Wachtel, 2016).

Fourth grader Nathan had four ACEs. After witnessing his father physically and verbally abuse his mother, his parents got a divorce. Nathan was scared to stay with his dad and be apart from his mom. He worried about her and her safety while he was gone. At his dad's house, Nathan witnessed community violence, even once seeing his dad assault his mom's new boyfriend in front of him. Nathan's dad had PTSD and used substances to cope with his mental illness. After watching his dad use a knife to threaten a neighbor, Nathan brought a utility knife to school. After showing it to other students in his class and using it to open his lunch, Nathan was sent to the principal's office and suspended.

In many school districts, bringing a knife to school at any age is a zero-tolerance offense, resulting in multi-day suspension or expulsion. Fortunately for Nathan, his school did not adhere to these policies. After a one-day suspension and parent meeting, Nathan was allowed to return to school. Before rejoining his class, Nathan participated in three restorative conferences with other students who saw the knife. Those students shared with Nathan how seeing a knife at school scared them and made them afraid to be his friend. They told Nathan that their parents were scared and they worried that he would bring it again. Nathan got a chance to apologize and vow to never bring a knife again. Using the restorative conference gave both Nathan and the victims a chance for closure and reassurance. Nathan was reaccepted into his classroom community and has had no further issues of violence or antisocial behavior.

For more information about specific RPs or for additional training for yourself or school staff, visit IIRP's website, www.iirp.edu

Best Practices for Alignment with Trauma-Sensitivity

Enrique was 6. As a first grader, he already had three ACEs. Divorced parents, a father in jail, and an emotionally abusive mother was more stress than he could tolerate. His toxic stress led him to be aggressive, impulsive, and easily agitated. When Enrique was in fight-or-flight mode, he would withdraw under desks and tables, run from the classroom or hide in other areas of the school. As adults approached him, prompting him to return to class or come out from under a table, he would hit, kick, and scream.

Instead of responding to Enrique's need for safety and self-regulation skills, his school responded with discipline. Suspending him and repeatedly punishing him for aggression during his stress response did nothing to curb the behavior. In fact, it made it worse. One day, after Enrique refused again to come out from under a teacher's desk, the school called the police. The police arrested Enrique and walked him in handcuffs through the school parking lot. The handcuffed 6-year-old waited in the back of a police car that day while other students watched and played at recess. Instead of meeting his needs with positive reinforcement (SWPBIS), teaching self-regulation (SEL), or using a restorative approach to discipline (RP), the school chose to re-traumatize a

98 Develop Trauma-Sensitivity Schoolwide

student by arresting him just like he witnessed his father arrested months before.

In order to avoid re-traumatization of a student, school discipline models must be safe, effective, and build on mutual trust. When describing discipline models like zero-tolerance, suspensions, and detentions, these are some of the last words that come to mind. More often, words like aggressive, controlling, power, and shame come to mind. For a school to be trauma-sensitive, it must recreate its policies and procedures, including its discipline model. The trauma-sensitive discipline model reflects the understanding that traumatized students may not be in control of their behaviors, especially when escalated due to fear. What traumatized students need is to learn how to self-regulate and reflect on their behaviors. They must receive support to try again. RP, through its underlying theory of the social discipline window, and its overt practices to build trusting communities, is a match for trauma-sensitive schools.

RP and restorative discipline in schools hold offenders accountable for their actions, empower the voice of the victim, develop a deep sense of belonging and confidence among classmates, and increase student's participation and connectedness to school. Any trauma-sensitive school should think seriously about incorporating RPs into their discipline model. Without these, the discipline model has a high likelihood for re-traumatization and will seem disconnected from other trauma-sensitive philosophies.

The Role of the School Counselor

The school counselor is an integral part of the management and delivery for schoolwide social-emotional and positive behavior programs. As a part of the SEL, PBIS, RTI, or RP teams at a school site, counselors ensure that all students have equitable access to these programs. Counselors also ensure that the programs are implemented with fidelity to maximize the positive impact for students. One feature that many of these programs have in common is a data-driven and tiered approach to interventions. School counselors' knowledge of data-driven services and comprehensive program management makes them well suited for a leadership role within these programs. However, being the sole manager of all these programs would overwhelm any counselor and fall outside of the recommended counselor role according to ASCA. Counselors should be a part of the management team for these initiatives, but not be the manager. This team approach ensures that a mental health expert (the school counselor) is able to be an advocate for students' well-being, while an administrative leader handles logistics and other tasks.

When an administrator manages these programs alone, they could become a box to check instead of a trauma-sensitive program with immense benefits to students. Counselors can advocate for the consistent use of data in these programs. By ensuring that the data is collected objectively, through universal screenings with cut points, counselors can erase potential biases and subjectivity in school discipline and intervention referrals. By relying on the data and not just observations, students are less likely to fall through the cracks.

Students with ACE exposure may not always have large upset reactions and externalizing behaviors. They may be quiet, withdrawn, and disengaged. Students like these can frequently be overlooked and pushed along from grade to grade, not receiving the academic and social-emotional instruction they need. However, students exposed to ACEs who do have large, upset reactions and externalizing behaviors are much more likely to be punitively disciplined, especially students of color, for these actions outside of their rational control (Skiba, 2004). Students also need equitable protection to ensure that they receive social skills training and check-ins they need. These Tier 2 interventions give students feelings of support and connection instead of the abandonment, isolation, or shame from traditional suspensions and detentions.

School counselors can also advocate for the fidelity of these programs, especially PBIS and RPs by ensuring that all staff are trained in these philosophically unique programs. The concepts of teaching behavior expectations, rewarding the good instead of punishing the bad, and solving programs collaboratively instead of doling out discipline are new ideas for many educators and school staff. But it's not just teachers who have an impact on students each day at school. Paraeducators, cafeteria workers, campus aids, bus drivers, security guards, custodians, secretaries, and crossing guards all interact with students in a way that reinforces or damages the positive school climate and intervention programs. These staff members can add to a trauma-sensitive school, if they are trained appropriately, or hinder the universal approach if they are not given adequate guidance on these new strategies.

As school counselors, we must avoid the common trap of getting pigeon-holed into the "feel good only" category. This is more common in elementary and middle school counseling than high school counseling. Participating in academically focused programs like RTI gives counselors a broader reach. Not to mention, these academic teams need a social-emotional expert! Sometimes, RTI and intervention meetings focus only on the student's test scores and academic behaviors instead of considering underlying causes. School counselors can help RTI and SST teams to consider ACEs and trauma as an underlying cause for low academic achievement.

Counselors can advocate for interventions despite the student's externalizing behaviors. Instead of labeling a student lazy and overlooking them for an intervention, school counselors can advocate for that student's access to the assistance program. Being a part of the "academic only" meetings also ensures that both RTI and PBIS are incorporated together to form a true MTSS model, supporting students' academics, behaviors, and emotional needs all at the same time.

Aligning a comprehensive counseling program to these types of schoolwide programs can ensure the greatest success for students academically,

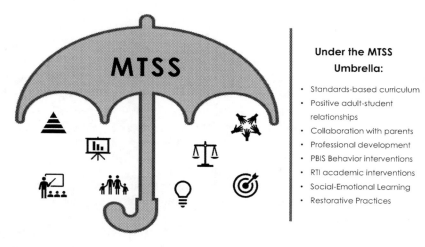

Figure 7.9 The umbrella of MTSS: A recipe for student success (Rawson, 2019).

behaviorally, and emotionally regardless of their past trauma. By providing a consistent, structured, and positive environment using schoolwide programs, counselors will decrease the need for reactive counseling services. Instead of moving from crisis to crisis, counselors can work preventatively to set up intervention frameworks, less traumatic discipline methods, and SEL skill building. Spending time on preventative work is time well spent. The work of a preventative counselor will reach more students with greater long-term impact. Students with ACEs need wraparound support, not just brief meetings. These programs can provide that support by bringing every staff member into the plan. Students with ACEs can achieve academic excellence through RTI, learn appropriate social behaviors through PBIS, gain emotional competence and self-regulation skills through SEL, and build trust and connection to their school community with RPs. This is an MTSS recipe for success (Figure 7.9).

References

Brodsky, S. (2016, June 28). Is Discipline Reform Really Helping Decrease School Violence?. *The Atlantic*. Retrieved from www.theatlantic.com/education/archive/2016/06/school-violence-restorative-justice/488945/
Carlton Hills School Staff. (2018). *Carlton Hills PBIS Matrix*. Santee, CA: Author.
CASEL. (2019). *CASEL: History*. Retrieved from CASEL: https://casel.org/history/
CASEL. (2019). *Core SEL Competencies*. Retrieved from CASEL: https://casel.org/core-competencies/
CASEL. (2019). *What is SEL*. Retrieved from CASEL: https://casel.org/what-is-sel/

Schoolwide Programs 101

Center on Response to Intervention at American Institutes for Research. (2019). *The essential components of RTI [Online image].* Retrieved from Center on Response to Intervention at American Institutes for Research: www.rti4success.org/

Dunning, C. (2019). *Incorporating Trauma into PBIS and Teacher Management.* Retrieved from Topeka Public Schools: www.topekapublicschools.net/cms/lib/KS02203960/Centricity/Domain/132/TRAUMA%20INTO%20PBIS.pdf

Durlak, J. A., Weissberg, R. P., Dymnicki, A. B., Taylor, R. D., & Schellinger, K. B. (2011). The Impact of Enhancing Students' Social and Emotional Learning: A Meta-Analysis of School-Based Universal Interventions. *Child Development, 82*(1), 405–432. Retrieved from https://casel.org/the-impact-of-enhancing-students-social-and-emotional-learning-a-meta-analysis-of-school-based-universal-interventions/

Greenberg, M. (2006). Promoting Resilience in Children and Youth: Preventative Interventions and their interface with neuroscience. *Annals of the New York Academy of Sciences, 1094*(1), 139–149.

Harris, N. B. (2018). *The Deepest Well: Healing the Long-Term Effects of Childhood Adversity.* New York, NY: Houghton Mifflin Harcourt.

Horner, R. H., Sugai, G., & Anderson, C. M. (2010). Examining the Evidence Base for School-Wide Positive Behavior Support. *Focus on Exceptional Children, 42*(8), 1–16.

McInerney, M., & Elledge, A. (2013). *Using a Response to Intervention Framework to Improve Student Learning: A Pocket Guide for State and District Leaders.* Washington, DC: American Institutes for Research.

McIntyre, T. (2019). *Functional Behavior Assessment.* Retrieved from Behavior Advisor: www.behavioradvisor.com/FBA.html

National Center for Response to Intervention. (2010). *Essential Components of RTI – A Closer Look at Response to Intervention.* Washinton, DC: U.S. Department of Education, Office of Special Education Programs, National Center on Response to Intervention.

Skiba, R. (2004). Zero Tolerance: The Assumptions and the Facts. *Education Policy Briefs, 2*, 1–8. Retrieved from https://files.eric.ed.gov/fulltext/ED488918.pdf

Taylor, R. D., Oberle, E., Durlak, J. A., & Weissberg, R. P. (2017). Promoting Positive Youth Development through School-Based Social and Emotional Learning Interventions: A Meta-Analysis of Follow-Up Effects. *Child Development, 88*(4), 1156–1171.

Trauma Learning and Policy Initiative. (2019). *The Solution: Trauma Sensitive School.* Retrieved from Trauma Learning and Policy Initiative: https://traumasensitive-schools.org/trauma-and-learning/the-solution-trauma-sensitive-schools/

van der Kolk, B. (2005). Developmental Trauma Disorder. *Psychiatric Annals, 35*, 401–408. Retrieved from Traumatic Stress Institute: https://traumaticstressinstitute.org/wp-content/files_mf/1276541701VanderKolkDvptTraumaDis.pdf

Wachtel, T. (2016). *Defining Restorative.* Retrieved from International Institute for Restorative Practices: www.iirp.edu/images/pdf/Defining-Restorative_Nov-2016.pdf

Watchel, T. (1999). Restorative Justice in Everyday Life: Beyond the Formal Ritual. *Reshaping Australian Institutions Conference: Restorative Justice and Civil Society.* Canberra, Australia: The Australian National University. Retrieved from www.iirp.edu/eforum-archive/4221-restorative-justice-in-everyday-life-beyond-the-formal-ritual

Step 3

Implement School Counseling Strategies to Support Students with ACEs

The TSC Model

8 Developing TSC

From neuroscience to school connectedness, and self-regulation to community partnerships, the information about trauma is wide and school counselors' time is thin. School counselors need a way to organize the good work we are already doing to address toxic stress and pinpoint gaps in practice. The TSC model for School Counseling at a trauma-sensitive school is an organizational framework to do just that.

By aligning research about the effects of trauma with evidence-based counseling interventions, school counselors are moving the needle for students with Adverse Childhood Experiences (ACEs). In the Santee School District, school counselors and social workers categorized their work around ACEs into three main themes – (1) Tiered Interventions; (2) Student Self-Regulation; (3) Creating Connectedness (TSC). By addressing these three themes, we were more likely to increase our students' ability to be socially, emotionally, and academically successful within a general education classroom. In the long term, we hope that TSC can reduce the need for special education services, the likelihood of suspensions, and the negative impact of trauma on student's self-concept.

A TSC School Counseling Program addresses the needs of students with ACEs by providing:

1 *Tiered Interventions* to objectively and thoroughly address students' academic, social-emotional, and behavioral needs.
2 *Student Self-Regulation* strategies to develop self-control, self-reflection, and self-efficacy skills.
3 *Connections* to school through meaningful adult relationships, engagement within the classroom, and opportunities for extracurricular involvement.

Within these three broad themes exist interventions and counseling practices that best meet the needs of both students with ACEs and the general population. In this way, counselors can ensure that their daily tasks such as teaching SEL lessons, facilitating counseling small groups, and reacting to student crises all serve a large purpose and work toward a common goal. For a complete list of interventions that align with TSC, see Appendix C.

The goal of TSC is to provide a comprehensive school counseling program that lessens the educational impact of childhood trauma.

106 *The TSC Model*

In this chapter, each of the three components of TSC will be addressed in further detail. In Chapters 9–11, examples of school counseling practices and interventions for each category are provided.

ARC: A Theoretical Model to Guide the Work

One theory that guided the development of TSC was the Attachment, Self-Regulation, and Competency (ARC) intervention framework for children with complex trauma (Kinniburgh, Blaustein, Spinazzola, & van der Kolk, 2005). The ARC model is a clinical model for use by psychologists and mental health therapists working with children and families. The TSC model adapts the concepts of ARC to be used by school counselors who do not provide long-term mental health therapy.

The ARC intervention framework is a "flexible model of intervention that is embedded in a developmental and social context and can address a continuum of trauma exposures" (Kinniburgh et al., 2005). This model connects the trauma research to the most effective clinical psychology and counseling treatments for traumatized children.

The ARC framework addresses gaps and areas of relative weakness created when ACE exposure interferes with normal child development (Kinniburgh et al., 2005). By focusing on skill building instead of only processing traumatic memories, this framework helps students transform the traumatic experience into something that propels them forward. The ARC model encourages "traumatic experience integration," which includes healthy mourning of a traumatic loss, making meaning from the trauma, developing coping skills, and a present-oriented mentality despite the past trauma. By focusing on skill building and meaning making, the ARC model develops resilience, a protective factor that prevents a negative impact from further traumatization (Cook, Blaustein, Spinazzola, & van der Kolk, 2003).

In addition to building skills in deficit areas, the ARC framework focuses on systemic change within the child's context. Interventions focus on the family and home environment, changes to routines and structures, and strengthening the secure attachment between the child and their caregivers (Kinniburgh et al., 2005). Utilizing this systems approach, therapists can ensure that the skills developed using the ARC framework and the therapeutic goals are generalizable outside of the therapy sessions. As this model focuses primarily on children, using a systems approach also ensures the application of skills and habits outside of the child's control. By educating parents about the effects of trauma and utilizing them as partners in the child's treatment, the therapist can increase the likelihood that the therapeutic goals are met.

There are three key areas of intervention in the ARC model: Attachment, Regulation, and Competency. Within each area, systemic, familial, and individual interventions can be effective. The ARC approach encourages clinicians to use many developmentally appropriate interventions. The ability for clinicians to choose from a wide variety of evidence-based tools allows the framework to be flexible and meet the needs of each specific child and context (Kinniburgh et al., 2005).

Attachment

The word attachment describes the relationship and interactions between children and their primary caregivers. Attachments are developed throughout childhood and have a substantial impact of the child's identity development, understanding of themselves and others, and their ability to regulate emotions. Secure attachments and nurturing caregiving promote healthy social and emotional development and have long-term, positive effects on relational health and resiliency (Kinniburgh et al., 2005).

Children who develop insecure attachments to their primary caregivers, as is common for maltreated children, have later difficulties in developing a complex emotion management system. Due to a lack of consistent and supportive caregiving, maltreated children are forced to manage their own emotions and traumatic experiences. They rely on simplistic and infantile coping skills such as crying, temper tantrums, or avoidance. As the child continues to grow in the absence of a secure attachment, they never learn any other ways to cope with emotions. These immature strategies become even more ingrained (Kinniburgh et al., 2005).

In the ARC model, the two main goals for attachment are to build or rebuild healthy attachment relationships with caregiving adults and to create a safe space for healthy recovery from trauma. While the home environment and primary caregiver-to-child relationship are of utmost importance, the attachment principles can be applied to all environments within the child's context and to all significant adults (e.g. using the principles at school with teachers).

These goals are achieved by:

1   Creating a stable and structured environment by establishing routines and habits.
2   Increasing the caregiver's ability and capacity to handle the child's "big emotions" and big reactions.
3   Improving the caregiver's ability to attune to the child's feelings rather than simply responding to the child's behaviors.
4   Increasing positive reinforcement and specific praise to enhance the child's self-esteem and ability to identify with their strengths rather than weaknesses.

(Kinniburgh et al., 2005)

Regulation

Students who are exposed to ACEs frequently enter "fight, flight or freeze." This automatic stress response turns on even when no true danger or stressor is present. Due to their past trauma, students with ACEs are hypervigilant and anticipate the worst outcomes. Since traumatic events have no clear "cause and effect" pattern, students with ACEs may struggle to assess the fault in a situation correctly. Instead, they may internalize negative emotions like shame, blame, and guilt due to a misunderstanding of why events occurred. They also may employ unhealthy emotion management, either externalizing ("exploding") or internalizing/withdrawing instead of appropriately calming themselves down (Figure 8.1).

Regulation refers to the process by which students return to a state of calm after a triggering event activates their stress response. Regulation also refers to the process by which students avoid engaging their stress response by proactively managing their emotions. In the ARC model, there are three primary self-regulation skills addressed:

1 *Emotion identification skills.* This is the ability to accurately recognize one's own feelings and connect these feelings to experience. It also involves being able to identify emotions in others by reading their expressions and cues.
2 *Emotional expression skills.* This includes the ability to express and communicate feelings and the personal feelings experience. This includes how a student physically experiences emotions or a reflection on the emotions and why they occurred. For example, if a student can tell the teacher "I am feeling really hot and red, I know I am mad." Or "I felt sad today when Lily told me I was bossy."

- Aggression
- Hyperactivity
- Out of seat
- Eloping (Running from class)
- Excessive Talking
- Blurting/ Interrupting
- Impulsivity
- Loud Volume
- Distracts others
- Irritates others with noises, touching or proximity
- Tantrums
- Hostile/ Defiant Behavior
- Compulsive behaviors
- Obscene language and gestures

Externalizing Behaviors

- Extreme shyness
- Socially withdrawn
- Isolates self
- Rarely participates in discussions
- Low self-esteem
- Depressed mood/ sadness
- Fears/ phobias
- "shuts down" and refuses school work
- Missing assignments
- Freezes on tests
- Neglected or forgotten by peers
- Excessive worries/ anxiety
- Eating disorders

Internalizing Behaviors

Figure 8.1 ACEs impact student behaviors. Students cope with toxic stress by internalizing and externalizing their experience (Rawson, 2019).

Developing TSC 109

3   *Emotional management (modulation)*. Modulation is the ability to identify triggers that shift emotions to a more aroused state, detect the shift in mood, and then return to a calm state. This can occur using coping skills like taking a break or listening to music or regulation tools such as stress balls, fidgets, etc.

(Kinniburgh et al., 2005).

Competency

Child development is a continuous process that is broken down into stages by developmental theorists. The stages help us understand what tasks should be occurring at various points throughout the child's life. Using acquired skills as developmental markers, parents and teachers can understand the developmental stage of a child compared to peers. Skills such as developing abstract reasoning in adolescence or using expressive language in toddlerhood are common milestones.

Children move through the developmental stages by using the newly developed skills in combination with previously acquired skills. This progressive learning builds competency from infancy through adulthood in four domains – cognitive, emotional, interpersonal, and intrapersonal (Kinniburgh et al., 2005). Failure to find success in one of these four developmental areas can derail this skill-acquisition process. Developmental delays may decrease a child's sense of competency and their confidence in their own abilities.

The four domains of competency are defined as follows:

1   *Cognitive*: academic performance and achievement, language development and executive functioning skills.
2   *Emotional*: frustration tolerance, problem-solving skills and attention.
3   *Interpersonal*: building secure attachments, building positive friendships, building mature adult relationships.
4   *Intrapersonal*: awareness of internal emotions and states, development of positive self-concept, realistic assessment of their own competencies.

(Kinniburgh et al., 2005)

Competency development is key to building resilience in children with ACEs. Through achieving competencies, children can enhance self-worth, build perseverance, make connections with teachers or mentors, build normal developmental skills that were lost or never gained, and enhance their ability to plan ahead, set goals, and control impulses (Kinniburgh et al., 2005). The ARC model achieves competency development and builds resilience by:

1   Creating opportunities for children to find success and mastery.
2   Creating opportunities for healthy connection to other peers, adults, and community members.

110　*The TSC Model*

3　Identifying personal strengths and applying them to enhance positive self-concept.
4　Encouraging self-reflection and self-evaluation of outcomes in order to develop a sense of control and a belief in their own abilities.

(Kinniburgh et al., 2005)

ARC and TSC

Implementing aspects of the ARC model throughout my own career solidified my belief in its importance. As a school counselor, I do not provide long-term mental health therapy. I do provide brief, skill- or goal-based interventions to improve students' personal-social and academic outcomes. The ARC model provided general categories through which I could organize my school counseling program.

When I began to attempt to align my program with ARC, I found much of it to be useful, but a few things didn't match my school counselor scope of practice. For example, throughout the ARC model, it is recommended to work directly with families to implement trauma-sensitive strategies at home. In the ARC model, this includes parent-child interaction therapy, other attachment-based therapies, and wraparound services in the home (Kinniburgh et al., 2005). School counselors do not provide these services but can refer families to these services within each local community.

ARC was never meant to be a framework for school counselors. Using the concepts of ARC and adding school counseling specific practices, TSC was born. The self-regulation components of each model lineup directly, and the attachment component of ARC is similar to the connectedness component of TSC. One component of ARC that differs from TSC is competency vs. tiered interventions. I have chosen tiered interventions in the TSC model to emphasize that within a comprehensive school counseling program, there is an essential responsibility to meet the needs of students systemically and not simply individually. While enhancing student's competency and, in turn, their self-esteem is an integral part of a school counselor's role, competency is embedded within the other two components of self-regulation and connections.

The ARC model recommends working directly with families to implement trauma-sensitive strategies at home. In the ARC model, this includes parent-child interaction therapy, other attachment-based therapies, and wraparound services in the home (Kinniburgh et al., 2005). School counselors do not provide these services but can refer families to these services within each local community.

My hope is that TSC helps school counselors to organize their trauma-sensitive program. Through organization, counselors can ensure that their program is both preventative and wide-reaching. Many school counselors become ineffective when their systemic and preventative school counseling program becomes a reactionary program for a small number of students.

A common complaint from school counselors is that they are simply "putting out fires." When implementing a trauma-sensitive program, this idea of not just "putting out fires" becomes even more important. Trauma-sensitive school counselors do NOT just respond to explosive behaviors in the classroom

Developing TSC 111

or deescalate students in the counseling office. Trauma-sensitive counselors must be leaders on their campus. They are developing and implementing tiered interventions that ensure the safety and belonging of all students in order to prevent the fire.

We are Smokey the Bear, NOT the firefighter.

Tiered Interventions

RTI.
MTSS.
PBIS.
Alphabet soup?

Tiered-intervention systems are the framework on which the TLC school counseling model is built. Often labeled by confusing acronyms and filled with educational jargon, school counselors can get easily confused by the myriad of tiered-intervention options. Unfortunately, this confusion leads some school counselors to either misuse or misrepresent the system they create. While RTI (an academically focused tiered system) and PBIS (a behaviorally focused tiered system) both have a role to play in the school by themselves, school counselors need to be focusing on the overlap of the two systems. The acronym MTSS commonly refers to this cross-section of RTI and PBIS.

These academic and behavioral interventions are incredibly important to ensure trauma-sensitivity and advance the core academic mission of the school. School counselors should play an active role in supporting MTSS (Figure 8.2).

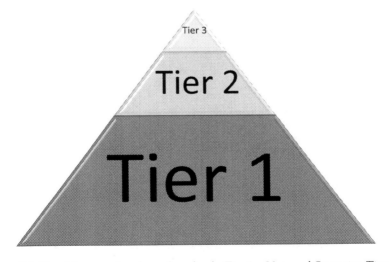

Figure 8.2 Tiered Interventions have three levels: Tier 1 – Universal Strategies; Tier 2 – Targeted Support; Tier 3 – Intensive, Individualized Intervention (Rawson, 2019).

112   *The TSC Model*

But school counselors also live in another world of standards and acronyms. Creating a counseling program using the ASCA National Model to address the ASCA Mindsets and Behaviors for Student Success is the core mission of a school counselor.

The *ASCA National Model: A Framework for School Counseling Programs* guides school counselors to develop a program that goes beyond reactive counseling or individual student meetings. The school counseling program outlined in the ASCA National Model is an integral part of the school's academic mission. The model was created to enhance school counselors' abilities to have a meaningful impact on the outcomes of academic achievement, attendance, and student behavior/discipline (American School Counselor Association, 2019). The model has four key components to develop a comprehensive counseling program:

1   Define the program through the student and professional counselor standards addressed.
2   Manage the program through planning, goal setting, and evaluation.
3   Deliver the program through direct access to students in classroom lessons, small groups, and individual meetings, as well as consultation and collaboration with teachers and administrators to provide student support.
4   Assess the programs' impact on student's perceptions of school and school-related outcomes of attendance, academic achievement, and discipline.

(American School Counselor Association, 2019)

The ASCA National Model helps counselors ensure that they are staying true to the role of a professional school counselor and not becoming a secretary, campus supervisor, data entry clerk, or on the other end of the spectrum, an additional school administrator. When addressing trauma, it is easy as a school counselor to end up as a mental health therapist, only working with a few high-need students for a long period of time. This is also not a role of a professional school counselor.

While the ASCA Model is not a tiered-intervention system, using a tiered-intervention system is a great way to address some of its core components. First, the ASCA Model recommends that 80% of counselor's time be spent on direct or indirect student services. Using a tiered-intervention model ensures that the services you directly provide address the needs of all students and your direct student services are not focused on only a few students. While long-term counseling, crisis response, or student deescalation would still be in line with ASCA's use of time recommendations, it is not effective or in line with the professional counseling goal to impact the academic achievement and well-being of ALL students on campus.

Second, a tiered-intervention system ensures that school counselors are delivering content and services in multiple ways. If school counselors only facilitate social skills in small groups, their expertise and leadership are

Developing TSC   113

being under-utilized. Students with ACEs have greater needs than one intervention can address. In the same way, if school counselors only deliver SEL classroom lessons, many students with higher level needs are being underserved.

Lastly, a tiered-intervention system is informed by data, which is also integral to assessing the impact of the counseling program. Using universal academic screenings, school climate surveys, discipline referral data, attendance rates, and GPAs, a school counselor can determine areas of student need and close the gap between where students are currently and where they could be with appropriate interventions.

For the complete list of the ASCA Mindsets and Behaviors for Student Success, see Appendix D (American School Counselor Association, 2014).

MTMDSS and TSC – Tiered-Interventions and Trauma-Sensitivity in a Comprehensive Counseling Program

The ASCA National Model recommends school counselors address students' needs in the college/career domain just as they would address academic or social-emotional needs. But MTSS tiered interventions rarely address career counseling. In 2017, Trish Hatch – author, professor, and school counseling advocate – created a tiered-intervention model that addresses all three domains of school counseling practice – academic, social-emotional, and college/career. She called it the Multi-tiered Multi-domain Model for Student Support (MTMDSS). This model incorporates the format of tiered interventions, while ensuring student access to all domains of an ASCA school counseling program (Hatch, 2017b).

Including the college/career domain from the ASCA National Model alongside the traditional MTSS model ensures that all students have access to future-oriented planning with their school counselors. Using this model, students have the chance to broaden their awareness of future opportunities, guarantee their access to these opportunities, and receive personalized interventions to reach their college/career goals. Incorporating the college/career domain is both an excellent strategy to motivate students and an essential component in building competence and student engagement (Hatch, 2017a) (Figure 8.3).

Using the MTMDSS diagram to map out a school counseling program identifies its strengths and weaknesses (Hatch, 2017b). In 2019, my school district counselors attended a training by Trish Hatch to implement our own MTMDSS model. Here are two examples of MTMDSS models from our district. While many interventions are similar, some are very different, showing that even within the same district, school sites have a variety of unique needs (Figure 8.4).

MTMDSS models also align with trauma-sensitivity. By ensuring access to a comprehensive school counseling model at all tiers, school counselors can preventatively and reactively address the educational impact of childhood

114 The TSC Model

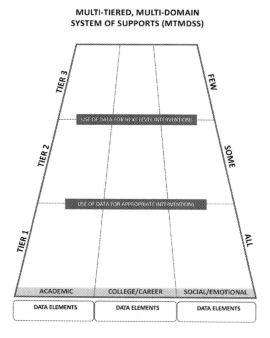

Figure 8.3 MTMDSS aligns both the ASCA National Model and an MTSS Tiered-Intervention System (Hatch, 2017).

adversity. But some common school counseling duties and programs do not align with trauma-sensitivity. For example, data entry, substitute teaching, coordinating state testing, and supervising detention. When analyzing an MTMDSS model, the counselor should ask themselves – "Does this intervention help our school achieve the goal of trauma-sensitivity?" and "Is this an appropriate use of my time?" Every intervention should be answered with a resounding "YES!"

In my own practice, I use the MTMDSS framework to ensure compliance with three distinct frameworks:

1   An MTSS academic/behavioral tiered-intervention model.
2   The ASCA National Model for a comprehensive school counseling program that addresses the academic, social/emotional, and college/career domains.
3   The TLC model for trauma-sensitivity in school counseling.

To ensure fidelity to the TLC model, mark each intervention on my MTMDSS chart with a "T" "S," or a "C." All interventions should fall into one of these

Developing TSC 115

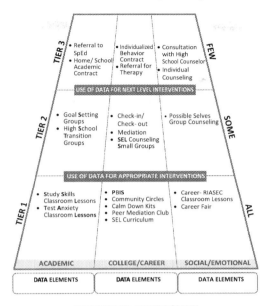

Figure 8.4 (a) Example of Elementary/Middle School Counseling MTMDSS organizational system (Hatch, 2017). (b) Example of High School Counseling MTMDSS organizational system (Hatch, 2017).

116 The TSC Model

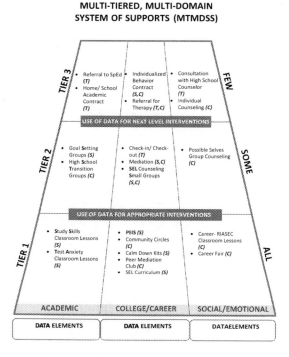

Figure 8.5 Alignment of MTMDSS and TSC for an Elementary/Middle School Counseling Program (Hatch, 2017).

three categories to align the program with research-based best practices for interventions to address the educational impact of trauma (Figure 8.5).

T: Any direct or indirect counseling service that supports the tiered-intervention framework without directly addressing self-regulation or developing connections to school. This includes SST meetings, parent conferences, and referrals to community resources.

S: Any intervention or service that supports the learning of self-regulation skills. This includes small groups for anger management, SEL core-curriculum, behavioral crisis response interventions, and more.

C: Any intervention or service that builds students' connections to the school community, including adults, peers, academic content, and extracurricular activities. This connection to school increases opportunities for students to build competence, self-efficacy, and self-worth.

In a model like this, all students have access to a broad variety of universal interventions, regardless of their need. This allows for a school-wide culture to

Developing TSC   117

develop and ensures consistency across the campus. This consistency provides a feeling of the security, predictability, and routine for our students with ACEs. Universal screenings and progress monitoring provide the feedback necessary to move students from tier to tier. Tier 2 services are provided to 10–15% of the student population based on the needs identified in the data. Whether behavioral, academic, or social-emotional, these interventions target specific gaps in skills in order to bring students up to speed with their peers and help them find success within Tier 1/General classroom environment. Tier 3 services are intensive services offered to the 1–5% of students who do not succeed with Tier 2 services. These wraparound-style services offer personalized interventions, thorough assessments and community-based resource referrals.

Within a tiered system, students receive preventative services like SEL to prepare for common childhood challenges. But for students who need more than prevention, a tiered system provides additional, accessible interventions. The use of data such as universal SEL screeners, counseling program needs assessments, and individual student progress monitoring ensures that interventions are distributed based on true need, and not swayed by any biases or subjective opinions such as "this student is lazy," when really ACEs are the true cause for their distractibility. Or when teachers brush students aside by saying "they are so sweet, they will be just fine," when internalizing anxiety is pushing the student farther and farther behind.

Student Self-Regulation

Teaching self-regulation is essential to building the social-emotional capacity of students with ACEs. Due to lack of coping skill development and lack of secure attachments, many students with ACEs struggle to express their emotions, read the emotions of others, and cope with uncomfortable feelings. Growing up with ACEs, students may never see healthy emotion management modeled at home. They may struggle to perceive the cause and effect patterns in an emotional response. Students with ACEs who frequently return to the "fight, flight or freeze" response even when no stressor is present need help learning how to recognize their body's fear response and shut it down when it is not needed. This allows them more control of their own emotions and behavior.

In Jax's family, there were lots of kids and lots of chaos. With five siblings – including a twin sister and a severely disabled brother – and two divorced parents who both worked full time, home felt more stressful than helpful. Jax and his sister were often "babysat" by their iPads and video games as their parents tended to the needs of their brother. Still, the hours per day of screen time wasn't as bad as being left physically alone, emotionally alone and without necessary food or care. That also happed to Jax. He and his twin sister Dakota regularly came to school dirty, with worn-out clothes and a lack of medical care.

In addition to the signs of physical neglect, both Jax and his sister Dakota struggled with self-regulation due to emotional neglect. Jax's parents let him and Dakota fight verbally and physically. The twins were often putted against

118   *The TSC Model*

each other, one feeling like the "good twin" or "bad twin" on any given day. Anytime Jax didn't get his way, or especially when he lost a game at recess, he became angry and aggressive. He would scream, elope, hit himself, hide, and kick. To deescalate him, it took many adults and many hours. Dakota was anxious, often crying in class, panicking and shutting down when schoolwork was too hard, or when she feared getting in trouble.

Jax's school counselor worked individually with Jax for two years before seeing any progress toward improved self-regulation. Slowly but surely, techniques like mindfulness, grounding, thought stopping, positive self-talk, and coping skills began working for Jax. He was able to reduce his stress and fear at school, allowing him to function more successfully in a typical 5th-grade class.

At the root of many frequent classroom challenges is the same common thread: Student "misbehavior." From what we know about trauma and its impact on learning and development, this "misbehavior" is not a choice or a willfully defiant act, but instead the effect of an overloaded stress response system. Many behavior management techniques only focus on the surface behaviors and not on the root causes. But when the root cause is trauma, very little behavior modification is going to work without decreasing the student's stress first. Only then can the student be reengaged in learning. Learning self-regulation skills gives students tools in their own tool box. These skills allow students to manage their own behavior. Whether it's in a classroom, a home, or in the community, students with self-regulation skills will be more adaptable, forward-thinking, and self-controlled.

Self-regulation "refers to the energy expended when we respond to stress and then recover" (Shanker & Hopkins, 2017, p. 33). Teaching students to self-regulate involves both direct instruction about regulation strategies and a shift in focus from addressing misbehavior to addressing stress behavior. When a student acts out at school, we must ask ourselves "What just happened that stressed this student?" Once a trigger is determined, then we must reflect. Asking ourselves "How can I decrease this student's stress and increase their feelings of safety?" is a good place to begin (Shanker & Hopkins, 2017).

When children are developing their attachment relationships in infancy, self-regulation is still undeveloped. Infants have no coping skills or ability to regulate their stress alone; they rely completely on the caregiver to rock, soothe, feed, or otherwise comfort them until their stress level returns to normal. Through this back-and-forth relationship of becoming stressed and then regulated over and over, the infant begins to learn the natural process of self-regulation. For students with ACEs, this developmental process may have never occurred or may have been interrupted due to trauma. This leaves many students with underdeveloped self-regulation skills and difficulty returning to higher-order thinking and learning once they enter a stressed out "fight-or-flight mode" (Shanker & Hopkins, 2017).

Teachers, counselors, and other caring adults teach students to regulate their current stress and decrease potential stress. Through adult vigilance, the stressors of the school environment can be eliminated or greatly reduced.

Developing TSC   119

But some stressors will still exist. Inevitably, there are unstructured time, a distracting classmate, and high-stakes testing. Teaching our students specific self-regulation strategies will benefit them both in the moment of stress and in the future when stress appears at home, in college, or at their workplace.

Tanner was a typical 5th-grade boy. He loves sports, You Tube, and aspired to be a film director one day. But Tanner's behavior was not typical. He struggled with self-regulation and had no models for regulation at home. After a traumatic early childhood and parent's divorce, Tanner brought his "fight-or-flight" instincts with him to school each day. When he felt embarrassed, singled out, or overwhelmed, he would shout out, make inappropriate noises, use vulgar language, and refuse work. Many days a week, he was kicked out of class, furthering his belief that school was an unsafe and unhelpful place. After a referral to the school counselor, some self-regulation interventions were put in place for Tanner. First, the school counselor advocated for a change of placement, and Tanner was moved to another classroom for a fresh start. The counselor used Check-In/Check-Out for daily behavior monitoring and allowed Tanner to pursue his passions of TV and video broadcasting by making films about the school rules for other struggling students. Tanner connected with the curriculum *The ZONES of Regulation* and even began teaching younger students how to regulate themselves using the program.

Creating Connectedness

Lastly, TLC focuses on developing connections between students and school. These connections include both secure attachments to adults at the school site and engagement with school activities. Developing at least one secure adult relationship is the single most influential factor in developing student resiliency (National Scientific Council on the Developing Child, 2015).

While healthy attachment relationships, for most students, start at home, teachers can also have a positive impact on student well-being and academic achievement. By creating a positive sense of belonging, love, and acceptance at school, teachers can form the healthy attachment relationships with students in addition to or in lieu of a parent.

In early infancy and childhood, every child develops a type of attachment to their primary caregiver. Whether secure, avoidant, resistant, or a mix of styles (called disorganized attachment), this attachment style can impact later attachments in adult relationships. There is an extensive body of literature demonstrating associations between child-teacher relationships and the impact on academic achievement. The general consensus is that when children develop securely attached relationships to teachers, there are positive effects on their long-term academic outcomes (Bergin & Bergin, 2009; Klem, 2004). Additionally, when children feel safe within the classroom environment, there are similar positive effects. The quality of the teacher-student relationship is a stronger predictor of academic achievement than either peer relationships or maternal attachment style (O'Connor & McCartney, 2007). It is highly likely that teachers can develop strong, securely attached relationships with students despite any ACEs or insecure attachments to primary caregivers.

Strong emphasis should be placed on boosting the quality of teacher-student relationships due to their strong positive association with student achievement through student engagement. Children who have higher-quality teacher relationships need less teacher attention to complete tasks. They can use the teacher as a "secure base," being able to independently explore new ideas and take on challenges within the classroom context. Children with lower-quality teacher relationships need more direct teacher attention and redirection, which is negatively associated with academic achievement (O'Connor & McCartney, 2007).

This concept of teacher/student relationships affecting learning is commonly referred to as school connectedness. School connectedness was officially defined in 2004 by the Wingspread Declaration on School Connectedness as "the belief by students that adults in the school care about their learning as well as about them as individuals" (Wingspread Declaration on School Connections, 2004). School connectedness falls within the broader category of protective factors – individual and environmental characteristics that buffer students from the effects of trauma and ACEs. School connectedness is a promising protective factor due to its robust research backing and the ability of schools to affect lasting change in this area (Centers for Disease Control and Prevention, 2009).

Within the six attributes of a trauma-sensitive school, five attributes specifically highlight the importance of the emotional connection to school and relationships between children and adults in the school:

- "The school supports all children to feel safe physically, socially, emotionally, and academically."
- "The school addresses students' needs in holistic ways, taking into account their relationships, self-regulation, academic competence, and physical and emotional well-being."
- "The school explicitly connects students to the school community and provides multiple opportunities to practice newly developing skills."
- "The school embraces teamwork and staff share responsibility for all students."
- "Leadership and staff anticipate and adapt to the ever-changing needs of students" who have experienced trauma.

Due to this emphasis for trauma-sensitive schools to prioritize positive relationships, I consider connectedness to be foundational to the TSC model. Before creating interventions or teaching skills, students must feel connected and safe.

School Connectedness: Three-Part Impact

School connectedness involves three components: High academic standards and appropriate learning supports; positive adult-student relationships; and physical and emotional safety (Wingspread Declaration on School Connections, 2004).

High Standards and Learning Supports

Holding students to high academic standards and expecting grade-level appropriate work increase the students' connection to school. But the high expectations themselves are not sufficient to increase school connectedness. They must be coupled with a teacher or counselor's beliefs that all students can learn, that educational gaps can close, and that students benefit from working in collaborative groups on challenging and engaging tasks (Biag, 2014).

Classrooms must be supported to reach high expectations. Counselors and administrators communicate these expectations to parents, create incentives for student progress, and develop school-wide programs to support the classroom learning (Biag, 2014). Tiered interventions, professional development, and collaborative work time support teachers in their pursuit of high expectations for all students. Interventions must be available for students who are not meeting the standards so that the bar isn't lowered.

Some educators have personal beliefs that interfere with their ability to hold all students to high expectations. Unfortunately, some educators believe that students from low-income communities, students with ACEs, or students from minority racial backgrounds can't learn as well as students from a racial majority or higher socio-economic level. These educators will, in turn, require less of these students. They will not challenge them academically or expect quality work output. This lack of challenge and adult belief leads to school disconnectedness and decreased motivation to learn (Biag, 2014).

Caring Relationships

School connectedness is improved when students know that adults care about both their individual and academic achievements. Teachers and counselors who build positive and authentic relationships with students can shape the way that students see their own academic abilities and personal identities (Centers for Disease Control and Prevention, 2009). Students feel supported when they see adults who devote their time, energy, attention, and emotional capacity to helping them. Adults who become confidants, role models, and mentors, in addition to their role as "teacher," have a greater capacity to promote resilience than those who are simply instructional leaders (Wang, Haertel, & Walberg, 1994). Even small strategies like handshakes and positive morning greetings can go a long way in developing a sense of authentic care and concern.

According to the guidebook *The Heart of Learning and Teaching: Compassion, Resiliency and Academic Success* (Wolpow, Johnson, Hertel, & Kincaid, 2009), there are six principles for educators to follow in order to develop high-quality relationships with students:

1   Always empower, never disempower
2   Provide unconditional positive regard
3   Maintain high expectations

122   The TSC Model

4   Check assumptions, observe and question
5   Be a relationship coach
6   Provide guided opportunities for helpful participation

ALWAYS EMPOWER, NEVER DISEMPOWER

By its nature, the educator-student relationship is one of unequal power. The teacher, as the authoritative figure, must work to empower the voices of students or risk disempowering them by default. Students who are exposed to ACEs may already feel fearful around people of authority. Any attempts by the educator to wield additional control through yelling, force, coercion, or threats typically worsen the student's already heightened fight-or-flight response. This can increase disruptive behavior or even worse, cause additional trauma.

Educators can empower their students and yield their power to create a more respectful, caring, and harmonious environment. Educators' responses to student behavior should reflect their understanding that many externalizing behaviors are outside of the students' conscious awareness and ability to control (Wolpow et al., 2009). Collaborative expectation setting, restorative practices, and community building all empower students and create mutual respect and trust within the classroom. Students who trust their teachers will respect the teacher's use of authority when necessary and will comply with instructions more easily.

PROVIDE UNCONDITIONAL POSITIVE REGARD

Unconditional positive regard (UPR) is a concept that counselors may recognize from the work of Carl Rogers and the practices of Client-Centered therapy. UPR is the genuine acceptance of and respect for a person regardless of their words, actions, beliefs, or other circumstances. In other words, unconditional love. Students with ACEs may have never experienced UPR from caregivers. Educators who effectively show UPR toward their students can escape the commonly re-traumatizing experience of the "reenactment triangle" (Bloom & Farragher, 2013, p. 91). In the reenactment triangle, students with past ACEs unconsciously reenact trauma in neutral settings. By escalating their behavior against those in power, students force those in power to engage with the student in many of the same ways that the perpetrator of their trauma engages them.

Caleb didn't believe anyone loved him. His parents were too busy paying attention to their contentious divorce and his much younger half-siblings to pay attention to Caleb. He felt abandoned by his dad who he rarely saw and was verbally abused by his mother. For as long as he could remember, he was also bad at school. He hated reading, thought his teachers hated him, and had very few friends. The only thing he felt good at was getting the teacher's attention – and not in a good way. This is how Caleb got attention at home too. The more trouble he could cause, the more his parents paid attention to him. So it made sense to him that the more outlandish the behavior at school, the more one-on-one time he got with the vice principal or school counselor. Caleb was bringing his teachers right into the reenactment triangle. He treated them the same way he treated his parents, he expected them to respond the same way (with negative attention and verbal abuse), and many times he got what he expected. The more teachers yelled at him, the more it fueled his fear and negative self-talk.

Counselors and teachers can help themselves get into the habit of using UPR by consistently using *I-feel statements* when discussing misbehavior with students. For example: "I feel surprised when you raise your voice in the classroom because our expectation is to use indoor voices." Or "I feel concerned when you cry in class. I am here to help you. Whenever you need help, just raise your hand."

Counselors and teachers can also *reflect* to engage with students through UPR. Reflecting paraphrases and repeats back the students' feelings and concerns so the student feels heard and understood. For example, if a student says "You are the worst counselor ever!" a response could be "I'm sorry you feel that way. I hear you saying that I have upset you. I would like to work together to solve this problem whenever you are ready."

MAINTAIN HIGH EXPECTATIONS

According to Wolpow et al. (2009, p. 73), having "consistent expectations, limits and routines sends the message that [students are] worthy of unconditional positive regard and attention." Consistency within the classroom environment allows students to feel safe due to the sense of routine and their ability to anticipate the future outcomes. This sense of environmental safety helps to lessen their hyperarousal and fight-or-flight instincts. It increases the likelihood that students can engage in the academic material using the pre-frontal cortex and critical thinking regions of the brain.

Holding consistent academic expectations while using scaffolds to support gaps in learning allows students to recognize their own abilities and develop self-efficacy, confidence, and self-esteem. Seeing themselves succeed on the same academic level as other peers serves as a motivator toward more pro-social and pro-academic behaviors.

CHECK ASSUMPTIONS, OBSERVE, AND QUESTION

All educators come into their roles with their own personal biases. These may be racially, culturally, religiously, or personally motivated. No matter the origin of these biases, they are typically out of our realm of consciousness. Compassionate educators differentiate themselves because they purposefully bring their biases into their conscious awareness. This decreases bias and increases UPR for their students. They catch themselves making assumptions about students. When they catch one, they acknowledge it and move toward

124   *The TSC Model*

more objective observations of their students. Through listening and making reflective changes, compassionate educators make their classroom emotionally safe for all students. They ask thoughtful questions, acknowledge their own mistakes, and apologize.

BE A RELATIONSHIP COACH

Educators should think of themselves as not only academic coaches – facilitating learning of reading and math – but as relationship coaches – facilitating learning of friendship building and problem solving. In elementary education, this comes naturally. Elementary educators frequently teach the rules to playground games, guide students toward functional group work, and use turn-taking activities like community circles to build trust and enhance socialization. But by middle school, many educators assume that the work of "relationship coaching" has already been done.

Even in secondary education, teachers can still be relationship coaches by teaching students about perspective taking, debate decorum, civic behavior, respectful advocacy, and continuing the elementary lessons of turn-taking, conflict resolution, and collaboration.

PROVIDE GUIDED OPPORTUNITIES FOR HELPFUL PARTICIPATION

Lastly, compassionate educators help students make meaningful contributions to the well-being of others in order to improve their own sense of self-worth and resiliency. The ability to give back empowers students with ACEs to see themselves outside of the victim role. It gives them opportunities to practice being a helper instead of always being helped or helpless. For students with ACEs, there may be a lack of selfless and civic behavior modeled at home. Due to this, any types of service learning or participatory activities should be thoughtful, supervised, and guided to ensure that students follow expected norms for behavior (Wolpow et al., 2009). This sense of meaningful participation builds school connectedness, attachment to the teacher, and peer relationships, all of which have a strong impact on academic achievement throughout a child's educational career.

As counselors, we impact school connectedness each time we meet with a student. Giving students one-on-one attention, personalized information, and active listening enhances their feelings of belonging and emotional safety at school. Effective counseling relies more on the attachment and relationship between the counselor and the client (student in this case) than the specific curriculum, intervention, or plan. Skills such as nonverbal communication, creating realistic expectations, responding empathetically, forming a positive therapeutic relationship, and flexibility in administration of counseling techniques have better outcomes than a strict treatment plan or curriculum guide (Schore & Schore, 2008).

Caring educators recognize student strengths and seek to develop those strengths. Resilience is developed when individuals learn to engage their own inner strengths and tap into community resources to overcome adversity. Unfortunately, focusing on deficits, gaps, and weaknesses is common in academic settings. It does not serve the student well to think of their weaknesses when developing a connection to school or personal resilience (Hurlington, 2010). Once strengths are identified using assessments or observations, efforts should be made to teach students about their own strengths and opportunities should be provided for students to apply their strengths on behalf of their own learning and the learning of others.

Physical and Emotional Safety

The perceptions of both physical and emotional safety impact students' feelings of connectedness to their education (Centers for Disease Control and Prevention, 2009). A clean and well-maintained physical environment sets the stage for a healthy social and academic environment housed within the physical space.

Schools should be clean. Cleanliness includes both good hygienic components such as disinfected bathrooms and hallways free from litter, and aesthetic components like graffiti free walls and updated landscaping, paint, and facilities. Schools should also be safe from intruders and community violence. Setting expectations that students and staff clean up after themselves and look after the campus builds a sense of connectedness to the school environment and prepares the way for positive school climate to develop (Centers for Disease Control and Prevention, 2009).

Emotional safety is also influenced by a variety of factors. School discipline policies, opportunities for students to participate in decision making, schoolwide values, classroom management, and the frequency of bullying behaviors can all impact students' perceptions of emotional safety. For example, schools that had a harsher and more traditional, punitive discipline policy had lower rates of school connectedness. Classrooms that have predictable routines, clear behavioral expectations, fair consequences, and engaging lessons feel emotionally safer, more positive, and have more connected students (Centers for Disease Control and Prevention, 2009).

School should be free from bullying, harassment, and intimidation between students and between teachers and students. Classrooms that encourage student participation and develop norms like "we learn from our mistakes" allow students to be vulnerable and open without fear of humiliation or teasing. Many children from traumatic backgrounds, such as those in foster care or involved in the juvenile justice system, lack daily, consistent positive relational interactions. Classrooms can make up for positive relational deficits in other areas of the child's life by encouraging healthy peer relationships, healthy adult relationships, and healthy interactions with relative strangers such as volunteers or support staff on campus (Perry & Ludy-Dobson, 2010).

126   *The TSC Model*

Outcomes of Connectedness

School connectedness is widely considered one of the most important protective factors for youth. A wide body of research supports that having just one positive, committed adult relationship outside of the home can shield children from many of the adverse effects of childhood trauma.

In this section, we will discuss the research regarding the protective qualities of school connectedness and the positive outcomes related to high connection at school.

Improved Teen Wellness

Self-esteem and general feelings of "mattering" are strong predictors of teen wellness. But they aren't the only predictors. School connectedness also contributes to the holistic wellness of teens (Watson, 2018). Poor teen wellness, a precursor to poor adult mental and physical wellness, is also associated with delinquency, social issues, and mental illness. School counselors can reduce the impact of ACEs through interventions that enhance social skills and self-management skills. These interventions, in turn, enhance students' self-esteem and sense of belonging, leading to holistic wellness (Watson, 2018).

Improved Attendance

Positive school climate and school connectedness are linked to better attendance at both the individual and school-wide levels (Van Eck, Johnson, Bettencourt, & Lindstrom Johnson, 2016). Research clearly shows this linkage in one direction – attendance leads to connection. When students attend school, they are more connected to teachers and peers and more likely to engage academically (Catalano, Oesterle, Fleming, & Hawkins, 2009). But is the opposite also true? Does school connectedness lead to improved attendance? In short, YES.

When asked a series of questions about their perceptions of school climate and connectedness, students who rated their school climate and connectedness as "positive" were less likely to have chronic absenteeism. Chronic absenteeism refers to a student missing more than 10% of the school days in any given year, excused or unexcused. Similarly, when the student body collectively rated the level of school connectedness and school climate low, the school-wide rate of chronic absenteeism was higher (Van Eck et al., 2016).

Levels of school connectedness were determined in this study based on students rating of statements such as "students feel safe at this school" and "I would choose to stay at this school even if I had the opportunity to transfer." Activities to improve attendance should also include a relationship component to improve school connectedness. Interventions such as teachers mentoring students, home visits, parenting workshops, and check-ins will accomplish this task.

Renee didn't like school. Academics were hard due to her learning disability and focusing felt impossible because of her ADHD. She received special education services and often felt singled out and stupid. She struggled to make friends, often finding herself in more "drama" than true friendships.

Renee's mom worked nights and her dad was in jail. Each morning, Renee was in charge of waking herself up, getting dressed and ready for school, and boarding the school bus on time. When it came time to wake up, Renee rarely wanted to put in the effort to get dressed and out the door. Her absences and tardies piled up.

It was only after the vice principal made a special connection with Renee that she began wanting to come to school. Each morning, the VP waited at the front gate for Renee, greeting her with a big hug and a pep talk. Renee earned punches on a punch card system for being on time – working her way toward a small gift card to her favorite restaurant. The combination of incentives, personal connection, and positive attention gave Renee the motivation she needed to make school a priority.

Decreased Behavior Concerns and Violence

There are negative associations between school connectedness and both violent behavior and risk-taking behavior. Improved school connectedness is associated with less motor vehicle risks, including motorcycle accidents and being a passenger with a reckless or intoxicated driver. Additionally, positive school connections were associated with lower levels of aggression and victimization, less physical fighting, less change of using a weapon, and lower chances of being injured due to physical violence (Chapman, Buckley, Sheehan, Shochet, & Romaniuk, 2011).

Better Mental Health

School connectedness is a moderating factor between improvements in social skills and improved mental health. This means that the more students are connected to school, the greater the likelihood that interventions like social skills training can positively impact their mental health (Carney, Kim, Hazler, & Guo, 2018). Training students to improve their social skills by decreasing aggressive behavior and improving communication allows students to more easily build relationships with other students and with adults.

The more connected a student is to school, the less symptoms of mental illness they display. School connectedness was also positively linked to future reports of mental well-being and negatively associated with future diagnoses and symptoms of mental illness. For example, for both boys and girls, a lack of school connectedness one year prior predicted depressive symptoms. For girls, it also predicted symptoms of anxiety (Shochet, Dadds, Ham, & Montague, 2006).

128 The TSC Model

Linked to Adult Health Outcomes

Just as adversity in childhood is associated with poor health outcomes as adults, so do other childhood phenomena. In the case of protective factors like school connectedness, the higher the protective factor, the lower the chances of risk-taking behaviors and emotional distress as an adult (Steiner et al., 2019).

Having connections to the school community produces effects that endure well past high school graduation. When combined with family connectedness, school connectedness was associated with 48–66% lower odds for health risk behaviors in adulthood (Steiner et al., 2019). According to Steiner et al. (2019), school connectedness reduces adult:

- Emotional distress
- Odds of suicidal ideation
- Physical violence
- Victimization by physical violence
- Sexually transmitted infection diagnoses
- Substance abuse, including prescription drug misuse and illegal drug use.

Connection to Academic Achievement

School connectedness improves students' academic motivation. School connectedness is positively associated with students' internal feelings toward school and their belief in its usefulness (Gillen-O'Neel & Fuligni, 2013). The more connected a student is to school, the more enjoyable they say it is. Students are more likely to report that high school is useful when they feel a strong positive connection to their school. While school connectedness is not directly responsible for academic achievement, connectedness helps students view school as useful and enjoy coming to school even when their grades are low (Gillen-O'Neel & Fuligni, 2013). This sense of educational persistence prevents students from dropping out or giving up when school gets harder each year.

School connectedness, through the specific aspects of student/teacher relationships and reports of bullying, is linked to academic achievement. Students who reported that they were being bullied (an all too common reason why students feel disconnected from school) had lower achievement scores in both math and reading on standardized tests. Students who reported positive relationships with teachers and staff were very likely to score higher on both math and reading assessments (Konishi, Hymel, Zumbo, & Li, 2010).

In 2017, the Tubbs Fire burned through northern, CA As a fast-moving and unpredictable wildfire, it forced many families to flee from their homes in the middle of the night with only moments to spare. Leilani's family was one of these. Her family heeded the warning, woke their children at 3 am, and left everything behind. Their home burned as did many homes in their neighborhood. Family friends and neighbors lost their lives and Leilani couldn't stop thinking about it. Before the fire, Leilani was a cheerleader, an ASB school

Developing TSC 129

leader, and President of the Bullying Prevention club at school. After the fire, she couldn't handle any of those responsibilities anymore. She became distant, sensitive, fearful, and preoccupied. Leilani referred herself to the school counselor and began a process of healing. She created a connection with her counselor that was deeper and more authentic than her relationships with teachers. She trusted her counselor and her counselor supported her. When other teachers told her "Everyone's house burned, its time to get over it," her school counselor said "Your timeline is different and that's ok." Because of the connection with her counselor, Leilani did learn self-regulation strategies, process her traumatic experience, and move forward in her own time. She was accepted into a top tier college and has a bright academic future.

Resilience: The Outcome of the Work

Anytime someone brings up the word trauma, another word is sure to follow: Resilience. But what is resilience? How does someone attain it? These questions are hotly debated. Following the flood of ACE studies in the 2010s, the misunderstood idea of resilience came to the surface as the "silver bullet." "If only those kids were resilient, then…" or "if only those kids could get over it…" are the beginnings of many well-meaning but misleading remarks about the effects of ACEs and the role of resilience.

So then what is the difference between students who seem to overcome their adversity and those who don't? While resilience is the answer, resilience is not just a character trait of strength or emotional stability. It is a mix of biological tendencies, environmental factors, and learned skills. Resilience is not a starting point, or a skill in itself, but instead an outcome of the work. Through the TSC model with its relationships, self-regulation interventions, and feelings of safety, children with ACEs can turn their toxic stress into tolerable stress and become resilient adults.

Resilience has many definitions. In researching resilience for this book, I found more than 15 different definitions of the word. For our purposes, we are defining resilience the way it is defined by the National Scientific Council on the Developing Child as "a positive, adaptive response in the face of significant adversity" (National Scientific Council on the Developing Child, 2015).

The research is clear that not all students who experience ACEs struggle with the effects written about in this book. Not every abused child has executive functioning concerns. Not every neglected teenager struggles with anxiety. Not every child of divorced parents is hypervigilant. So how does a child acquire this magical ability to be O.K.? Despite their background, despite how toxic stress affects the developing brain, despite the overwhelming odds against them, why do some children seem unscathed by ACEs?

The most common finding in resilience research is that children who have this positive adaptive response despite their ACEs also have at least one positive, stable relationship with a supportive adult. This adult could be a parent, caregiver, pastor, teacher, or any other adult who is committed to the

130 *The TSC Model*

child and can buffer them from the negative effects of toxic stress (National Scientific Council on the Developing Child, 2015). These secure attachment relationships can make up for insecure attachments to an abusive mother, neglectful caregiver, absent father, or any other negative primary attachment relationship. Having a supportive, committed adult also helps children develop skills to respond to adversity. These skills like goal setting, self-reflection, self-regulation, and adaptability are taught by emotionally available and caring adults. This combination of committed, supportive relationships, skill building for self-regulation, and positive experiences builds the foundation for resilience (National Scientific Council on the Developing Child, 2015).

When I list those three components of resilience – supportive relationships, self-regulation, and positive experiences, I instantly make the connection back to TSC. The three key areas of TSC – tiered interventions, self-regulation, and connectedness – match almost exactly. Resilient students are the *outcome* of a TSC counseling program, or a similar program promoting the three resilience components. Contrary to popular belief, resilience is not a "pull-yourself-up-by-your-bootstraps" mentality and a lack of resilience is not a moral failure.

In their analysis of resilience research, the National Scientific Council on the Developing Child (2015) observed nine common themes and findings about the scientific nature of resilience:

1   *It is biological and environmental.* Resilience results from a combination of both an innate resistance to difficulty and external supportive factors like committed, caring adults and the development of coping skills.
2   *It is observable.* Resilience is scientifically observable in the brain, immune response, and genetic response to adversity in childhood.
3   *It is predisposed.* There are a common set of external factors that predispose children to more positive outcomes despite toxic stress and ACEs:

   a   The presence of at least one stable, caring adult relationship in a child's life.
   b   The belief in an internal locus of control and mastery over circumstances (i.e. "I can overcome difficulty and am in control of what happens in my future.").
   c   The development of self-regulation and executive functioning skills to manage their own behavior and cope with difficult challenges.
   d   The support of a faith, hope, or cultural context to ground the child in shared traditions and meaning.

4   *It is teachable.* Learning coping skills to handle stress develops resilience as the stress response changes over time to turn toxic stress into tolerable stress.
5   *It is harder for sensitive kids.* Some children display more heightened sensitivity to both positive and negative experiences.
6   *It is context-specific.* Children can show resilience in some situations and not in others.

Developing TSC 131

7 *It doesn't help in the worst-case scenarios.* The individual response to stress is incredibly variable; however, extreme adversity such as genocide or environmental catastrophe almost always creates physical and/or mental health impairments that require treatment in the short-term or long-term.

8 *It can't be developed alone.* Resilience requires caring adult support and relationships. It cannot be established through self-reliance or grit alone.

9 *Resilience can be developed through skill building at any age.*

While science continues to prove that resilience cannot develop in isolation, policy hasn't caught up. Many social and educational policies still rely on the faulty belief that an individual with enough grit can overcome adversity with little to no help. The reality is that no one can just tough it out without a supportive environment of relationships and a toolbox of healthy coping skills. In a school environment, building trauma-sensitivity can promote resilience development by creating a context of caring support where children can thrive.

Schools are also in a unique position to systemically address risk-factors for low resilience and include resilience-building components:

- When schools promote positive school climate and a sense of belonging, they allow children to develop the committed adult-child relationships required for resilience.
- Schools have opportunities in their structured learning environments to embed lessons about self-regulation and coping skills. Having these lessons ensures that every child has access to knowledge about healthy stress responses.
- Lessons about growth mindset in the classroom encourage students to examine their own sense of mastery over difficult challenges, and a college/career focus propels students to consider their future and their role in creating the future they envision for themselves (Masten, Herbers, Cutuli, & Lafavor, 2008).
- Schools offer early screenings for academic concerns such as kindergarten readiness assessments. Intervening early to develop reading and language skills can boost a child's self-confidence in academic settings.
- Before the child creates a negative association with learning or a belief that they are not a good reader/student/test taker, etc., schools can scaffold content so that every student can access it.
- Schools can also address basic needs like providing healthy foods for breakfast and lunch. This leads to better physical health and improved mood.
- Schools counterbalance the risks created by homelessness, foster care, or transiency by providing stability of environment through the same classroom, teacher, peer group, and routines throughout the school year (Masten et al., 2008).

132   *The TSC Model*

- Schools provide opportunities for students to develop competence in both academic and extracurricular areas.
- Schools provide an asset-rich environment that gives children access to art, music, literature, science, nature, athletics, mentoring, and leadership in a way that home may not be able to.
- Schools provide opportunity to learn about places, people, careers, and possibilities beyond the boundaries of a violent neighborhood or a toxic home environment.

(Masten et al., 2008)

Among many professional helpers, there is an innate desire to stimulate positive outcomes in the lives of children. But we must be careful. The strategies discussed in this book such as providing caring and stable relationships and developing self-regulation skills must be always accomplished within the professional scope of our role as an educator. School counselors cannot expect to be the one caring adult for every student at their school, nor can a teacher or principal "save" a student from adversity at home.

We are not saviors. We are educators following the scientific research to provide optimal learning environments for students.

When we act as saviors outside of professional boundaries, we can do more harm than good. As educators, we will typically NOT be around for a student's entire life. We should NOT be deeply involved in what happens outside of school hours. We are NOT a parent replacement. Our best work is done while supporting the positive and protective factors a child does have, and providing equitable, engaging learning opportunities at school.

References

American School Counselor Association. (2014). *ASCA Mindsets and Behaviors for Student Success: K-12 College-and Career-Readiness Standards for Every Student*. Retrieved from American School Counselor Association: www.schoolcounselor.org/asca/media/asca/home/MindsetsBehaviors.pdf

American School Counselor Association. (2019). *ASCA National Model: A Framework for School Counseling Programs* (4th ed.). Alexandria, VA: American School Counselor Association.

Bergin, C., & Bergin, D. (2009). Attachment in the Classroom. *Educational Psychology, 21*(2), 141–170.

Biag, M. (2014). A Descriptive Analysis of School Connectedness: The Views of School Personnel. *Urban Education, 51*(1), 1–28. doi:10.1177/0042085914539772

Bloom, S., & Farragher, B. (2013). *Restoring Sanctuary: A New Operating System for Trauma-Informed Systems of Care*. New York, NY: Oxford Unviersity Press.

Carney, J. V., Kim, H., Hazler, R. J., & Guo, X. (2018). Protective Factors for Mental Health Concerns in Urban Middle School Students: The Moderating Effect of School Connectedness. *Professional School Counseling, 21*(1), 1–9. doi:10.1177/2156759X18780952

Catalano, R. F., Oesterle, S., Fleming, C. B., & Hawkins, J. D. (2009). The Importance of Bonding to School for Healthy Development: Findings from the Social Development Research Group. *Journal of School Health, 74*(7), 252.

Centers for Disease Control and Prevention. (2009). *School Connectedness: Strategies for Increasing Protective Factors Among Youth.* Atlanta, GA: U.S. Department of Health and Human Services.

Chapman, R. L., Buckley, L., Sheehan, M. C., Shochet, I. M., & Romaniuk, M. (2011). The Impact of School Connectedness on Violent Behavior, Transport Risk-Taking Behavior, and Associated Injuries in Adolescence. *Journal of School Psychology, 49*(4), 399–410.

Cook, A., Blaustein, M., Spinazzola, J., & van der Kolk, B. (2003). *Complex Trauma in Children and Adolescents.* Retrieved from National Child Traumatic Stress Network: www.nctsn.org/sites/default/files/resources//complex_trauma_in_children_and_adolescents.pdf

Gillen-O'Neel, C., & Fuligni, A. (2013). A Longitudinal Study of School Belonging and Academic Motivation across High School. *Child Development, 84*(2), 678–692.

Hatch, T. (2017a, March 8). *MTMDSS Template.* Retrieved from Multi Tiered, Multi-Domain System of Supports by Trish Hatch, PhD. Hatching Results, LLC: www.hatchingresults.com/blog/2017/3/multi-tiered-multi-domain-system-of-supports-by-trish-hatch-phd

Hatch, T. (2017b, March 8). *Multi Tiered, Multi-domain System of Supports, by Trish Hatch, PhD.* Retrieved from Hatching Results: www.hatchingresults.com/blog/2017/3/multi-tiered-multi-domain-system-of-supports-by-trish-hatch-phd

Hurlington, K. (2010, February). *Bolstering Resilience in Students: Teachers as Protective Factors.* Retrieved from Ontario Ministry of Education: www.edu.gov.on.ca/eng/literacynumeracy/inspire/research/ww_bolstering_students.pdf

Kinniburgh, K., Blaustein, M., Spinazzola, J., & van der Kolk, B. (2005). Attachment, Self-Regulation and Competency: A Comprehensive Intervention Framework for Children with Complex Trauma. *Psychiatric Annals, 35*, 424–430. Retrieved from http://psychrights.org/research/digest/CriticalThinkRxCites/kinniburgh.pdf

Klem, A. (2004). Relationships Matter: Linking Teacher Support to Student Engagement and Achievement. *Journal of School Health, 74*, 262–273.

Konishi, C., Hymel, S., Zumbo, B., & Li, Z. (2010). Do School Bullying and Student-Teacher Relationships Matter for Academic Achievement? Multilevel Analysis. *Canadian Journal of School Psychology, 25*, 19–29. doi:10.1177/0829573509357550

Masten, A., Herbers, J., Cutuli, J., & Lafavor, T. (2008). Promoting Competene and Resilience in the School Context. *Professional School Counseling, 12*(2). doi:10.1177/2156759X0801200213

National Scientific Council on the Developing Child. (2015). *Supportive Relationships and Active Skill-Building Strengthen the Foundations of Resilience: Working Paper No. 13.* Retrieved from www.developingchild.harvard.edu.

O'Connor, E., & McCartney, K. (2007). Eamining Teacher-Child Relationships and Achievement as a Part of an Ecological Model of Development. *American Educational Research Journal, 44*(2), 340–369.

Perry, B., & Ludy-Dobson, C. (2010). The Role of Healthy Relational Interactions in Buffering the Impact of Childhood Trauma. In E. Gil (Ed.), *Working with Children to Heal Interpersonal Trauma: The Power of Play* (pp. 26–43). New York, NY: Guiliford Press.

Schore, J., & Schore, A. (2008). Modern Attachment Theory: The Central Role of Affect Regulation in Development and Treatment. *Clinical Social Work Journal, 36*(1), 9–20.

134 *The TSC Model*

Shanker, S., & Hopkins, S. (2017). On Becoming a Self-Reg Haven. In W. Steele (Ed.), *Optimizing Learning Outcomes: Proven Brain-Centric Trauma-Sensitive Practices*. New York, NY: Routledge.

Shochet, I. M., Dadds, M., Ham, D., & Montague, R. (2006). School Connectedness Is an Underemphasized Parameter in Adolescent Mental Health: Results of a Community Prediction Study. *Journal of Clinical Child and Adolescent Psychology, 35*(2), 170–179.

Steiner, R. J., Sheremenko, G., Lesesne, C., Dittus, P. J., Sieving, R. E., & Ethier, K. A. (2019). Adolescent Connectedness and Adult Health Outcomes. *Pediatrics, 144*(1), e20183766. doi:10.1542/peds.2018-3766

Van Eck, K., Johnson, S., Bettencourt, A., & Lindstrom Johnson, S. (2016). How School Climate Related to Chronic Absence: A Multi-Level Latent Profile Analysis. *Journal of School Psychology, 61*, 89–102. doi:10.1016/j.jsp.2016.10.001

Wang, M., Haertel, G., & Walberg, H. (1994). Educational Resilience in Inner Cities. In M. Wang, & E. Gordon, *Educational Resilience in Inner-City America: Challenges and Prospects* (pp. 45–72). Hillsdale, NJ: Erlbaum.

Watson, J. (2018). Examining the Relationship between Self-Esteem, Mattering, School Connectedness, and Wellness among Middle School Students. *Professional School Counseling, 21*(1), 108–118.

Wingspread Declaration on School Connections. (2004). *Journal of School Health, 74*(7), 233–234.

Wolpow, R., Johnson, M., Hertel, R., & Kincaid, S. (2009). *The Heart of Learning: Compassion, Resiliency, and Academic Success*. Retrieved from Compassionate Schools Initiative at the Office of Public Instruction: www.k12.wa.us/CompassionateSchools/HeartofLearning.aspx

9 Tiered Interventions
Putting It All Together

This chapter is a comprehensive resource guide of trauma-sensitive tiered interventions for use by school counselors. These resources were chosen because they align with a trauma-sensitive philosophy and their use is supported by research, best practices, and/or ASCA standards. Interventions address at least one of the 11 roles of a trauma-sensitive school counselor:

- "Recognize the signs of trauma in students"
- "Focus on resilience and strengths so that trauma does not predict individual failure"
- "Avoid practices that may re-traumatize students"
- "Create connected communities and positive school climates"
- "Implement effective academic and behavioral practices, such as positive behavioral interventions and supports and social and emotional learning"
- "Promote safe, stable and nurturing relationships"
- "Provide community resource information to students and families dealing with trauma"
- "Educate staff on the effects of trauma and how to refer students to the school counselor"
- "Collaborate with community resources to provide support for students"
- "Promote a trauma-sensitive framework for policies, procedures and behaviors to entire staff"
- "Recognize the role technology can play in magnifying trauma incidents for students"

(American School Counselor Association, 2016)

Any reference in this chapter to any person, organization, activities, products, or services, or any linkages from this book to the website of another party do not constitute or imply the endorsement, recommendation, or favoring of the person, organization, activities, products, or services over other trauma-sensitive school counseling interventions.

Trauma-Sensitive Tier 1 interventions for School Counselors

The following section contains examples of Tier 1 interventions that are both trauma-sensitive and within the scope of the professional school counselor

136   *The TSC Model*

role. These interventions support the use of a tiered framework without directly addressing self-regulation or school connectedness. The interventions in this section are as follows:

- Administrator-Counselor Collaboration
- Community Education
- Equity and Access to Courses and Services
- School-wide Awareness Initiatives
- Trauma Training
- Data Collection: Universal Screening to move from Tier 1 to Tier 2

Administrator-Counselor Collaboration

The administrator-counselor relationship is central to the success and effectiveness of any comprehensive counseling program. Especially in a trauma-sensitive program or tiered intervention program, the counselor cannot work alone. The scope of the program is too vast and requires whole-school buy-in. The school administrator sets the tone and the vision for their school. Without the administrator's support, a school-wide program of any type is impossible. Administrators must be philosophically aligned with the trauma-sensitive mission for the TSC program to flourish.

That is not to say that administrators must always be on board from the very beginning. In many cases, they aren't. It takes a bold school counselor leader to advocate for trauma-sensitivity and get a program started. School counselors can voice their opinions and concerns, as well as bring big ideas to the school. So take a step. Implement one trauma-sensitive intervention. Share one ACEs article with a colleague. Advocate hard for one student with ACEs. It could be our counselor passion that changes an administrator's mind and moves the school toward trauma-sensitivity. According to ASCA, there are three keys to a successful administrator-counselor relationship:

1   Mutual trust and respect
2   Principal-counselor communication
3   Shared vision and decision-making
                              (American School Counseling Association, 2009)

School counselors have a responsibility to bring their expertise in student advocacy, mental health, and social-emotional perspectives to this collaborative relationship. Most principals work with school counselors. But many have never worked with a school counselor leader. Asking for a regularly scheduled meeting time is a great first step toward a collaborative administrator-counselor relationship.

Once a weekly or bi-weekly meeting is set, counselor leaders must prepare for these meetings. What information or data should the principal know? What topics should be on the agenda? Here are a few to consider:

Tiered Interventions   137

- New research about social-emotional topics and their impact on learning.
- Information about current and potential counseling interventions.
- Counseling data from a recent intervention, a use-of-time study, or other data source.
- Questions for the administrator.

Creating an agenda that is bigger than a few "red flag kids" to discuss shows leadership and systems-level thinking. Show administrators that counselors deserve a seat at the leadership table.

This intervention meets the ASCA recommendations for trauma-sensitivity by:

- "Educat[ing] staff on the effects of trauma and how to refer students to the school counselor"
- "Promot[ing] a trauma-sensitive framework for policies, procedures and behaviors to entire staff"

(American School Counselor Association, 2016)

More information or resources for this intervention:

- *Finding a Way: Practical Examples of How an Effective Principal-Counselor Relationship Can Lead to Success for All Students* – College Board www.schoolcounselor.org/asca/media/asca/home/FindWay.pdf
- *A Closer Look at the Principal–Counselor Relationship: A Survey of Principals and Counselors* – College Board www.schoolcounselor.org/asca/media/asca/home/CloserLook.pdf

Community Education

Tier 1 services can extend beyond the student body to include parents, families, and community members into the trauma-sensitive mission. Just as school staff needs trauma-sensitivity training, so do parents/guardians and the school community. Community education can happen both formally, through workshops and large meetings, and informally, through phone calls and conversations. While many counselors provide parent/guardian support about academic issues (e.g. how to access a student's grades online) or about college going (e.g. holding a FAFSA information night), counselors should also consider how their community education workshops address the social-emotional needs of the families.

Informal community education infuses trauma-sensitive practices and language into every conversation we have with families. We want to ensure that families feel safe with school personnel, just as we hope their children feel safe with us. We do not know every student's background before speaking with their family. If trauma red flags come up in conversation, school counselors

138   *The TSC Model*

may ask about trauma in order to understand a more well-rounded picture of why the student is displaying the concerning behaviors. If trauma is known in the student's background, conversations with families should include information about ACEs and the impact of trauma.

Trauma-sensitive community workshops could include the following topics:

- Creating a positive learning/homework environment at home
- Positive discipline
- ACEs and the impact of trauma
- How to access community resources
- Why attendance matters and strategies to improve attendance
- How to help your child cope and de-escalate
- Build a calm down kit with your child
- How to build resiliency and growth mindset at home

This intervention meets the ASCA recommendations for trauma-sensitivity by:

- "Recogniz[ing] the signs of trauma in students"
- "Focus[ing] on resilience and strengths so that trauma does not predict individual failure"
- "Provid[ing] community resource information to students and families dealing with trauma"

(American School Counselor Association, 2016)

More information or resources for this intervention:

- *Factsheet: Parenting a Child who has Experienced Trauma* – Child Welfare Information Gateway www.childwelfare.gov/pubPDFs/child-trauma.pdf

Equity and Access to Courses and Services

All students deserve a fair shot. All students deserve an equal opportunity to try. One important role of the school counselor is as a student advocate, ensuring that students' best interests are at the center of all school decisions. Unfortunately, not all students get this equal shot. Sixty-three percent of all students will experience at least one ACE before their 18th birthday. In low-income, urban communities, ACEs and community violence are even more common. We know that these communities have disproportionately high levels of people of color, whose toxic stress can be compounded by racial and historic stress (National Child Traumatic Stress Network, Justice Consortium, Schools Committee, and Culture Consortium, 2017).

Students of color are regularly exposed to racism through their own personal experiences, media coverage of current events, and social media.

Tiered Interventions 139

School environment and curriculum should not add to the list of traumatic or oppressive daily influences. Instead, schools can build students' resilience to oppression by:

- Opening "avenues of discussion and information that are factual, compassionate, open, and safe" within the classroom (National Child Traumatic Stress Network, Justice Consortium, Schools Committee, and Culture Consortium, 2017, p. 3).
- "Creating an environment that acknowledges the role of systemic racism inside and outside of school" (National Child Traumatic Stress Network, Justice Consortium, Schools Committee, and Culture Consortium, 2017, p. 3).
- Helping "students and colleagues understand the connection between historical trauma, systemic racism, and community trauma in communities of color" (National Child Traumatic Stress Network, Justice Consortium, Schools Committee, and Culture Consortium, 2017, p. 8).
- Understand the culture of the school community and find cultural references, stories, and activities that will connect with your students.
- Help students think big! They have unique and powerful opportunities for leadership. "Support student-led activism to help students experience teachers as allies. This can further enhance the learning experience, applying lessons learned in a meaningful manner as well as deepening trusting relationships" (National Child Traumatic Stress Network, Justice Consortium, Schools Committee, and Culture Consortium, 2017, p. 8).

This intervention meets the ASCA recommendations for trauma-sensitivity by:

- "Focus[ing] on resilience and strengths so that trauma does not predict individual failure"
- "Avoid[ing] practices that may re-traumatize students"
- "Creat[ing] connected communities and positive school climates"
(American School Counselor Association, 2016)

More information or resources for this intervention:

- *Addressing Race and Trauma in the Classroom: A Resource for Educators* – National Child Traumatic Stress Network www.schoolcounselor.org/asca/media/PDFs/FINAL-Race-and-Trauma-in-the-Classroom-Factsheet.pdf
- *Pursuing Social and Emotional Development Through a Racial Equity Lens: A Call to Action* – The Aspen Institute www.aspeninstitute.org/publications/pursuing-social-and-emotional-development-through-a-racial-equity-lens-a-call-to-action/
- *Applying an Equity Lens to Social, Emotional, and Academic Development* – Robert Wood Johnson Foundation www.rwjf.org/en/library/research/2018/06/applying-an-equity-lens-to-social-emotional-and-academic-development.html

140　*The TSC Model*

School-wide Awareness Initiatives

Awareness weeks and months are an important Tier 1 intervention. Red Ribbon Week, Black History Month, Attendance Awareness Month, and National Coming Out Day are all examples of awareness events. They create a positive community and a shared understanding of important topics that affect students and their families. These celebrations extend beyond the school walls. They provide opportunities to collaborate with community leaders, business, and non-profits in the community.

Topics like suicide prevention, drug prevention, bullying prevention, mental health, military issues, and racial and ethnic diversity and heritage are an important part of a comprehensive counseling program. Awareness events bring attention to these and other topics which may not otherwise be discussed during the school year. Awareness weeks/months give calendar opportunities to schedule community education, assemblies, guest speakers, and events. While awareness weeks/months should be engaging, and in many cases celebratory, they are also educational. It is important that these events are used to further their unique causes and do not just become a "spirit week" or a day out of class.

Some examples include:

- Red Ribbon Week, A drug-prevention event – October: Deliver classroom lessons from Project Alert or other drug-prevention curriculum to teach students about the dangers of teenage drug use and how to resist the peer pressure to use drugs.
- National Bullying Prevention Month – October: Plan large bullying prevention events or assemblies to raise awareness of the bullying reporting procedures at the school. Teach students ways to confront bullying and support victims.
- Suicide Prevention Awareness Month – September: Use an evidence-based curriculum like Signs of Suicide to teach students how to notice red flags for suicide risk, the symptoms of teenage depression, and how to report their suspicions.

This intervention meets the ASCA recommendations for trauma-sensitivity by:

- Creat[ing] connected communities and positive school climates"
- "Provid[ing] community resource information to students and families dealing with trauma"

(American School Counselor Association, 2016)

More information or resources for this intervention:

- *2019–2020 National Educational and Health Awareness Dates Calendar –* ASCA www.schoolcounselor.org/asca/media/asca/home/2019-20 AwarenessCalendar.pdf

Tiered Interventions 141

- Suicide Prevention Awareness Month: www.nami.org/get-involved/awareness-events/suicide-prevention-awareness-month
- National Bullying Prevention Month: www.pacer.org/bullying/nbpm/
- Red Ribbon Campaign: http://redribbon.org/

Trauma Training

Prior to beginning whole-school, trauma-sensitive work, all staff must be trained. Training should include a broad overview of ACEs, the effects of ACEs on learning and classroom behavior, and trauma-sensitive strategies they can implement immediately. While teachers and specialists will deliver most of the interventions, ALL staff members have a role to play. Office staff, campus aides, nutrition workers, and security guards should receive this first level of training. Completing this training is essential to gain buy-in for the trauma-sensitive philosophy. Teachers and staff must understand the WHY of what they are doing before they will fully participate. Trauma training gives purpose to the program.

Not all staff members will initially be on board with the trauma-sensitive philosophy. Common reasons for lack of buy-in include feeling untrained or unprepared for the emotionality of a trauma-sensitive approach or feeling like "it's not my job." Secondary training should include information about compassion fatigue (secondary trauma) to address the emotional concerns. It should also include an alignment of trauma-sensitive practices and current teaching practices. When teachers realize that so much of what they are already doing is trauma-sensitive, they will feel less overwhelmed about implementing this new approach.

This intervention meets the ASCA recommendations for trauma-sensitivity by:

- "Educat[ing] staff on the effects of trauma and how to refer students to the school counselor"
- "Promot[ing] a trauma-sensitive framework for policies, procedures and behaviors to entire staff"

(American School Counselor Association, 2016)

More information or resources for this intervention:

- *Trauma Sensitive Schools Training Package* – National Center for Safe Supportive Learning Environments https://safesupportivelearning.ed.gov/trauma-sensitive-schools-training-package

Data Collection: Universal Screening to move from Tier 1 to Tier 2

Data collection is essential in tiered intervention programs. In order to move students between the tiers of the program, school counselors and program leaders match students with appropriate interventions to close gaps and find

142   *The TSC Model*

success. At the Tier 1 level, two types of data pinpoint which Tier 2 services are needed and for whom they are needed.

First, a needs assessment is conducted to determine which *interventions* are needed. Needs assessments allow teachers, staff, parents, and students to identify areas of concern and areas of relative success. For school counselors, a needs assessment may include questions about students' perception of school climate, students' knowledge of SEL topics, and teacher's perception of social-emotional and behavioral concerns. Needs assessments can also take a deep dive into existing data to look for gaps or discrepancies. Data commonly used in needs assessments include GPA, course enrollment, number of college applications, suspensions, and attendance based on race, gender, socioeconomic status, or other grouping.

Next, universal screenings pinpoint which *students* need Tier 2 services. For the purposes of this book, we will focus on data that can be universally collected and points to a need for behavioral or social-emotional support, not academic. Collecting universal data ensures that no student is overlooked because someone assumes "They will be fine. They have a good family." Or "She never speaks up, so she must not need help." Universal screenings allow counselors and school leaders to look for trauma red flags, lack of social-emotional skills, attendance concerns, or frequent discipline. Students whose data is "high" in multiple categories may need an even higher level of intervention.

Examples of universal screenings:

- *Office referral data*: Which students have been referred for more than two office referrals this week? More than four this month?
- *Grades/GPA data*: Which students are under a 2.0 GPA? Do any students have noticeable declines compared to their GPA the previous year?
- *Attendance data*: Which students are chronically absent (missing more than 10% of the total school days)? Chronically tardy? Truant?
- *Nurse data*: Which students have seen the nurse more than twice this week? More than four times this month? Which students are visiting the nurse for symptoms of anxiety such as shortness of breath, panic attacks, headache, or dizziness? For symptoms of depression – low mood, fatigue, stomachache, lack of appetite?
- *Special populations*: Which students deserve added support based on their special population category such as special education, foster/homeless, English language learner, international student, or free lunch recipient?
- *School climate survey*: Which classrooms or grade levels have the lowest perceptions of school climate? Which areas need to be addressed more strategically?
- *Participation data (FAFSA completion, extracurricular attendance, etc.)*: Which students have not completed recommended forms like FAFSA? Which students are missing graduation requirements? Which students have not joined a club on campus? Which families did not attend parent-teacher conferences?

More information or resources for this intervention:

- Ripple Effects: https://rippleeffects.com/uses/#tiered-interventions
- Panorama Education: www.panoramaed.com/
- Attendance Works: www.attendanceworks.org/
- *Using Action Plans and Results Reports* – By Mark Kuranz and Karen Griffith, New Jersey School Counselor Association School Counselor News www.schoolcounselor.org/newsletters/october-2018/using-action-plans-and-results-reports?st=NJ

Trauma-Sensitive Tier 2 Interventions for School Counselors

The following section contains examples of Tier 2 interventions that are both trauma-sensitive and within the scope of the professional school counselor role. These interventions support the use of a tiered framework and meet student needs without directly addressing self-regulation or connection to school. The interventions in this section are as follows:

- Behavior Contracts
- Check-In/Check-Out
- Small Group School Counseling
- Student Study Team Meetings
- Teacher Workshops: Opt in
- Progress Monitoring: Using Data to Move from Tier 2 to Tier 3

Behavior Contracts

Behavior contracts are an agreement between a teacher and a student that clearly outlines desired goal behaviors and rewards for displaying those desired behaviors at school. Behavior contracts go by many names, including behavior progress report, sticker chart, or daily behavior log. Ideally, this behavior contract is also a communication instrument between the teacher and the parent/guardian. It should go back and forth each day to ensure consistency and accurate reporting of behaviors.

Behavior contract goals reflect the 2–3 highest priority behaviors to address. Behavior contracts with too many expectations or expectations that are not priorities can lead to student and teacher frustration using the contract. Students should be invested in the contract process by helping to determine the contract rewards and making other small decisions such as what the contract looks like (color, pictures, font, etc.).

Behavior contracts can also include a self-monitoring or self-reflection component. This component allows students to know how they are doing and requires adults to discuss the student's progress with them throughout the day. Conversations about the student's self-monitoring include questions like

144   *The TSC Model*

"What is going well?" "What could be better?" and "How do you plan to come back from this mistake?"

This intervention meets the ASCA recommendations for trauma-sensitivity by:

- "Implement[ing] effective academic and behavioral practices, such as positive behavioral interventions and supports and social and emotional learning"
- "Promot[ing] safe, stable and nurturing relationships"
                              (American School Counselor Association, 2016)

More information or resources for this intervention:

- *Behavior Contracts* – PBIS World www.pbisworld.com/tier-2/behavior-contract/
- Self and Match: http://selfandmatch.com/self-and-match/

Check-In/Check-Out

Check-In/Check-Out (CICO) is an intervention developed by Deanne A. Crone, Leanne S. Hawken, and Robert H. Horner. It is a Tier 2 intervention for students who are not abiding by school-wide expectations and are not successful with other Tier 2 interventions such as social-emotional small groups. CICO uses one-on-one adult interaction to begin and end each day positively. Through CICO, a student starts their day with a positive check-in with a teacher, counselor, administrator, or other adult on campus. This person offers the student brief encouragement and gives them a daily behavior contract. The student must be encouraged by the adult's feedback and attention, so making the mentor a person who already has a positive relationship with the student is a win-win. In my experience, former teachers who were "favorite teachers" work great as CICO mentors since the time commitment is low and the relational commitment is already well established.

Throughout the day, the student uses the behavior contract within their classroom, doing self-monitoring and -reflection with the classroom teacher. At the end of the day, the student "checks out" with the same adult, for more positive encouragement and reflection on the day's behaviors. If a reward is attached to the behavior contract, the reward is delivered during the "check out." The student then takes home the behavior contract to be signed by a parent and returned during the next morning's check-in. CICO's daily contract signing builds a strong home-school connection.

CICO develops a sense of belonging at school and a sense of safety through consistently structured and positive adult interaction. This intervention also builds positive rapport between adults and students. These students may typically distrust authority figures on campus and need this personalized intervention to build trust.

Tiered Interventions 145

CICO must be implemented with fidelity for it to work well. If a mentor is frequently absent, or the student does not report to them morning and afternoon, the reinforcement breaks down. Students who are not already motivated by adult feedback but more motivated by escape are not the best candidates for CICO (Vanderbilt University: Department of Special Education, 2013).

This intervention meets the ASCA recommendations for trauma-sensitivity by:

- "Implement[ing] effective academic and behavioral practices, such as positive behavioral interventions and supports and social and emotional learning"
- "Promot[ing] safe, stable and nurturing relationships"
                              (American School Counselor Association, 2016)

More information or resources for this intervention:

- *Tip Sheet: Check-In/Check-Out (CICO)* – Vanderbilt University https:// my.vanderbilt.edu/specialeducationinduction/files/2013/07/Tip-Sheet-Check-In-Check-Out.pdf
- *How To: Manage Problem Behaviors: Check-In/Check-Out* – Intervention Central www.interventioncentral.org/behavior_management_check_in_check_out
- *Check-In/Check-Out* – PBIS World www.pbisworld.com/tier-2/check-in-check-out-cico/
- *Responding to Problem Behaviors in Schools* – By Deanne A. Crone, Leanne S. Hawken, and Robert H. Horner www.guilford.com/books/Responding-to-Problem-Behavior-in-Schools/Crone-Hawken-Horner/9781606236000

Small Group School Counseling

Small group school counseling is an effective, efficient, and research-based practice to enhance specific skills common to a group of students (American School Counselor Association, 2014). School counseling small groups allow students to gain self-awareness while also learning to communicate, self-regulate, and improve specific behaviors. These behavioral improvements lead to personal-social success and academic achievement. Counseling small groups are a Tier 2 intervention that is short-term and brief. School counselors should not provide long-term mental health therapy or facilitate long-term support groups for students. Common topics for small groups include anger management, coping skills, self-regulation, organizational skills, executive function skills, conflict resolution, listening skills, and social skills.

146   *The TSC Model*

Small group participants need both a personal commitment to the group and parent permission to join the group. Groups abide by the expectation of confidentiality and mutual trust in order to make the group a safe space for all participants. Data is collected before and after the school counseling small group to determine its effectiveness. Data such as office disciplinary referrals, GPA, and attendance data are called "outcome data" and held as the most significant measure of student improvement. Other data such as shifts in perception, attitude, and application of skills learned are also important and are collected from students directly or from teachers.

This intervention meets the ASCA recommendations for trauma-sensitivity by:

- "Focus[ing] on resilience and strengths so that trauma does not predict individual failure"
- "Implement[ing] effective academic and behavioral practices, such as positive behavioral interventions and supports and social and emotional learning"
- "Promot[ing] safe, stable and nurturing relationships"
                                    (American School Counselor AssSociation, 2016)

More information or resources for this intervention:

- *Position Statement: The School Counselor and Group Counseling* – ASCA www.schoolcounselor.org/asca/media/asca/PositionStatements/PS_ Group-Counseling.pdf

Student Study Team Meetings

Student Study Team (SST) meetings are a Tier 2 intervention that brings together specialists, interventionists, general education teachers, counselors, and administrators to discuss the unique needs of one student. SST meetings are part of the data collection process between Tier 1 and Tier 2, or Tier 2 and Tier 3. The purpose of an SST is to gather historical and current information about a student in order to develop effective interventions to address that student's needs. SST meetings should include specialists from a variety of expertise areas, including speech and language, academic interventions, special education, and school counseling. The school nurse, behavior specialist, or English Language Development instructor could also participate when needed. These meetings generally include the parent/guardian and possibly the student based on age.

Students are referred for an SST meeting based on teacher observations, parent requests, or due to a data-driven cut point. For example, "After the first report card, the school will convene an SST for any student under a 2.0 GPA." Or, "After 100 days of school, there will be an SST for any student who has missed more than 10 days" (10% of total days in chronically absent).

This intervention meets the ASCA recommendations for trauma-sensitivity by:

- "Recogniz[ing] the signs of trauma in students"
- "Focus[ing] on resilience and strengths so that trauma does not predict individual failure"
- "Avoid[ing] practices that may re-traumatize students"
- "Promot[ing] a trauma-sensitive framework for policies, procedures and behaviors to entire staff"

(American School Counselor Association, 2016)

More information or resources for this intervention:

- Beyond SST – SST Management System: www.beyondsst.org/Account/Features
- *SST Best Practices Manual* – Sacramento City Unified School District www.scusd.edu/sites/main/files/file-attachments/sst_best_practices_manual_0.pdf

Teacher Workshops: Opt-in

Leading social-emotional professional development is a Tier 1 responsibility of school counselors. In this model, professional development is a "one-size-fits-all" model. Teachers and faculty are required to attend staff meetings and listen to one topic regardless of what the school staff needs or desires to learn about. This model of professional development can lead to low staff morale and frustration over wasted time. Teachers and faculty, just like students, need their voices to be heard and valued. They need to be a part of the decision-making process to be engaged. Specialists like school counselors or school psychologists may also feel out of place at staff meetings that are focused on academic curriculum that is not within their scope of practice.

One way to ensure that professional development meets the needs of staff is to offer differentiated workshop-style professional development courses or coaching opportunities. Specialized professional development and coaching is considered a Tier 2 service. For example, at Hill Creek School in Santee, California, three professional development meetings each year are set aside for teacher-led workshops. Veteran teachers, counselors, and other specialists lead various professional development sessions. These sessions are selected based on teacher preference data. Administrators survey teachers to determine topics of interest and then create a menu of options. During the professional

148 *The TSC Model*

development block, teachers choose 1–2 sessions to attend from the menu based on time. Topics led by the school counselor may include advanced learning in restorative practices, creating a safe classroom environment, behavior contracts/check-in/check-out, building better relationships with students, self-care and reducing burnout, or managing students in crisis.

In addition to a teacher choice model of professional development, there is a teacher needs-based model. Workshops may be assigned to teachers based on data, such as high office discipline referrals, low perceptions of a caring classroom environment, or for new teachers who haven't learned about the Tier 2/Tier 3 practices at the school site. Who attends each session is an administrative decision; however, school counselors may play a role in facilitating the workshops and following up with teachers after the session is over. Working with a few teachers to enhance their classroom social-emotional practices can eliminate the need to work with large amounts of students from those classes.

This intervention meets the ASCA recommendations for trauma-sensitivity by:

- "Educat[ing] staff on the effects of trauma and how to refer students to the school counselor"
- "Collaborat[ing] with community resources to provide support for students"
- "Promot[ing] a trauma-sensitive framework for policies, procedures and behaviors to entire staff"

(American School Counselor Association, 2016)

More information or resources for this intervention and school counselor leadership:

- *School Counselors as Program Leaders: Applying Leadership Contexts to School Counseling,* By Colette Dollarhide www.schoolcounselor.org/asca/media/asca/LeadershipSpecialist/Dollarshide.pdf
- ASCA-U Training: School Counseling Leadership Specialist www.schoolcounselor.org/school-counselors/professional-development/asca-u-specialist-trainings/school-counseling-leadership-specialist

Progress Monitoring: Using Data to Move from Tier 2 to Tier 3

After the implementation of Tier 2 services, data is collected to determine whether the services were successful. Did the intervention improve students' classroom behavior? Increase attendance? Decrease office referrals? Building a social-emotional skill? Or Improve GPA? The data will determine if the 6–8-week intervention was:

1 *Successful!* The student does not need the intervention again.
2 *Working.* The student needs another round of the intervention to achieve the goals.

3   *Not working.* The student needs more individualized intensive interventions (Tier 3).

This type of data is called progress monitoring data. Progress monitoring data shows trends over time, pre- and post-intervention comparison, and frequency, intensity, or duration of behaviors. Progress monitoring data is typically more thorough and time-consuming to collect than universal screening data because it paints a more specific picture. Screening data takes information from one point in time. But progress data is longitudinal. It reveals what is changing, in what ways it is changing, and what is still left to change.

Examples of progress monitoring data include:

- *Teacher observation of SEL attitudes and skills (perception data)*: Teachers' observations of students are a great source of data for school counselors. Teachers directly interact with students where problem behaviors occur most – in academic classes. Their rating scales, before and after an intervention, or at set intervals during an intervention, help determine the success of the intervention as a whole or of specific portions. If a student's difficulties are occurring during unstructured times such as recess and lunch, a campus aide or supervisor may fill out these observation forms instead.
- *Homework/assignment tracker*: Students complete daily or weekly assignment tracking checklists or planner checks to determine progress in work completion rates.
- *Scatterplot*: A scatterplot determines both the frequency of an undesired behavior and the patterns in time of day or activity during which the behavior occurs.
- *Antecedent, Behavior, Consequence Chart*: This data collection chart can be part of a larger functional behavior analysis (FBA) or used on its own. It identifies specific triggers for behavior or specific functions of the behavior. In other words, why is the behavior occurring and what is the behavior accomplishing for the student? Understanding the immediate triggers and the functions can help counselors and behavior specialists create personalized interventions to implement replacement behaviors and eliminate triggers.
- *Pre/post-data*: Student data used in universal screenings such as GPA, attendance, and office discipline referrals can be compared to pre- and post-intervention to give a snapshot of the intervention's impact on the student's education. The application of skills learned in the group should lead to favorable educational outcomes; however, this may take more time to appear than one intervention cycle. Data in these outcome areas is collected for Tier 2 students well after they have completed interventions and are no longer in need of Tier 2 services. This longitudinal data helps school counselors see backslides and re-intervene quickly to reduce the impact.

150 *The TSC Model*

More information or resources for this intervention:

- ASCA-U Specialist Training: School Counseling Data Specialist www.schoolcounselor.org/school-counselors/professional-development/asca-u-specialist-trainings/school-counseling-data-specialist
- *When to use Functional Behavioral Assessment? A State-by-State Analysis of the Law* – PBIS World www.pbis.org/resource/when-to-use-functional-behavioral-assessment-a-state-by-state-analysis-of-the-law
- *Data Tracking* – PBIS World www.pbisworld.com/data-tracking/
- *Functional Behavior Assessment* – PBIS World www.pbisworld.com/tier-2/functional-behavior-assessment-fba/
- *Organizational Tools* – PBIS World www.pbisworld.com/tier-2/organizational-tools/

Trauma-Sensitive Tier 3 Interventions for School Counselors

The following section contains examples of Tier 3 interventions that are both trauma-sensitive and within the scope of a professional school counselor role. These interventions support the use of a tiered framework and meet student needs without directly addressing self-regulation or connection to school. The interventions in this section are as follows:

- Crisis Interventions
- Referral to SPED
- Referral for Community Resources
- Solution-Focused Brief Therapy
- Tier 3 Data: Developing a Wrap-around Plan

Crisis Interventions

School counselors play a pivotal role in ensuring that students, especially those with ACEs, feel safe at school. Part of that role is to implement programs and services that prevent school violence, such as SEL and PBIS. Another key element to ensuring safety is having an available school counselor for reactive services. Reactive counseling includes responding to school violence and the threat of potential violence (American School Counselor Association, 2019a). School counselors help diffuse potentially violent situations, refer students for community mental health services, facilitate conflict mediation, and participate in a team-based approach to assess for risk and threats (American School Counselor Association, 2019b).

Student violence toward other students is not the only safety concern on campus. School counselors are vital in response to suicidal ideation and self-harm, including cutting, eating disorders, substance abuse, and other risk-taking behaviors. School counselors serve a unique purpose by ensuring appropriate crisis response at school and making mental health referrals as needed. In the case of suicidal ideation, counselors also have an ethical responsibility to contact the student's parents/guardians. If parents/guardians do not take the suicidal threat seriously and do not get their child necessary mental health assistance, school counselors must contact child protective services (American School Counselor Association, 2018).

This intervention meets the ASCA recommendations for trauma-sensitivity by:

- "Recogniz[ing] the signs of trauma in students"
- "Avoid[ing] practices that may re-traumatize students"
- "Provid[ing] community resource information to students and families dealing with trauma"
- "Collaborat[ing] with community resources to provide support for students"

(American School Counselor Association, 2016)

More information or resources for this intervention:

- *Position Statement: The School Counselor and Suicide Prevention/Awareness –* ASCA www.schoolcounselor.org/asca/media/asca/PositionStatements/ PS_Suicide.pdf
- *ASCA Ethical Standards for School Counselors:* www.schoolcounselor.org/ asca/media/asca/Ethics/EthicalStandards2016.pdf
- *Position Statement: The School Counselor and Safe Schools and Crisis Response –* ASCA www.schoolcounselor.org/asca/media/asca/Position-Statements/PS_SafeSchools.pdf
- The Columbia-Suicide Severity Rating Scale: http://cssrs.columbia.edu/
- Sandy Hook Promise: www.sandyhookpromise.org/prevention_programs

Referral to SPED

When students are not responding to Tier 1 and Tier 2 interventions, Tier 3 interventions offer a more personalized and intensive focus on rehabilitating the student. Special Education (SPED) is a service offered by all the U.S. public schools that is saved for this purpose. But it is not a catch-all for anyone who learns differently, nor is it magic bullet for students with disabilities. According to the U.S. Department of Education, the purpose of the Individuals with Disabilities Education Act (IDEA) and special education in schools is to "make available to [children with disabilities] a free, appropriate public education that emphasizes special education and related services designed to meet their unique needs and prepare them for further education, employment, and independent living" (U.S. Department of Education, 2019).

152   The TSC Model

According to IDEA, environmental or economic disadvantage (i.e. many ACEs such as neglect or household dysfunction) is not a disability. Therefore, it does not automatically qualify a student for SPED services. However, as research shows, ACEs may lead to disabilities, changes in brain architecture, and developmental delays in children, thus qualifying them to receive the specialized assistance (Jonson-Reid, Drake, Kim, Porterfield, & Han, 2004).

If a learning or other disability is suspected, a referral to the special education assessment process is a necessary next step. Through this process, school psychologists, resource specialists, speech and language pathologists, and other specialists complete extensive individual testing to determine if a disability exists, and if so, how it is affecting the student's educational performance (Individuals with Disabilities Education Act, 2004).

A referral for a special education assessment does not mean that the student will qualify for SPED services, only that the SPED team has 60 days to assess the student for the possibility of a disability that is affecting educational performance. If such a disability is found, then the team will present the student's family with a draft of an Individualized Education Program (IEP). An IEP is the school's offer of services to accommodate the student's disability and educate the student using strategies that specifically address the gaps caused by the disability.

This intervention meets the ASCA recommendations for trauma-sensitivity by:

- "Focus[ing] on resilience and strengths so that trauma does not predict individual failure"
- "Implement[ing] effective academic and behavioral practices, such as positive behavioral interventions and supports and social and emotional learning"

(American School Counselor Association, 2016)

More information or resources for this intervention:

- *Protecting Students with Disabilities* – Office of Civil Rights, U.S. Department of Education www.ed.gov/about/offices/list/ocr/504faq.html
- United States Code – Education of Individuals with Disabilities: https:// uscode.house.gov/browse/prelim@title20/chapter33/subchapter1&edition= prelim

Referral for Community Resources

School counselors often function in a similar capacity to school social workers. Both counselors and social workers make student and family referrals to community resources as needs arise. Making referrals is important because counselors cannot solve student concerns alone.

School counselors are a bridge between the school and the community. For many families, a lack of resources like a cell phone or home internet service is a barrier to accessing needed resources. From housing vouchers to food pantries, domestic violence shelters to legal clinics, and immigration assistance to tutoring, wonderful services exist within every community. Unfortunately, many families who need them have no idea where to go for help.

Creating a community referral list is a great first step. This website gives students, families, and school staff members access to updated community resource information. Families do not need to rely on a liaison or other gatekeeper to get information. They can access it on their own if they desire. The resource guide also allows school counselors to find the needed information quickly when assisting a family.

Resource guides must include the name of the agency, phone number, and services offered at minimum. Adding a location map, hours of operation, service fees, languages spoken, and insurances accepted adds to the usefulness of the list. And of course, make sure that the list is updated frequently. Due to high turnover and restructuring in community non-profits, contact information should be checked at least annually.

Once a need is identified and a referral is made, the school counselor's job is not done. Following up with both the referral source and the family closes the communication loop and ensures a true connection was made. This follow-up confirms that the student's and family's needs are addressed or gives counselors another chance to re-refer or refer to a different resource. School counselors create a system for referral tracking to make the process of assessing a need, referring for service, collecting necessary documentation, and following up both seamless and efficient.

This intervention meets the ASCA recommendations for trauma-sensitivity by:

- "Provid[ing] community resource information to students and families dealing with trauma"
- "Collaborat[ing] with community resources to provide support for students"

(American School Counselor Association, 2016)

More information or resources for this intervention:

- *Bridging Students to the Community*, By Jacqueline Zeller, PhD, New Jersey School Counselor Association School Counselor News www.schoolcounselor.org/newsletters/october-2017/bridging-students-to-the-community?st=NJ
- Riverside Unified School District Resource Guide: http://riversideunified.org/common/pages/DisplayFile.aspx?itemId=2212380

154 The TSC Model

Solution-Focused Brief Therapy

Solution-focused brief therapy is a widely used theoretical orientation for individual school counseling interventions. Developed in the 1970s, solution-focused brief therapy is future-oriented and goal-led. It centers on the basic principle that clients (students) already have the capacity, knowledge, and skills to make positive changes in their life. They just need some clarification and direction (Institute for Solution-Focused Therapy, 2019).

Rather than focusing on the past and the problems that brought the student into the counselor's office, solution-focused counselors direct the student's attention toward how they can make positive changes in their future to solve the problem that brought them to counseling. This therapeutic technique is ideal for school counselors due to our large caseloads and limited time to spend with students individually. School counselors do not provide long-term therapy. Setting a goal and working toward a specific solution allows students to see noticeable positive changes in a short amount of time. It builds their confidence to continue making changes even after the counseling intervention is complete.

Solution-focused brief counseling employs techniques such as scaling questions, the "Miracle Question," goal setting, complimenting, cheerleading, future-oriented questions, looking for previously used solutions, and coping questions (Institute for Solution-Focused Therapy, 2019). Solution-focused brief therapy can be used for nearly any problem that brings a student to seek individual counseling.

This intervention meets the ASCA recommendations for trauma-sensitivity by:

- "Implement[ing] effective academic and behavioral practices, such as positive behavioral interventions and supports and social and emotional learning"
- "Promot[ing] safe, stable and nurturing relationships"
- "Focus[ing] on resilience and strengths so that trauma does not predict individual failure"
- "Avoid[ing] practices that may re-traumatize students"
  (American School Counselor Association, 2016)

More information or resources for this intervention:

- *What is Solution-Focused Therapy?* – The Institute for Solution Focused Therapy https://solutionfocused.net/what-is-solution-focused-therapy/
- *Solution-Focused Brief Counseling in Schools: Theoretical Perspectives and Case Application to an Elementary School Student,* By May Sobhy and Marion Cavallaro, American Counseling Association VISTAS www.counseling.org/resources/library/VISTAS/2010-V-Online/Article_81.pdf

Tier 3 Data: Developing a Wrap-around Plan

Using data to move students into Tier 3 services is a key component in the tiered intervention model. This data ensures that only the highest need students receive these highly specialized interventions. Much time, money, and human capital are wasted when Tier 3 services are offered to too many students or to students who do not need these interventions. Evidence-based assessments that are both valid and reliable are the best forms of data at this high level. These are some of the same assessments used in the special education assessment process. They must be administered by someone with adequate training such as a school psychologist, resource specialist, or speech/language pathologist, depending on the type of assessment.

As a student advocacy leader, school counselors should be a part of multidisciplinary teams to refer students for special education assessments or Tier 3 data collection. We should participate in analyzing the results of the data collection. However, school counselors should not be individually responsible for making special education or Tier 3 eligibility decisions, coordinating the IEP process or 504 process, assessing students, or acting as a testing coordinator.

More information or resources for this intervention:

- www.counseling.org/docs/default-source/vistas/article_427cfd25f16116603 abcacff0000bee5e7.pdf?sfvrsn=e2eb452c_4
- www.schoolcounselor.org/asca/media/asca/PositionStatements/PS_ Disabilities.pdf

References

American School Counseling Association. (2009). *Finding a Way: Practical Examples of How an Effective Principal-Counselor Relationship Can Lead to Success for All Students.* Alexandria, VA: American School Counseling Association.

American School Counselor Association. (2014). *The School Counselor and Group Counseling.* Retrieved from American School Counselor Association: www. schoolcounselor.org/asca/media/asca/PositionStatements/PS_Group-Counseling.pdf

American School Counselor Association. (2016, August). *The School Counselor and Trauma-Informed Practice.* Retrieved from American School Counselor Association: www. schoolcounselor.org/asca/media/asca/PositionStatements/PS_TraumaInformed.pdf

American School Counselor Association. (2018). *The School Counselor and Suicide Prevention/Awareness.* Retrieved from American School Counselor Association: www.schoolcounselor.org/asca/media/asca/PositionStatements/PS_Suicide.pdf

American School Counselor Association. (2019a). *ASCA National Model: A Framework for School Counseling Programs* (4th ed.). Alexandria, VA: American School Counselor Association.

American School Counselor Association. (2019b). *The School Counselor and Safe Schools and Crisis Response.* Retrieved from American School Counselor Association: www. schoolcounselor.org/asca/media/asca/PositionStatements/PS_SafeSchools.pdf

Individuals with Disabilities Education Act, 20 U.S.C. § 1401 (2004)

156   *The TSC Model*

Institute for Solution-Focused Therapy. (2019). *What is Solution-Focused Therapy?* Retrieved from Institute for Solution-Focused Therapy: https://solutionfocused.net/what-is-solution-focused-therapy/

Jonson-Reid, M., Drake, B., Kim, J., Porterfield, S., & Han, L. (2004). A Prospective Analysis of the Relationship between Maltreatment and Special Education Eligibility among Poor Children. *Child Maltreatment, 9*(4), 382–394.

National Child Traumatic Stress Network, Justice Consortium, Schools Committee, and Culture Consortium. (2017). *Addressing Race and Trauma in the Classroom: A Resource for Educators.* Los Angeles, CA and Durham, NC: National Child Traumatic Stress Network. Retrieved from American School Counselor Association: www.schoolcounselor.org/asca/media/PDFs/FINAL-Race-and-Trauma-in-the-Classroom-Factsheet.pdf

U.S. Department of Education. (2019). *About IDEA.* Retrieved from U.S. Department of Education: https://sites.ed.gov/idea/about-idea/#IDEA-Purpose

Vanderbilt University: Department of Special Education. (2013, July). *Tip Sheet: Check-In/Check-Out (CICO).* Retrieved from Vanderbilt University: Department of Special Education: https://my.vanderbilt.edu/specialeducationinduction/files/2013/07/Tip-Sheet-Check-In-Check-Out.pdf

10 Self-Regulation
Developing Strategies through Skill-Building Lessons

This chapter is a comprehensive resource guide of trauma-sensitive, school counseling interventions that develop students' self-regulation. These resources were chosen because they align with a trauma-sensitive philosophy and their use is supported by research, best practices, and/or ASCA standards. Interventions address at least one of the 11 roles of a trauma-sensitive school counselor:

- "Recognize the signs of trauma in students"
- "Focus on resilience and strengths so that trauma does not predict individual failure"
- "Avoid practices that may re-traumatize students"
- "Create connected communities and positive school climates"
- "Implement effective academic and behavioral practices, such as positive behavioral interventions and supports and social and emotional learning"
- "Promote safe, stable and nurturing relationships"
- "Provide community resource information to students and families dealing with trauma"
- "Educate staff on the effects of trauma and how to refer students to the school counselor"
- "Collaborate with community resources to provide support for students"
- "Promote a trauma-sensitive framework for policies, procedures and behaviors to entire staff"
- "Recognize the role technology can play in magnifying trauma incidents for students"

(American School Counselor Association, 2016)

Any reference in this chapter to any person, organization, activities, products, or services, or any linkages from this book to the website of another party do not constitute or imply the endorsement, recommendation, or favoring of the person, organization, activities, products, or services over other trauma-sensitive school counseling interventions.

158   *The TSC Model*

Self-Regulation Tier 1 Interventions

The following section contains examples of Tier 1 interventions that are both trauma-sensitive and within the scope of a professional school counselor role. These interventions help students self-regulate. Interventions included in this section are:

- Brain Breaks, Exercise, and Yoga
- Calm Down Kits and Spaces
- Flexible Environments
- Mindfulness and Meditation
- Modeling Emotion Management and Healthy Communication
- Positive Behavior Interventions and Supports (PBIS)
- Social Emotional Learning (SEL)
- Sensory Opportunities

Brain Breaks, Exercise, and Yoga

As an important component of any stress-reduction regimen, exercise is beneficial in helping students regulate themselves during the school day. While research has shown physical benefits of exercise for many decades, newer research supports a wider range of advantages. Exercise builds new neural connections, increases memory, improves problem-solving and decision making, and regulates the stress response (Harris, 2018).

In schools, exercise can be a component of student self-regulation. Getting students up and moving improves their overall daily functioning, decreases behavior referrals, improves academics, and improves students' ability to pay attention (Harris, 2018). Incorporating movement into the school's daily routine by walking laps before school, adding a recess break in the afternoon, or allowing time for yoga after lunch will improve students' ability to self-regulate.

This intervention meets the ASCA recommendations for trauma-sensitivity by:

- "Creat[ing] connected communities and positive school climates"
- "Implement[ing] effective academic and behavioral practices, such as positive behavioral interventions and supports and social and emotional learning"
- "Promot[ing] a trauma-sensitive framework for policies, procedures and behaviors to entire staff"

(American School Counselor Association, 2016)

More information or resources for this intervention:

- Yoga in Schools: https://yogainschools.org/
- Go Noodle: www.gonoodle.com/
- Cosmic Kids: www.cosmickids.com/

Self-Regulation Strategies   159

- The Kids Guide to Staying Awesome and In Control: Simple Stuff to Help Children Regulate their Emotions and Senses, By Lauren Brunker www.amazon.com/Kids-Guide-Staying-Awesome-Control/dp/1849059977

Calm Down Kits and Spaces

A Calm Down Kit is a small bin or bucket filled with sensory stimulating items. These items help students regulate their emotions by grounding them and re-directing their energy. The tools give students tangible ways to physically re-lease stress like using a fidget. They also provide opportunities for mindfulness through tools like bubbles or visual timers. Some tools that could be included in a Calm Down Kit include:

- Stress ball
- Fidgets
- Weighted beanbag or small wrist weight
- Various textured items
- Bubbles
- Play-Doh
- Index cards for drawing or journaling
- Visual timers
- Stretchable items to pull
- Pinwheels

Calm Down Spaces allow students an opportunity to remove themselves from a visually or auditorily stimulating environment. A Calm Down Space is a place within the classroom or counseling office that is safe and quiet. There, students can regain composure or take a break from an otherwise stressful environment. This space could be a corner of the classroom, a tent or covered area, a back room (with an adjacent door to allow for constant supervision), or other space the teacher creates. The area should have self-regulation tools and calming visuals to reduce stimulation and increase feelings of safety. Calm Down Kits and spaces provide opportunities for students to practice newly learned self-regulation skills in a safe and supportive environment.

As a Tier 1 intervention, school counselors provide Calm Down Kits to all classrooms and spaces for students (including the main office, specialist offices, health office, and after-school programs). For this strategy to be most effective, counselors also provide classroom lessons and direct instruction on the proper use of the calm down tools, mindfulness, and Calm Down Spaces.

This intervention meets the ASCA recommendations for trauma-sensitivity by:

- "Avoid[ing] practices that may re-traumatize students"
- "Creat[ing] connected communities and positive school climates"

160   *The TSC Model*

- "Implement[ing] effective academic and behavioral practices, such as positive behavioral interventions and supports and social and emotional learning"
- "Promot[ing] safe, stable and nurturing relationships"
- "Promot[ing] a trauma-sensitive framework for policies, procedures and behaviors to entire staff"

(American School Counselor Association, 2016)

More information or resources for this intervention:

- *15 Great Ideas for Your Classroom Calm Down Kit*, By Kathryn Trudeau – We Are Teachers www.weareteachers.com/calm-down-kit-products/
- *Calm Down Kit for Anxious Kids*, By Stephanie Oswald – Parenting Chaos https://parentingchaos.com/calm-kit-anxious-kids/
- *The Classroom Calming Corner* – The Watson Institute www.thewatson-institute.org/watson-life-resources/situation/classroom-calming-corner/

Flexible Environments

The strategy of flexible seating allows students to learn in an environment unique to their needs. Students are empowered to choose and control small portions of their day such as their location within the classroom and the furniture they use while working. Flexible seating refers to alternative classroom arrangement and alternative furniture instead of simply rows of desks and chairs. These alternatives could include sitting on the floor or on cushions; using a standing desk, stool, or high back chair; accessing wobble seats and exercise balls for moment; or enjoying the comfort of living room furniture and benches. Flexible seating also refers to classrooms with movable furniture to allow for student grouping and collaboration.

Flexible seating gives students options. Options and choice lead to more engagement in their own learning and a sense of safety in choosing what feels right to them. However, for traumatized students, flexible seating could feel overwhelming due to its ever-changing nature or overstimulation. Care should be taken to explain the expected and unexpected behaviors for each flexible seating option and create systematic procedures for students to move between seating options in the room.

This intervention meets the ASCA recommendations for trauma-sensitivity by:

- "Avoid[ing] practices that may re-traumatize students"
- "Creat[ing] connected communities and positive school climates"
- "Implement[ing] effective academic and behavioral practices, such as positive behavioral interventions and supports and social and emotional learning"
- "Promot[ing] safe, stable and nurturing relationships"

(American School Counselor Association, 2016)

More information or resources for this intervention:

- *Designing Flexible Seating With Students*, By Tom Deris – Edutopia www.edutopia.org/article/designing-flexible-seating-students
- *How K-12 Schools Can Create Flexible Seating in the Classroom*, By Eli Zimmerman – Ed Tech Magazine https://edtechmagazine.com/k12/article/2019/02/how-k-12-schools-can-create-flexible-seating-classroom-perfcon

Growth Mindset: Thinking Successfully

Carol Dweck, Stanford professor and world-renowned motivation researcher, has a theory. She believes that the way people think about challenges affects their chance of overcoming them. In schools, she believes that the way students think about learning and what they believe about their own intelligence can change how much they learn and their academic success. Her theory holds true. Years of her own research show that people who find extreme success all have a similar thought pattern about how they achieved excellence. She calls this pattern "growth mindset" (Dweck, 2006).

Dweck defines growth mindset as the belief that "even basic talents and abilities can be developed over time through experience" (Harvard Business Review, 2012). People with growth mindset desire to take on challenges, "not worried about how smart they are, how they'll look, what a mistake will mean. They challenge themselves and grow" (Harvard Business Review, 2012). A fixed mindset, by contrast, is "when people believe their basic qualities, their intelligence, their talents, their abilities are just fixed traits. They have a certain amount and that's it" (Harvard Business Review, 2012).

A growth mindset leads students to tackle challenges, try new things, see difficulties or failures as a chance to grow and learn, and focus on the process of improvement. This mindset allows students to think more positively about their future opportunities and present experiences.

> They can be in control of their ultimate destiny through the way they TRY, not the way they ARE.

As school counselors, we cultivate this growth mindset by praising students' progress and process instead of their talent or ability. This may sound like:

- "I like how you asked for help when you didn't know the answer."
- "I saw you go back to the text and look for the answer again, that was so resourceful."
- "I'm proud of you for making a change to wake up 15 minutes earlier each day. You were on time for school 3 days out of 5 this week instead of 1."

> Students must know that we value their effort, grit, resilience, and persistence, not just their test score, GPA or perfection.

(Harvard Business Review, 2012)

162   The TSC Model

School counselors have dozens of student conversations each week. With the right tweaking, these conversations could easily cultivate a growth mindset. Counseling techniques like goal setting, progress monitoring, and solution-focused brief therapy all promote growth mindset. Conversations about attendance, course completion, GPA, office referrals, or college applications can be framed through the lens of growth mindset. Students can monitor their own successes and attempts at success by documenting "what's working/not working" as they work toward overcoming challenges.

Dweck specifically researched children. She wanted to know how growth mindset is developed at a young age. And what she learned is now implemented in classrooms across the country. To develop growth mindset in children, we teach students that the brain is a muscle. That it grows stronger connections each time we learn something new. As the brain makes connections, it is "growing" and getting smarter with time. It's not the brain they were born with but the one they created (Harvard Business Review, 2012). This explanation is especially important for our students with ACEs who are struggling due to their depleted neural connections. While they can't erase what happened to them, they have a chance each day to learn new ways of thinking, new skills and new talents they never had before.

This intervention meets the ASCA recommendations for trauma-sensitivity by:

- "Recogniz[ing] the signs of trauma in students"
- "Focus[ing] on resilience and strengths so that trauma does not predict individual failure"
- "Creat[ing] connected communities and positive school climates"
- "Implement[ing] effective academic and behavioral practices, such as positive behavioral interventions and supports and social and emotional learning"

(American School Counselor Association, 2016)

More information or resources for this intervention:

- Mindset Works: www.mindsetworks.com/
- Carol Dweck's Official Growth Mindset Website: https://mindsetonline.com/
- Growth Mindset Videos – Class Dojo: https://ideas.classdojo.com/b/growth-mindset
- Mindset Scholar's Network (research collaborative for growth mindset): https://mindsetscholarsnetwork.org/about-the-network/

Mindfulness and Meditation

The practice of mindfulness is rooted in Buddhist meditation and more recently morphed into a Westernized practice of "present-focused, non-judgmental

Self-Regulation Strategies   163

awareness" (Ortiz & Sibinga, 2017). Mindfulness can ease the adverse effects of toxic stress by both reducing the impact of current stress and developing long-term coping skills to reduce future stress (Ortiz & Sibinga, 2017). Many studies have confirmed the evidence that mindfulness is an effective practice for children and youth exposed to trauma.

Benefits of mindfulness among children and youth include:

- Decreased anxiety
- Decreased negative, intrusive, or repetitive thoughts
- Decreased stress regarding school performance
- Decreased physical (somatic) complaints related to stress such as headaches and stomachaches
- Improved classroom behavior
- Decreased suicidal ideation and self-harm
- Improved social functioning
- Decreased conflict with peers
- Decreased aggression
- Improved attention
- Improved sense of well-being

(Ortiz & Sibinga, 2017)

Tier 1 mindfulness programs are beneficial for all students, but for students with ACEs, they are especially positive. For students with ACEs, schoolwide mindfulness interventions increased cognitive abilities, reduced physical health complaints linked to mental health issues, increased coping skills, reduced PTSD symptoms, and enhanced resilience. Mindfulness training is also effective for improving teacher well-being and decreasing teacher burnout (Ortiz & Sibinga, 2017).

This intervention meets the ASCA recommendations for trauma-sensitivity by:

- "Creat[ing] connected communities and positive school climates"
- "Implement[ing] effective academic and behavioral practices, such as positive behavioral interventions and supports and social and emotional learning"
- "Promot[ing] safe, stable and nurturing relationships"

(American School Counselor Association, 2016)

More information or resources for this intervention:

- David Lynch Foundation: www.davidlynchfoundation.org/schools.html
- Mind Yeti (Committee for Children): www.mindyeti.com/v2/s/
- Mindfulness in Schools Project: https://mindfulnessinschools.org/
- Mindful Schools: www.mindfulschools.org/

164　*The TSC Model*

Modeling Emotion Management and Healthy Communication

Adults across school campuses model healthy emotion management, communication, and healthy conflict. When adults model, students will repeat these practices in their daily interactions with other students and adults. But modeling will not be successful alone. Emotion management and communication skills must be directly taught before modeling will reinforce appropriate behaviors.

Many of our students with ACEs have never seen adults manage their emotions in a healthy way and need both skills and examples. At school, students learn emotion management skills like self-talk, deep breathing, and communicating feelings. They can also learn healthy conflict skills like active listening, validation of others' emotions, and problem-solving.

Watching adults have civil conflict, solve problems, forgive, and take ownership of wrongdoing provides students the healthy examples they need. Within community circles or class meetings, teachers and counselors may share some of their own emotions (within healthy and safe boundaries), and throughout the day, adults should use the same healthy communication when speaking with other adults on campus, including parents and staff. Students are always watching.

This intervention meets the ASCA recommendations for trauma-sensitivity by:

- "Avoid[ing] practices that may re-traumatize students"
- "Creat[ing] connected communities and positive school climates"
- "Promot[ing] safe, stable and nurturing relationships"
(American School Counselor Association, 2016)

More information or resources for this intervention:

- *Preparing Youth to Thrive: Promising Practices in Social & Emotional Learning –* The Forum for Youth Investment www.selpractices.org/standard/modeling-emotion-management

Positive Behavior Interventions and Supports (PBIS)

Through the implementation of school-wide PBIS, students receive explicit training on the differences between expected and unexpected behaviors in the school setting. Many students with ACEs come from homes and/or neighborhoods that function on a set of rules very different than a typical elementary school. The idea of reporting the bothersome behaviors of others instead of defending yourself physically, or the idea of raising your hand to participate instead of cheerfully exclaiming an idea may be foreign to some children.

While not all students are unfamiliar with these rules, all students need explicit behavior instructions before they can be expected to follow a set of school-wide behavior expectations. Even without ACEs, students are sometimes unaware of behavior expectations at school due to lack of school experience or lack of positive school experiences.

A key component in self-regulation is the ability to feel safe and calm. Predictable routines and behaviors allow for students to experience the feeling of safety. When schools implement PBIS with fidelity, students with ACEs see what predictability of behavior, consequences, and rewards look like. They can learn the pattern of cause and effect. For example, "If follow the rules I learned, then I earn a prize." Or "If I follow the rules I learned, then the teacher is happy." This repetitive process of positive reinforcement will help engrain the concept that following the expected behaviors and the rules leads to preferred outcomes.

This intervention meets the ASCA recommendations for trauma-sensitivity by:

- "Focus[ing] on resilience and strengths so that trauma does not predict individual failure"
- "Avoid[ing] practices that may re-traumatize students"
- "Creat[ing] connected communities and positive school climates"
- "Implement[ing] effective academic and behavioral practices, such as positive behavioral interventions and supports and social and emotional learning"
- "Promot[ing] a trauma-sensitive framework for policies, procedures and behaviors to entire staff"

(American School Counselor Association, 2016)

More information or resources for this intervention:

- PBIS World: www.pbisworld.com/
- OSEP Technical Assistance Center on Positive Behavioral Interventions and Supports: www.pbis.org/
- *School Counselors' Role in Coordinating and Implementing Positive Behavior Intervention and Supports (PBIS)*, By Erin Matheson and Jacob Olsen www.wa-schoolcounselor.org/Files/OlsenTIER1.pdf

Social Emotional Learning (SEL)

SEL curriculums like Second Step, Positive Action, Caring School Community, or Sanford Harmony address a variety of social emotional traits. All of them share a similar goal: To increase pro-social behavior and decrease school violence. One common trait between most SEL curriculums is the inclusion of self-regulation lessons. These include feelings identification, coping skills, and assertiveness/communicating feelings. According to CASEL's five core competencies of SEL, self-regulation is embedded in all aspects of SEL. It is a foundational skill needed to access all higher-level thinking skills such as

166   The TSC Model

developing a growth mindset, goal setting, problem-solving, and paying attention (CASEL, 2019).

SEL is implemented at the Tier 1 level through school counseling core curriculum or as it is taught by teachers within their own classrooms. In addition to the direct instruction of these skills, teachers, counselors, and administrators can reinforce these skills in their interactions, counseling conversations, discipline, or academic content area. When SEL is embedded throughout the school day, students see the purpose and connection between SEL and real-life.

This intervention meets the ASCA recommendations for trauma-sensitivity by:

- "Creat[ing] connected communities and positive school climates"
- "Implement[ing] effective academic and behavioral practices, such as positive behavioral interventions and supports and social and emotional learning"
- "Promot[ing] safe, stable and nurturing relationships"
- "Promot[ing] a trauma-sensitive framework for policies, procedures and behaviors to entire staff"

(American School Counselor Association, 2016)

More information or resources for this intervention:

- CASEL: https://casel.org/what-is-sel/
- Second Step® (Committee for Children): www.secondstep.org/
- Caring Schools Community Curriculum: www.collaborativeclassroom.org/programs/caring-school-community/
- Positive Action® Curriculum: www.positiveaction.net/
- Sanford Harmony™: www.sanfordharmony.org/
- Kelso's Choice https://kelsoschoice.com/home/
- SEL Children's Literature (for use with Second Step): https://iassw.org/wp-content/uploads/2014/10/2nd_step_booklist.pdf

Sensory Opportunities

Students with ACEs can have challenges with sensory processing due to their early trauma and lack of normal childhood development. It is estimated that 16% of school-aged students have sensory processing difficulties (Biel, 2017). Children with sensory challenges experience extremely high or extremely low sensitivity to their senses of vision, hearing, touch, smell, and taste.

Students with trauma may be sensitive to sensory sensations due to the potential trauma reenactment it triggers. For example, students who were physically or sexually abused may be hypersensitive to touch. They may respond by pulling away, pushing, or yelling when accidentally bumped or tapped on the shoulder. Auditorily, students with trauma may be sensitive to loud noises, including alarms, whistles, sirens, harsh voices, or yelling.

As a Tier 1 intervention, teachers and counselors should be aware of the potential sensory issues of traumatized students. By raising their own awareness of sensory concerns, educators reduce the sensory stress in the learning environments. Taking down visually busy posters, turning off background music, and providing flexible seating are easy fixes to reduce sensory stress. Students should feel safe to voice their opinions when something is uncomfortable and empowered to choose an option that works for them and the classroom (Biel, 2017).

This intervention meets the ASCA recommendations for trauma-sensitivity by:

- "Recogniz[ing] the signs of trauma in students"
- "Focus[ing] on resilience and strengths so that trauma does not predict individual failure
- "Avoid[ing] practices that may re-traumatize students"
- "Educat[ing] staff on the effects of trauma and how to refer students to the school counselor"
- "Promot[ing] a trauma-sensitive framework for policies, procedures and behaviors to entire staff"
- "Recogniz[ing] the role technology can play in magnifying trauma incidents for students"

(American School Counselor Association, 2016)

More information or resources for this intervention:

- *Understanding Sensory Processing Disorder* – The Star Institute www.spd-star.org/basic/understanding-sensory-processing-disorder
- *How Sensory Processing Issues Affect Kids in School* – The Child Mind Institute https://childmind.org/article/how-sensory processing-issues-affect-kids-in-school/
- *Sensory Screening Tool: School,* By Lindsay Biel OTR/L https://sensoryprocessingchallenges.com/images/Sensorytoolschool.pdf

Self-Regulation Tier 2 Interventions

The following section contains examples of Tier 2 interventions that are both trauma-sensitive and within the scope of a professional school counselor role. These interventions help students self-regulate. Interventions included in this section are:

- Cognitive Behavioral Therapy in School Settings
- CBITS
- Coping Skills Training
- Visual Support Strategies
- Superflex®
- Trauma-sensitive Psychoeducation
- The ZONES of Regulation®

168   *The TSC Model*

Cognitive Behavioral Therapy (CBT) in School Settings

CBT is a form of counseling and psychotherapy that is evidence-based for a variety of diagnoses and conditions, including anxiety, depression, PTSD, and relationship problems. The methods used in the practice of CBT techniques are proven to produce changes for child and adolescent clients, and improve quality of life and social/behavioral functioning (American Psychological Association, 2019).

CBT is based on the core principle that the client's (student's in our case) presenting problems are based in part on unproductive and unhelpful thoughts and thought patterns. These thought patterns lead to patterns of unhelpful learned behaviors and negative coping strategies. A student's life can be significantly improved as they learn more helpful and positive ways of thinking, which lead to more helpful and positive behaviors and ultimately reduce the symptoms of the problems in their life (American Psychological Association, 2019).

CBT techniques to address unhealthy thought and behavior patterns include:

- Learning to recognize the thoughts which are creating problems.
- Learning to re-evaluate thoughts for their truth and their capacity to be realistic.
- Developing an understanding of the behaviors of others and the motives behind their behaviors.
- Implementing problem-solving skills and coping skills.
- Developing a sense of self-efficacy and a confidence in their own abilities and strengths.
- Applying role-playing to practice strategies and hypothetical conversations.
- Using mindfulness and relaxation techniques to calm the mind and body.
- Emphasizing "homework" and work outside of sessions to reinforce the learning inside the sessions.
- Focusing on the present and future instead of what brought the person to counseling. CBT techniques help the student move forward and make changes instead of processing past events.

(American Psychological Association, 2019)

School counselors can use CBT strategies in individual, group, and classroom settings. The techniques of role-play, problem-solving, learning coping skills, and evaluating self-talk for truthfulness are common practices of school counselors. For students with ACEs, employing CBT techniques during short-term, brief counseling is an appropriate way to address unhealthy learned behaviors without delving into "trauma therapy." Long-term trauma therapy is not appropriate in the school setting or within the scope of practice for school counselors.

Self-Regulation Strategies   169

This intervention meets the ASCA recommendations for trauma-sensitivity by:

- "Recogniz[ing] the signs of trauma in students"
- "Focus[ing] on resilience and strengths so that trauma does not predict individual failure"
- "Promot[ing] safe, stable and nurturing relationships"
- "Collaborat[ing] with community resources to provide support for students" (American School Counselor Association, 2016)

More information or resources for this intervention:

- Trauma-Focused CBT (for licensed therapists) https://tfcbt.org/
- *Cognitive Behavioral Play Therapy Techniques in School-Based Group Counseling: Assisting Students in the Development of Social Skills,* By Laura J. Fazio-Griffith and Mary B. Ballard – American Counseling Association VISTAS www.counseling.org/docs/default-source/vistas/article_18.pdf?sfvrsn=10
- *Using Cognitive Behavioral Therapy with Younger Students,* By Laura Driscoll – Social Emotional Workshop https://socialemotionalworkshop.com/2018/01/cognitive-behavioral-therapy-with-younger-students/

CBITS

Cognitive Behavioral Intervention for Trauma in Schools (CBITS) is group or individual trauma counseling designed for use in schools. The goals of CBITS include reducing behavioral problems, symptoms of depression, and symptoms of PTSD among middle and high school students who have experienced trauma (Cognitive Behavioral Intervention for Trauma in Schools, 2019). CBITS uses cognitive behavioral therapy techniques such as mindfulness, thought processing, psychoeducation, and problem-solving to improve educational functioning for students who experienced trauma. Educational functioning includes attendance, grades, classroom behavior, and student well-being.

CBITS offers training for school-based mental health professionals in person and on its website. The training gives counselors, social workers, and therapists information about the 10-session group or individual counseling intervention and provides video model examples of implementation. School counselors who are licensed mental health clinicians or work in conjunction with a licensed clinician can use this intervention once the training is complete.

CBITS was created specifically for students who experienced trauma and should not be used for students with "suspected ACEs" or simply for behavioral concerns. CBITS is an evidence-based program with proven results, including reductions in PTSD and depression symptoms among students who experienced trauma and participated in the intervention (Cognitive Behavioral Intervention for Trauma in Schools, 2019).

170 The TSC Model

This intervention meets the ASCA recommendations for trauma-sensitivity by:

- "Educat[ing] staff on the effects of trauma and how to refer students to the school counselor"
- "Focus[ing] on resilience and strengths so that trauma does not predict individual failure"
- "Promot[ing] safe, stable and nurturing relationships"
- "Collaborat[ing] with community resources to provide support for students"
  (American School Counselor Association, 2016)

More information or resources for this intervention:

- CBITS Training: https://cbitsprogram.org/

Coping Skills Training

In order for students to self-regulate their emotions, they must have a toolbox full of skills and strategies to calm themselves down. These self-calming strategies are referred to as coping skills and can be either healthy or unhealthy. Teaching students healthy coping skills is an essential Tier 2 intervention, especially for students with ACEs. If students are not taught healthy coping skills like deep breathing, sensory soothing, positive self-talk, or structured breaks, they frequently fall into unhealthy coping patterns. Unhealthy coping skills are strategies the student uses to regulate their emotions in the short-term that also have long-term negative consequences. Unhealthy strategies include self-harm, substance abuse, skipping school, physical aggression, or age-inappropriate temper tantrums.

Teaching coping skills is commonly part of a school counselor's role through small group counseling. Many great coping skills curriculums exist, and almost all counseling theories involve the use of coping skills. I like to use bibliotherapy to teach coping skills. Through the exploration of characters in the story, students identify coping skills. At a higher level, they can analyze if the coping skill in the story was healthy or unhealthy and discuss why. Through expressive arts therapy, students can design and build their own coping tools. Coping tools such as stress balls, calming jars, and paintings of positive visual imagery can help students at home and school.

Curriculums like *The ZONES of Regulation* also teach students to connect coping skills with emotions. Students choose different coping skills based on the emotion they feel. Through trying a wide variety of coping skills in the classroom, students gain awareness of which ones work for them. Some students need assistance applying coping skills in the classroom. A visual aid, or as I call it a "coping skills menu" helps them choose a strategy in the moment of extreme emotion.

This intervention meets the ASCA recommendations for trauma-sensitivity by:

- "Focus[ing] on resilience and strengths so that trauma does not predict individual failure"
- "Implement[ing] effective academic and behavioral practices, such as positive behavioral interventions and supports and social and emotional learning" (American School Counselor Association, 2016)

More information or resources for this intervention:

- *Teaching Coping Skills* – PBIS World www.pbisworld.com/tier-1/teach-coping-skills/
- *How to Teach Kids Coping Skills to Manage Big Feelings* – Coping Skills for Kids https://copingskillsforkids.com/blog/how-to-teach-kids-coping-skills-for-dealing-with-big-feelings
- Coping Skills in Children's Literature: https://copingskillsforkids.com/books

Visual Support Strategies

Within the classroom, many students need visual support to improve behavior and emotional functioning. Individualized schedules and self-monitoring systems ensure feelings of safety, behavioral compliance, and academic engagement. School counselors are often tasked with creating these charts and schedules. Counselors also coach teachers on the implementation of visual supports. Implementing these systems helps to bring predictability and consistency of expectations to a student's day. This boosts their sense of safety in the classroom and their trust of the teacher.

Visual schedules are just what they sound like – daily schedule charts with images. They cue students to what comes next throughout the day. Visual schedules decrease feelings of uneasiness about transitions and increase feelings of control and security in the school environment. The schedules look different based on the student's reading level and age. Some include only visuals, some have a combination of visuals and words, and some are only words. Schedules can be laminated and taped to the student's desk if they are consistent each day. If the schedule is fluid, the visual schedule should match by using Velcro or other fasteners to change the schedule from day to day or week to week.

First-Then is a behavioral compliance technique based on the Premack Principle. The Premack Principle was discovered in 1959 by Professor David Premack during his behavioral and psychological studies on monkeys. He discovered that a low desirability action was more likely to occur when its completion elicited a higher desirability action (Premack, 1959). The Premack Principle is used frequently when moms across the world say "first eat your broccoli, then you can have ice cream." Better examples from education include "First, finish your math worksheets, then you can go get a drink of water." Or "First, finish your test, then you can have 5 minutes of free time."

172   *The TSC Model*

Anytime the students are given contingencies to elicit an expected behavior that is of low desirability to the student, we are enacting the Premack Principle. This contingency allows students to learn cause-and-effect relationships and build trust with their teacher or counselor. A visual support helps some students better see the relationship between their compliance and their desired reward.

Self-monitoring systems are behavior charts that allow both the student and the teacher/counselor to keep track of the student's behavior. Having the student track their behavior alongside an adult allows for student self-reflection and student voice to be a part of the behavior management process. Many behavior charts are based solely on the teacher's observation or subjective opinion of "how the day went." Self-monitoring charts provide students the opportunity to collect their own data about their behavior and then compare their results to the results of the teacher.

Examples of self-monitoring include when students tally how many times they blurted out during a lesson, or how many times the teacher asked them to please return to their seats during work time. Another example is a type of behavior chat called Self and Match. A Self and Match chart helps teachers/counselors set specific behavior expectations for a student and then track that student's compliance. Students and teachers each have a rating scale and discuss their ratings together. This discussion helps students better understand the discrepancies and improves their ability to self-reflect.

This intervention meets the ASCA recommendations for trauma-sensitivity by:

- "Focus[ing] on resilience and strengths so that trauma does not predict individual failure"
- "Creat[ing] connected communities and positive school climates"
- "Implement[ing] effective academic and behavioral practices, such as positive behavioral interventions and supports and social and emotional learning"
- "Promot[ing] safe, stable and nurturing relationships"
- "Educat[ing] staff on the effects of trauma and how to refer students to the school counselor"
- "Collaborat[ing] with community resources to provide support for students"
- "Promot[ing] a trauma-sensitive framework for policies, procedures and behaviors to entire staff"

(American School Counselor Association, 2016)

More information or resources for this intervention:

- Goalbook Toolkit for Instructional Support: https://goalbookapp.com/toolkit/v/browse/strategies?subject=Behavior%20%26%20SEL
- *Self-Monitoring* – PBIS World www.pbisworld.com/tier-2/self-monitoring/
- *Visual Schedules* – PBIS World www.pbisworld.com/tier-2/individual-visual-schedules/
- Self and Match Self-Monitoring System: http://selfandmatch.com/

Self-Regulation Strategies   173

- *How to Make a Visual Schedule*, By Meg Proctor – The Inspired Treehouse https://theinspiredtreehouse.com/how-to-make-a-visual-schedule/
- First-Then Board and Visual Schedule Flipbooks: www.teacherspayteachers.com/Product/First-Then-Board-Visual-Schedule-Flip-Books-EDITABLE-3253360
- Editable Visual Schedules: www.teacherspayteachers.com/Product/EDITABLE-Visual-Schedules-for-SPED-with-Self-Reg-Class-Inclusion-2295890

Superflex®

Superflex is a social thinking curriculum developed by expert Speech and Language Pathologist Michelle Garcia Winner. The Superflex curriculum teaches students to understand self-regulation, social behavior, and social cogitation. That means students learn how to think about others' behavior and how other people think about their behavior. Using a team of comic book-style characters called the Unthinkables, this curriculum helps elementary-aged students recognize their own social thinking difficulties. Superflex teaches students strategies to improve their social awareness and social flexibility (Garcia Winner, 2015).

By framing these executive functioning, communication, and social skills by way of a fictional character, it brings abstract concepts to life in a way that young students can understand and discuss. For example, students learn about Rock Brain, an Unthinkable that causes students to get stuck on one activity or one way of thinking. Rock Brain disregards the directions of adults and the wants/needs of other students. Another Unthinkable is Energy Harry who causes students to have excessive energy and makes it difficult for them to sit still in class (Garcia Winner, 2015).

School counselors may use Superflex as a group curriculum to develop social skills and self-regulation, or as an individual counseling strategy. The curriculum teaches 14 Unthinkables, but students do not need to know all of them to engage in the learning. Matching a student with a few Unthinkables is a good way to introduce them to the concepts of social thinking and self-regulation without overwhelming them with too much information.

Garcia Winner also developed the "5 Step Power Plan" for cognition-based self-regulation. This strategy teaches students to become aware of their own body and actions and their actions' effect on others. Once they are aware, they use thought stopping and positive self-talk to regulate their emotions and social behavior, and apply socially expected behaviors (Garcia Winner, 2015).

This intervention meets the ASCA recommendations for trauma-sensitivity by:

- "Creat[ing] connected communities and positive school climates"
- "Implement[ing] effective academic and behavioral practices, such as positive behavioral interventions and supports and social and emotional learning"
- "Promot[ing] safe, stable and nurturing relationships"

(American School Counselor Association, 2016)

174   *The TSC Model*

More information or resources for this intervention:

- Superflex® five-step Power Plan: www.socialthinking.com/Articles?name=superflex-team-unthinkables-five-step-power-plan

Trauma-Sensitive Psychoeducation

Psychoeducation about trauma helps teens with ACE exposure to feel more at ease and in control of their own physical and emotional reactions. Psychoeducation is the process of providing specific research and information about a diagnosis or mental health concern to students or clients who are identified with that diagnosis or concern. In the case of ACEs and the role of school counselors, school counselors can be a source of psychoeducation in two ways:

1   As they provide general, age-appropriate information about the functions of the brain in emotion management and how traumatic experiences affect the brain. This would be a Tier 1 strategy.
2   As they provide specific information about toxic stress and trauma's impact on learning to students who disclosed their own ACEs to the counselor. This is a Tier 2 strategy.

School counseling interventions are typically brief and school counselors may not have adequate time or training to provide therapeutic services for students with ACEs. Therefore, school counselors should never directly ask a student if they have experienced trauma. Bringing up traumatic situations without adequate time to process them may derail a student's emotional functioning during the school day. Psychoeducation and directly discussing a student's ACEs should only be initiated by the student.

Psychoeducation for ACEs could include the following topics:

- Functions of the specific brain regions in emotion management such as the amygdala, prefrontal cortex, and hippocampus.
- Information about the ACE study and the prevalence of ACEs in the United States.
- Research about trauma's impact on learning and how a school counselor could help reduce the negative impact.
- Strategies to build resiliency.

This intervention meets the ASCA recommendations for trauma-sensitivity by:

- "Recogniz[ing] the signs of trauma in students"
- "Focus[ing] on resilience and strengths so that trauma does not predict individual failure"

- "Avoid[ing] practices that may re-traumatize students"
- "Promot[ing] safe, stable and nurturing relationships"
- "Provid[ing] community resource information to students and families dealing with trauma".
- "Educat[ing] staff on the effects of trauma and how to refer students to the school counselor"

(American School Counselor Association, 2016)

More information or resources for this intervention:

- Paper Tigers movie: https://kpjrfilms.co/paper-tigers/
- Resiliency Centers Classroom Guidance Lesson: www.teacherspay-teachers.com/Product/Resiliency-Centers-Classroom-Guidance-Lesson-Resilience-Activity-4050525

The ZONES of Regulation®

The ZONES of Regulation is a "concept to foster self-regulation and emotional control" (Kuypers, 2019). Based on a model of cognitive behavior management, *The ZONES of Regulation* teaches students to regulate their own behavior by first developing their skills of emotion identification, self-awareness, and social thinking. *The ZONES of Regulation* is based on the research of self-regulation for students with Autism Spectrum Disorder (ASD) and ADHD. It was also shown to be successful with students who experience emotional disturbances and trauma (Kuypers, 2019).

ZONES gives these students a concrete language to express their feelings and the knowledge of sensory regulation and coping strategies to re-regulate themselves (Kuypers, 2019). ZONES also incorporates social thinking strategies to assist students in understanding how their behavior affects the feelings and thoughts of others. This work develops the student's ability to take another's perspective, enhance empathy, and resolve conflicts.

The ZONES of Regulation **divides emotions into four categories based on levels of emotional alertness:**

- RED: Extremely high alertness, out-of-control of body, furious, angry, dysregulated, in fight-or-flight mode.
- YELLOW: High emotions and alertness, some dysregulation. This zone includes the emotions of frustration, worry, fear, silliness, stress, and excitement.
- BLUE: Low alertness, depressed emotions, including sadness, tiredness, boredom, and sickness.
- GREEN: A state of neutral emotion and alertness. In this ZONE, a student is considered "ready to learn" by being emotionally happy, calm, focused, and relaxed

(Kuypers, 2019).

176   *The TSC Model*

This intervention meets the ASCA recommendations for trauma-sensitivity by:

- "Focus[ing] on resilience and strengths so that trauma does not predict individual failure"
- "Creat[ing] connected communities and positive school climates"
- "Implement[ing] effective academic and behavioral practices, such as positive behavioral interventions and supports and social and emotional learning"
- "Promot[ing] safe, stable and nurturing relationships"

(American School Counselor Association, 2016)

More information or resources for this intervention:

- The ZONES of Regulation® book: http://zonesofregulation.com/index.html

Self-Regulation Tier 3 Interventions

The following section contains examples of Tier 3 interventions that are both trauma-sensitive and within the scope of a professional school counselor role. These interventions help students self-regulate. Interventions included in this section are:

- Referral to Behavior Specialist
- Section 504 Protection for Students with Disabilities
- Structured Breaks and Other Intensive Behavior Support Strategies

Referral to Behavior Specialist

As a part of a well-rounded special education team, public schools employ behavior specialists. A behavior specialist is certified in applied behavior analysis with a Board-Certified Behavior Analyst (BCBA) credential (Behavior Analyst Certification Board, 2020). Behavior specialists use the psychological theory of behaviorism. The premise of behaviorism is that all behavior follows predictable patterns and laws. Behaviorism believes that behavior can be changed or managed based on the immediate consequences or rewards for the behavior. Behavior specialists are experts in analyzing student behavior and creating plans to change behavior and improve students' social and behavioral functioning at school (Behavior Analyst Certification Board, 2020).

School counselors and educators make referrals to the behavior specialist as a part of a Tier 3 intervention plan for students with symptoms of toxic stress. Behavior specialists observe and track student behavior to identify specific functions of the behavior through a process called a Functional Behavior Analysis (FBA). The findings of the FBA lead the behavior specialist to create a plan called a Behavior Support Plan (BSP) when it is a stand-alone plan or a Behavior Intervention Plan (BIP) when it is part of an IEP. Strategies and goals identified through the BSP/BIP should be able to be implemented in a general education classroom as Tier 3 strategies. BSP/BIP plans fail when interventionists create plans that only work with one-on-one support and/or do not support the student through teaching behavior strategies or monitoring progress.

This intervention meets the ASCA recommendations for trauma-sensitivity by:

- "Collaborat[ing] with community resources to provide support for students"
- "Promot[ing] a trauma-sensitive framework for policies, procedures and behaviors to entire staff"

(American School Counselor Association, 2016)

More information or resources for this intervention:

- *Behavior Assessments* – OSEP Technical Assistance Center on Positive Behavioral Interventions and Supports www.pbis.org/resource-type/assessments
- Behavior Intervention Plan (BIP) – PBIS World www.pbisworld.com/tier-3/behavior-intervention-plan-bip/

Section 504 Protection for Students with Disabilities

Section 504 of the Rehabilitation Act of 1973 is a federal law that disallows discrimination based on a documented disability for anyone participating in a federally funded activity (Section 504 of the Rehabilitation Act of 1973). Public education is included in this category because all public schools receive federal funding. To comply with this federal law, public schools create 504 plans to document alterations to the student's education or educational environment. These alterations are referred to as accommodations. They are made to ensure equal access to a free and appropriate public education. Students qualify for a 504 plan if they have a mental or physical impairment which substantially limits at least one major life activity, have a prior record of a mental or physical impairment, or are considered to have such an impairment (Section 504 of the Rehabilitation Act of 1973).

504 accommodation plans are used only for students who do not qualify for an IEP. Students with a learning disability or other qualifying condition for an IEP have accommodations listed within their IEP and have no need for a separate 504 plan. Students who experience trauma may not qualify for an IEP and therefore may need a 504 plan. The 504 plan would accommodate for their self-regulation difficulties if the difficulties impair a major life activity and are diagnosed as a disability (or closely resemble a diagnosable disability). ACEs and toxic stress are not considered a disability or mental health disorder by themselves. But many symptoms of toxic stress mimic symptoms of other

178   The TSC Model

diagnoses like ADHD, anxiety, and PTSD, and therefore could be considered qualifiers for a 504 plan.

Psychoeducational or mental health evaluations should be conducted to determine the potential disabilities or symptoms that interfere with the student's life functioning. Accommodations made in the 504 plan are based on a team analysis of how to ensure equal education for the student. All 504 accommodation plans must be accepted and consented to by the student's parent/ guardian.

This intervention meets the ASCA recommendations for trauma-sensitivity by:

- "Implement[ing] effective academic and behavioral practices, such as positive behavioral interventions and supports and social and emotional learning"
- "Collaborat[ing] with community resources to provide support for students"
- "Promot[ing] a trauma-sensitive framework for policies, procedures and behaviors to entire staff"

(American School Counselor Association, 2016)

More information or resources for this intervention:

- *Nondiscrimination on the Basis of Handicap in Programs or Activities Receiving Federal Financial Assistance* – U.S. Department of Education www2.ed.gov/ policy/rights/reg/ocr/edlite-34cfr104.html
- *Frequently Asked Questions About Section 504 and the Education of Children with Disabilities – Office of Civil Rights*, U.S. Department of Education www2.ed.gov/about/offices/list/ocr/504faq.html
- *504 Education Plans* – Kids Health https://kidshealth.org/en/parents/504-plans.html

Structured Breaks and Other Intensive Behavior Support Strategies

When students are unable to communicate their self-regulation needs and frequently dysregulate, individualized interventions are used to prompt students to regulate their emotions when needed. Tier 2 interventions such as visual schedules, coping skills menus, First-Then contingency plans, and behavior contracts can be continued with modifications to make the intervention more intensive and appropriate for Tier 3. These modifications may include increased frequency of check-ins, increased desirability of reward, decreased demands for reward to be earned, or modification of behavioral goals to build different or more basic skills needed to achieve the original goals.

Another strategy used to help students who are frequently dysregulated is structured breaks. This system of building breaks into the student's daily

Self-Regulation Strategies 179

schedule helps the student to release energy through physical movement or rest without a break needing to be self-initiated. Structured breaks could look like "errands" to be run daily, walks to and from the school counselor's office, supervised laps around the track, time on approved exercise equipment like a trampoline or exercise ball, additional recess periods or rest time. Structured breaks may be used in conjunction with other schedule modifications such as shortened days or small group instruction. Once students are able to self-initiate breaks by communicating "I need a break" or using a break card/signal, the frequency of structured breaks can decrease and the student can be more in control of how they used their allotted number of breaks per day.

This intervention meets the ASCA recommendations for trauma-sensitivity by:

- "Creat[ing] connected communities and positive school climates"
- "Implement[ing] effective academic and behavioral practices, such as positive behavioral interventions and supports and social and emotional learning"
- "Promot[ing] safe, stable and nurturing relationships"

(American School Counselor Association, 2016)

More information or resources for this intervention:

- *Structured Breaks* – PBIS World

References

American Psychological Association. (2019). *What is Cognitive Behavioral Therapy?* Retrieved from American Psychological Association: www.apa.org/ptsd-guideline/patients-and-families/cognitive-behavioral

American School Counselor Association. (2016, August). *The School Counselor and Trauma-Informed Practice*. Retrieved from American School Counselor Association: www.schoolcounselor.org/asca/media/asca/PositionStatements/PS_TraumaInformed.pdf

Behavior Analyst Certification Board. (2020). *About Behavior Analysis*. Retrieved from Behavior Analyst Certification Board: www.bacb.com/about-behavior-analysis/

Biel, L. (2017). Students with Sensory Processing Challenges. In W. Steele (Ed.), *Optimizing Learning Outocmes: Proven Brain-Centric trauma Sensitive Practices* (pp. 74–94). New York, NY: Routledge.

CASEL. (2019). *What Is SEL*. Retrieved from CASEL: https://casel.org/what-is-sel/

Cognitive Behavioral Intervention for Trauma in Schools. (2019). *Home*. Retrieved from Cognitive Behavioral Intervention for Trauma in Schools: https://cbitsprogram.org

Dweck, C. (2006). *Mindset: The New Psychology of Success*. New York, NY: Ballentine Books.

Garcia Winner, M. (2015, May). *Superflex® the Team of Unthinkables and the Five-Step Power Plan*. Retrieved from Social Thinking: www.socialthinking.com/Articles?name=superflex-team-unthinkables-five-step-power-plan

180   *The TSC Model*

Harris, N. B. (2018). *The Deepest Well: Healing the Long-Term Effects of Childhood Adversity.* New York, NY: Houghton Mifflin Harcourt.

Harvard Business Review. (2012). The Right Mindset for Success. *The Right Mindset for Success.* Retrieved from https://hbr.org/2012/01/the-right-mindset-for-success

Kuypers, L. (2019). Retrieved from ZONES of Regulation: www.zonesofregulation.com/index.html

Ortiz, R., & Sibinga, E. (2017). The Role of Mindfulness in Reducing the Adverse Effects of Childhood Stress and Trauma. *Children, 4*(3), 16.

Premack, D. (1959). Toward Empirical Behavior Laws: I. Positive Reinforcement. *Psychological Review, 66*(4), 219–233. doi:10.1037/h0040891

Section 504 of the Rehabilitation Act of 1973. Retrieved from www2.ed.gov/policy/rights/reg/ocr/edlite-34cfr104.html#D

11 Creating Connectedness
Caring Matters

This chapter is a comprehensive resource guide of trauma-sensitive school counseling interventions that enhance school connectedness. These resources were chosen because they align with a trauma-sensitive philosophy and their use is supported by research, best practices, and/or ASCA standards. Interventions address at least one of the 11 roles of a trauma-sensitive school counselor:

- "Recognize the signs of trauma in students"
- "Focus on resilience and strengths so that trauma does not predict individual failure"
- "Avoid practices that may re-traumatize students"
- "Create connected communities and positive school climates"
- "Implement effective academic and behavioral practices, such as positive behavioral interventions and supports and social and emotional learning"
- "Promote safe, stable and nurturing relationships"
- "Provide community resource information to students and families dealing with trauma"
- "Educate staff on the effects of trauma and how to refer students to the school counselor"
- "Collaborate with community resources to provide support for students"
- "Promote a trauma-sensitive framework for policies, procedures and behaviors to entire staff"
- "Recognize the role technology can play in magnifying trauma incidents for students"

(American School Counselor Association, 2016a)

Any reference in this chapter to any person, organization, activities, products, or services, or any linkages from this book to the website of another party do not constitute or imply the endorsement, recommendation, or favoring of the person, organization, activities, products, or services over other trauma-sensitive school counseling interventions.

School Counseling Tier 1 Interventions

The following section contains examples of Tier 1 interventions that are both trauma-sensitive and within the scope of a professional school counselor

182 *The TSC Model*

role. These interventions support the development of school connectedness and perceptions of positive school climate. Interventions included in this section are:

- Attendance Awareness
- Award Ceremonies
- Bullying and Discrimination Prevention
- College/Career Counseling
- Community Circles
- Ensure Equity and Access
- Extracurricular Activities and Clubs
- Modeling Healthy Relationships and Connections
- Restorative Questions and Language
- Transition Programs

Attendance Awareness

School connectedness is positively associated with student attendance. The more connected students are to school, the more they want to attend. And conversely, the more they attend, the more connected they feel (Van Eck, Johnson, Bettencourt, & Lindstrom Johnson, 2016). School counselors can impact student attendance at all three levels of a tiered intervention system. Using resources from Attendance Works, an organization that seeks to reduce chronic absenteeism nationwide, school counselors can develop a plan to address attendance concerns within their comprehensive counseling program (Attendance Works, 2016).

At the Tier 1 level, counselors in collaboration with attendance clerks and administrators create incentives and awards to promote positive attendance. Additionally, they create messaging to address any misconceptions about attendance. For example, many parents and guardians underestimate the amount of days their student has missed. By sending "nudge letters" that compare their students' below average attendance to the days attended by the "average student" at the school (median days attended), parents are encouraged to increase their child's attendance to meet the norm, improving attendance by 10–15% compared to a control group (Shaw, 2018). Counselors can help in spreading the word to parents and community members about the importance of attendance and the misconception that excused absences are better than unexcused. Fact: A day missed is a day missed. Students who are chronically absent – missing more than 10% of school days for any reason – are more likely to have a lower reading level, feel less connected to school, have lower standardized test scores, and drop out of high school (Attendance Works, 2016).

At the Tier 2 level, school counselors make personalized connections with students and families who are at risk for chronic absenteeism, providing resources that reduce attendance barriers and promote factual information about student attendance. Interventions such as student attendance progress groups,

Creating Connectedness   183

mentoring programs, parent phone calls, and parent conferences would fit into this category.

At the Tier 3 level, counselors can collaborate with social workers and administrators to provide wraparound services and community resources to families with severe attendance concerns, especially for those with extreme barriers such as homelessness or chronic illness. Counselors and teams can facilitate home visits and implement attendance contracts to improve attendance in the most extreme cases.

This intervention meets the ASCA recommendations for trauma-sensitivity by:

- "Creat[ing] connected communities and positive school climates"
- "Provid[ing] community resource information to students and families dealing with trauma"
- "Collaborat[ing] with community resources to provide support for students" (American School Counselor Association, 2016)

More information or resources for this intervention:

- Attendance Works: www.attendanceworks.org/
- *Simple 'nudge' letters can boost school attendance, new research suggests,* By Neal Morton – Seattle Times www.seattletimes.com/education-lab/new-research-suggests-simple-nudge-letters-can-boost-student-attendance-in-schools/
- Attendance Activities School Year Plan: www.attendanceworks.org/wp-content/uploads/2019/06/Attendance-Planning-Calendar-K-12-rev-6-13-19-SAMPLE-ACTIVITIES.pdf

Award Ceremonies

Providing students with the opportunity to be recognized for school success can boost students' confidence in their abilities and their positive feelings toward school. Or it can shatter them. Typical award assemblies recognize a few high achieving students or a few students with consistently excellent behavior, discounting the rest of the students who are not achieving this perfect standard. When considering award ceremonies, school counselors and school leaders should be thoughtful about how and why awards are given, and to whom they are given. Here are a few questions to consider:

- Do awards recognize student excellence in a diverse variety of areas, including effort, academics, behavior, community service, attendance, sports, and leadership?
- Do awards recognize both process and excellence through "most improved" awards or awards based on goal achievement, not just Straight A's?

184 The TSC Model

- Do awards assemblies serve as a way for families to connect to the school through translated information and culturally meaningful practices?
- Are racial and ethnic groups equally represented? Or are implicit biases instead of accurate data influencing the award recipients?

Award assemblies that are carefully planned to reduce re-traumatization could enhance positive school climate and recognize the unique strengths and abilities of students. However, there is no research linking award ceremonies to school connectedness. This section is included to ensure that school counselors are thoughtful in the way award assemblies are implemented. This common practice should enhance school climate and not detract from it.

This intervention meets the ASCA recommendations
for trauma-sensitivity by:

- "Focus[ing] on resilience and strengths so that trauma does not predict individual failure"
- "Avoid[ing] practices that may re-traumatize students"
- "Creat[ing] connected communities and positive school climates"
(American School Counselor Association, 2016)

More information or resources for this intervention:

- *Building School Culture Where All Kids Feel Special*, By Sharon Chappell – Teaching Tolerance www.tolerance.org/magazine/building-school-culture-where-all-kids-feel-special

Bullying and Discrimination Prevention

Bullying may be the biggest buzz word in education this century. But it is more than just a hot topic; it has a deep impact on the perception of school safety and connection. Bullying is one of the most common complaints from both students and parents. It is also one of the most commonly misunderstood phenomena at schools. Bullying is the repeated, unwanted, and aggressive behavior of one or more students with perceived power toward one or more other students with less perceived power (U.S. Department of Health and Human Services, 2019). When bullying exists on a school campus, and students feel that adults around them are powerless to stop it, school connectedness and safety suffer. Bullying not only impacts the individual who is victimized, but also the community who witnesses to the harassment or violence.

Many evidenced-based bullying prevention interventions exist. Some notable ones include Olweus, Safe School Ambassadors, and Second Step. Implementing one of these evidence-based, bullying prevention programs is an obvious strategy to improve school connectedness. But it may not be the most cost- or time-effective. School counselors have many training opportunities such as the ASCA Bullying Prevention Specialist training or attending a conference through the International Bullying Prevention Association to learn about other effective strategies.

Teach students about the power of bystanders and the kid-friendly and safe ways they can intervene on behalf of the victim. This will decrease the opportunity for bullying by decreasing the power of the bully. The more that students are onboard by supporting the victim, the less students are available to create social power on behalf of the bully.

School-wide awareness programs such as National Bullying Prevention Month in October or the Great Kindness Challenge in January can raise awareness of bullying and can clear up any misconceptions for students and parents.

In addition to addressing bullying, schools must also address specific power-based discrimination, including racism, sexism, and discrimination based on sexual identity or disability. School counselors should train both students and teachers about the existence of microaggressions and how to create a more inclusive space for people of all backgrounds and identities.

This intervention meets the ASCA recommendations for trauma-sensitivity by:

- "Creat[ing] connected communities and positive school climates"
- "Implement[ing] effective academic and behavioral practices, such as positive behavioral interventions and supports and social and emotional learning"
- "Promot[ing] safe, stable and nurturing relationships"
                                        (American School Counselor Association, 2016)

More information or resources for this intervention:

- *Four Ways Teachers Can Reduce Implicit Bias,* By Jill Suttie – Greater Good Magazine https://greatergood.berkeley.edu/article/item/four_ways_teachers_can_reduce_implicit_bias
- International Bullying Prevention Association: https://ibpaworld.org/
- *Position Statement: The School Counselor and the Promotion of Safe Schools through Conflict Resolution and Bullying/Harassment Prevention* – ASCA www.schoolcounselor.org/asca/media/asca/PositionStatements/PS_Bullying.pdf
- ASCA U Bullying Prevention Specialist Training: www.schoolcounselor.org/school-counselors/professional-development/asca-u-specialist-trainings/bullying-prevention-specialist-en
- *Bullying: How counselors can intervene,* By Aida Midgett – Counseling Today https://ct.counseling.org/2016/06/bullying-counselors-can-intervene/
- Olweus Bullying Prevention Program: https://olweus.sites.clemson.edu/
- Safe School Ambassadors: https://community-matters.org/programs-services/youth-empowerment-programs/safe-school-ambassadors/

College/Career Counseling

Preparing students for college and career is a key role of any school counselor. From elementary school through high school, counselors should encourage students to consider their long-term plan and dream about what their future

186   *The TSC Model*

could look like. By providing necessary information about post-graduate opportunities, school counselors can help disengaged students feel like school is purposeful and beneficial.

Counselors explore students' strengths and interest, connecting those to career paths. They take students on college field trips to raise awareness about all that college has to offer. They open doors and build self-efficacy. Many students cannot rely only on their families for accurate information about college and career options. Counselors must ensure that they are giving every student an equal opportunity for success post-graduation.

This intervention meets the ASCA recommendations for trauma-sensitivity by:

- "Focus[ing] on resilience and strengths so that trauma does not predict individual failure"
- "Promot[ing] safe, stable and nurturing relationships"
- "Provid[ing] community resource information to students and families dealing with trauma"
- "Collaborat[ing] with community resources to provide support for students" (American School Counselor Association, 2016)

More information or resources for this intervention:

- *Position Statement: The School Counselor and Career Development* – ASCA www.schoolcounselor.org/asca/media/asca/PositionStatements/PS_ CareerDevelopment.pdf
- *Poised to Lead: How School Counselors Can Drive College and Career Readiness* – The Education Trust https://edtrust.org/wp-content/uploads/2013/10/Poised_ To_Lead_0.pdf
- *Eight Components of College and Career Readiness Counseling* – The College Board National Office for School Counselor Advocacy www. counseling.org/docs/default-source/library-archives/school-counselor-connection/8-components-of-college-and-career-readiness-counseling. pdf?sfvrsn=ee72442c_2

Community Circles

Community circles have one purpose: To build feelings of connectedness and trust within the classroom. Community circles are different than group discussions because they enhance feelings of togetherness, not just share information (Wachtel, 2016). First, in a community circle, all participants sit in a literal circle. By facing each other and sitting side by side, community circles physically show an equal level of importance among all members, including the teacher. Second, a community circle values the voices of all members. With a talking piece (a physical object that represents who has the floor to speak), all members of the community get a chance to share their ideas. By passing the talking piece from one to another in order, everyone is given equal time and representation.

Community circles should follow norms of behavior set by the group members. These shared norms ensure active listening and create a safe environment, free from bullying or embarrassment. Topic discussed in the circle should focus on the goal of connection and can include storytelling, check-ins about feelings, time to share interests and ideas, and make group decisions. Sometimes, after community trust is built, these circles can also serve as restorative circles to discuss harm within the classroom or misbehavior, but that shouldn't be the main purpose (Wachtel, 2016).

While school counselors do not typically teach their own classroom of students, community circles can be incorporated into guidance lessons or used within other communities at school, such as a community circle with club leaders, sports captains, or parents. School counselors who have been trained in the use of community circles (typically included in any restorative practices (RPs) training) can model circles for classroom teachers to use or co-facilitate circles in classrooms until teachers are more comfortable leading their own.

This intervention meets the ASCA recommendations for trauma-sensitivity by:

- "Creat[ing] connected communities and positive school climates"
- "Implement[ing] effective academic and behavioral practices, such as positive behavioral interventions and supports and social and emotional learning"
- "Promot[ing] safe, stable and nurturing relationships"
- "Promot[ing] a trauma-sensitive framework for policies, procedures and behaviors to entire staff"

(American School Counselor Association, 2016)

More information or resources for this intervention:

- *Building Community With Restorative Circles*, By Marieke van Woerkom – Edutopia www.edutopia.org/article/building-community-restorative-circles
- Goalbook Toolkit: Community Circles https://goalbookapp.com/toolkit/v/strategy/community-circle
- *Teaching Restorative Practices with Classroom Circles*, By Amos Clifford for San Francisco Unified School District www.healthiersf.org/Restorative-Practices/Resources/documents/RP%20Curriculum%20and%20Scripts%20and%20PowePoints/Classroom%20Curriculum/Teaching%20Restorative%20Practices%20in%20the%20Classroom%207%20lesson%20Curriculum.pdf

Ensure Equity and Access

School counselors are in a unique position as student advocates to ensure equity and access to educational opportunities in a system that is not always created for such equity. However, without purposefully advocating for students of color, seeking to understand their background and current realities, and reducing our own implicit biases, school counselors may inadvertently be gatekeepers instead of door-openers.

188   *The TSC Model*

According to the American School Counselor Association (2018), school counselors can enhance student equity and equitable treatment in the following ways:

- Using data to identify achievement and opportunity gaps or discrepancies.
- Advocating for college-going among minority student groups, including racial minorities, students with disabilities, and students with low socioeconomic status.
- Maintaining professional knowledge of students' diverse cultures and the current realities and news from these cultures.
- Maintaining skills and adequate training for working in a diverse school setting.
- Training school staff regarding different cultural groups within the school community.
- Collaborating to development of school policies around equitable treatment of all students.
- Promoting high academic standards for all students and the teaching of rigorous curriculum, academic courses, and college and career preparatory classes for all students.
- Developing plans to address over- or underrepresentation of specific groups in honors, AP, and other rigorous courses.
- Creating a safe and open environment that encourages any student to come forward with problems related to equity or discrimination.
- Collaborating with families in accessing community resources to assist them in removing barriers from their student's education.

(American School Counselor Association, 2018)

This intervention meets the ASCA recommendations for trauma-sensitivity by:

- "Focus[ing] on resilience and strengths so that trauma does not predict individual failure"
- "Avoid[ing] practices that may re-traumatize students"
- "Creat[ing] connected communities and positive school climates"
- "Collaborat[ing] with community resources to provide support for students"
- "Promot[ing] a trauma-sensitive framework for policies, procedures and behaviors to entire staff"

(American School Counselor Association, 2016)

More information or resources for this intervention:

- *Position Statement: The School Counselor and Equity for All Students* – ASCA www.schoolcounselor.org/asca/media/asca/PositionStatements/PS_Equity.pdf

Extracurricular Activities and Clubs

Involvement in extracurricular activities at school is a key strategy to improve students' connectedness and engagement (Centers for Disease Control and Prevention, 2009). Both sports and clubs allow students to feel a sense of belonging at

Creating Connectedness 189

school related to their specific interests. Clubs make a large and impersonal school campus feel smaller and more familiar. Elementary, middle, and high schools all have opportunities for students to be involved in extracurricular activities. Using parent volunteers and community organizations, schools without budgets and staff for clubs or sports can still offer these opportunities. For example, some school districts partner with sports organizations like the YMCA, or their local parks department to offer after-school sports at the school site or at nearby facilities. Community youth theaters, orchestras, and choirs also offer opportunities that can be brought to the school campus to increase opportunity and equity for students.

At schools where extracurricular activities are embedded into the school infrastructure, school counselors encourage participation through club fairs and follow up with students who have not joined a club or sport. At one California high school, the annual fall club fair is a required activity, hosted during the school day. All students are encouraged to enroll in a club during the fair. Students who do not sign up receive a follow-up meeting with a school counselor to discuss club opportunities and reduce barriers to entry. Students are also encouraged to create their own clubs if a club for their interests does not exist.

At elementary and middle school levels, school counselors work to bring club opportunities to campus and enhance students' feelings of belonging at a young age. Clubs like Safety Patrol, student government, and a welcoming committee for new students can give even young elementary students a responsibility and job within their school community.

This intervention meets the ASCA recommendations for trauma-sensitivity by:

- "Creat[ing] connected communities and positive school climates"
- "Promot[ing] a trauma-sensitive framework for policies, procedures and behaviors to entire staff"
                    (American School Counselor Association, 2016)

More information or resources for this intervention:

- *DOE Guidance on Legal Obligations for Extracurricular Activities* – Wright's Law www.wrightslaw.com/blog/doe-guidance-on-legal-obligations-for-extracurricular-activities/
- *The Extracurricular Edge* – College Board https://professionals.collegeboard.org/guidance/prepare/extracurricular
- *The Value of Extracurricular Activities* – National Education Association http://parents.nea.org/keeping-kids-curious/value-extracurricular-activities/

Modeling Healthy Relationships and Connections

It is the responsibility of all adults in the school setting to make all students feel welcomed, connected, and safe. By modeling healthy relationships and taking small steps to make students, parents, and visitors feel welcomed, each adult plays a role in boosting the perceptions of school climate and overall feeling of school connectedness.

190 *The TSC Model*

Students at school should feel like a part of a family, or a team. Addressing students by name, making eye contact when speaking to them, and greeting them with a handshake and a genuine welcome can go a long way in building school connectedness. School counselors can also form connections formally by having a check-in meeting with EVERY student on your caseload at least two times per year, or informally by being physically present at lunches, recesses, and before/after school. This strategy is commonly referred to as "minute meetings."

School staff frequently interact with each other in front of students. Staff should make a commitment to greet and communicate positively and genuinely with other adults. Simply saying "Hi Mrs. Smith, it's good to see you this morning!" is a powerful example of friendliness, hospitality, and care to all students watching.

School counselors can work with administrators to coach staff members, including school secretaries, attendance clerks, cafeteria workers, and campus supervisors to also display a warm and welcoming attitude. What a difference it makes to students who arrive tardy when they are greeted with a "We are so glad to see you Julian! Your class will be so happy you are at school today." Instead of the more typical "Sign in. Why are you late again? You better hurry up and get to class."

Positive and personalized greetings set students up for success in the classroom by decreasing their fears and increasing their sense of belonging. No matter how late, no matter the behavior, no matter the reputation, each child is still welcomed and is an important member of the team.

This intervention meets the ASCA recommendations for trauma-sensitivity by:

- "Promot[ing] a trauma-sensitive framework for policies, procedures and behaviors to entire staff"
- "Avoid[ing] practices that may re-traumatize students"
- "Creat[ing] connected communities and positive school climates"
- "Promot[ing] safe, stable and nurturing relationships"

(American School Counselor Association, 2016)

More information or resources for this intervention:

- *Welcoming Students With a Smile*, By Youki Terada – Edutopia www.edutopia.org/article/welcoming-students-smile
- *Positive Greetings at the Door: Evaluation of a Low-Cost, High-Yield Proactive Classroom Management Strategy*, By Clayton Cook et al. – Journal of Positive Behavior Interventions (February 19, 2018) https://journals.sagepub.com/doi/abs/10.1177/1098300717753831

Restorative Questions and Language

RPs include strategies to build community, repair harm within a community, and restore the community to a post-harm state of wellbeing (Wachtel, 2016). Within a school, RPs include many components which have been discussed

Creating Connectedness   191

previously in Chapter 7. One RP that is integral to enhancing school connectedness is the practice of affective statements and restorative questioning when talking to students about positive behavior and misbehavior.

We've probably all heard statements like these:

- "I've already told you to stop talking 10 times!"
- "You just hit her. Don't try to tell me why. I don't want to hear it."
- "Emily is so smart, why can't you be like Emily?"

These statements are too common in schools. The only outcome of comments like these are students who feel less connected, less heard, and less able to overcome challenges.

Affective statements are simple observations of positive or negative student behavior that remark on the way those behaviors AFFECTED another person (hence affective statements) or how the behavior affected the student themselves (Wachtel, 2016). Statements may sound like:

- "I am pleased to see you all working so quietly. That helps others in the classroom to concentrate."
- "I am appreciative that you all walked in a straight line in the hall. That leaves room for other classes to pass by."
- "I am concerned about the way you pushed in lunch line just now, I saw how it hurt Elliott's arm."
- "I am frustrated about the poor behavior report from the substitute. I felt embarrassed to hear how you didn't listen to him."

The affective statements seek to comment only on behaviors and not on the intrinsic worth or character traits of the student. They make students aware of their behaviors and should be delivered in as personalized a way as possible. Especially with correction, statements should be made in a whisper or privately to the student, never in front of peers or other adults on campus if possible.

Restorative questions seek to engage the student in a self-reflective process by encouraging them to think about how their misbehavior affected the others around them (Wachtel, 2016). Questions include:

1   "What happened, and what were you thinking at the time of the incident?"
2   "What have you thought about since?"
3   "Who has been affected by what happened and how?"
4   "What about this has been the hardest for you?"
5   "What do you think needs to be done to make things as right as possible?"
(San Francisco Unified School District, 2019)

School counselors can use these statements and questions in their direct work with students daily. Indirectly, school counselors can model restorative questions and affective statements for teachers and school staff. These statements and questions are easily incorporated into any training about school climate practices or many

192 *The TSC Model*

other professional development topics. Counselors can create restorative question cards or lanyard tags so that teachers and staff have a quick reference guide to this positive language in the moment of handling student misbehavior.

This intervention meets the ASCA recommendations for trauma-sensitivity by:

- "Avoid[ing] practices that may re-traumatize students"
- "Creat[ing] connected communities and positive school climates"
- "Implement[ing] effective academic and behavioral practices, such as positive behavioral interventions and supports and social and emotional learning"
- "Promot[ing] safe, stable and nurturing relationships"
- "Promot[ing] a trauma-sensitive framework for policies, procedures and behaviors to entire staff"

(American School Counselor Association, 2016)

More information or resources for this intervention:

- *Time to Think: Using Restorative Questions,* By Samantha White – International Institute for Restorative Practices News www.iirp.edu/news/time-to-think-using-restorative-questions
- *Restorative Practices Resources* – San Francisco Unified School District www.healthiersf.org/RestorativePractices/Resources/index.php
- Restorative Questions Cards: https://store.iirp.edu/restorative-questions-cards-pack-of-100-english-or-spanish/

Transition Programs

School counselors can promote school connectedness beginning even before the student's first day of school. Through successful transition programs, school counselors give students the opportunity to enter a new school with feelings of success, welcoming, safety, and confidence. Programs like this include peer-to-peer connection programs, open houses, orientations, summer bridge programs, and specialized programs for students who transition mid-year.

Transition programs can enhance feelings of safety by introducing students and families to school personnel and safety procedures. These programs increase connections by giving students a chance to meet peers, as well as older students serving in a leadership role as tour guides or activity leaders. Transition programs increase students' confidence in their ability to succeed at the new school. By giving them valuable information such as how to get from class to class, how to open a locker, or how to refer themselves to see a school counselor, students are set up for independent success. Older peers may even give personalized advice about turning in homework on time, joining a club, or attending tutoring.

This intervention meets the ASCA recommendations for trauma-sensitivity by:

- "Avoid[ing] practices that may re-traumatize students"
- "Creat[ing] connected communities and positive school climates"
- "Promot[ing] safe, stable and nurturing relationships"

(American School Counselor Association, 2016)

More information or resources for this intervention:

- Anchored 4 Life: https://anchored4life.com/
- Link Crew: www.boomerangproject.com/link/what-link-crew

School Counseling Tier 2 Interventions

The following section contains examples of Tier 2 interventions that are both trauma-sensitive and within the scope of a professional school counselor role. These interventions support the development of school connectedness and perceptions of positive school climate. Interventions included in this section are:

- College Application/FAFSA Support
- Counseling Small Groups for Friendship Building
- Counseling Small Groups for Transition
- Counseling Small Groups for Support
- Mentoring Programs
- Restorative Conferences

College Application/FAFSA Support

One way that high school counselors create school connectedness is by involving parents in their students' college-going process. While financial aid nights and college application workshops for parents are Tier 1 services in many high schools, Tier 2 follow-up is also a part of the process. This follow-up service increases parental connection to the school and decreases barriers to college-going. Follow-up should be provided to any families who did not respond to the universal interventions. For example, families who did not attend the FAFSA night, students who didn't take the SAT/ACT test before their senior year, who did not turn in required senior paperwork, etc.

Host a parent small group to complete applications or financial aid forms with a translator. Invite parents to small group discussions (sometimes called "Coffee with the Counselor") about higher education. Call families directly whose students are below a 2.0. Connecting with families will increase their trust in the school and the students' feelings of belonging and purpose (Centers for Disease Control and Prevention, 2009).

This intervention meets the ASCA recommendations for trauma-sensitivity by:

- "Creat[ing] connected communities and positive school climates"
- "Collaborat[ing] with community resources to provide support for students" (American School Counselor Association, 2016)

More information or resources for this intervention:

- Increasing Academic Achievement and College-Going Rates for Latina/o English Language Learners: A Survey of School Counselor Interventions,

By Amy Cook, Rachelle Pérusse Neag, and Eliana D. Rojas – *Journal of School Counselor Preparation and Supervision* (2012) https://repository.wcsu.edu/cgi/viewcontent.cgi?article=1008&context=jcps

Counseling Small Groups for Friendship Building

A common task for elementary school counselors and even some middle school counselors is to facilitate small groups for friendship building. Sometimes called Buddies or Lunch Bunch, the goal of this intervention is to enhance students' ability and desire to socialize through targeted skill building and opportunities to apply newly learned friendship skills.

Students who are on the margins of the school's culture could benefit from a group like this. These marginalized students may be new to the school, have behavioral challenges, or have disabilities such as Autism Spectrum Disorder that are causing them social difficulties. Friendship skills groups focus on a variety of topics from "how to introduce yourself" to "how to avoid bullying." Friendship groups are sometimes specialized based on student needs, for example, a group of new students, a group of students with autism, or a group of students who have behavioral issues on the playground.

One trauma-sensitive friendship group is an alternative recess group. Rather than having students sit out at recess as a punishment, students can attend a counselor-facilitated indoor recess. During this time, they enhance friendship skills such as cooperation, teamwork, and perspective taking by participating in structured team activities. Using a potentially negative situation to increase school connectedness benefits both the student and school community.

This intervention meets the ASCA recommendations for trauma-sensitivity by:

- "Focus[ing] on resilience and strengths so that trauma does not predict individual failure"
- "Avoid[ing] practices that may re-traumatize students"
- "Creat[ing] connected communities and positive school climates"
- "Implement[ing] effective academic and behavioral practices, such as positive behavioral interventions and supports and social and emotional learning"
- "Promot[ing] safe, stable and nurturing relationships"
                                        (American School Counselor Association, 2016)

More information or resources for this intervention:

- *Multimodal Counseling: Motivating Children to Attend School Through Friendship Groups*, By Donald B. Keat II, Kathy L. Metzgar, Deborah Raykovitz and James McDonald – The Journal of Humanistic Education and Development (June 1985) https://onlinelibrary.wiley.com/doi/abs/10.1002/j.2164-4683.1985.tb00269.x
- Friendship Small Group Resources – Counselor Keri www.counselorkeri.com/category/friendship/

Creating Connectedness 195

Counseling Small Groups for Transition

While transition programming is a Tier 1 school counseling function, some students may need additional support after the universal orientation or summer bridge program. One common practice to identify these students is for a sending counselor (such as a middle school counselor for outgoing 8th graders) to share with the receiving counselor (a high school counselor for incoming 9th graders) a list of "at-risk" students in hopes that these students receive extra support at their new school. This method is very subjective and may leave out students who need assistance or flag students who no longer need interventions. Instead, by using a universal screener, school counselors objectively determine who needs additional transition support. Screener questions may include an assessment of students' anxiety about the transition, knowledge of transition information, and barriers to a successful transition.

Small groups for transition support should directly address the needs of the students in the group. For example, at a South Carolina high school, Tier 2 transition students were divided into many small groups, including college application stress management and 1st-generation college-going. Both groups fall into the transition group category but serve students with different needs.

This intervention meets the ASCA recommendations for trauma-sensitivity by:

- "Collaborat[ing] with community resources to provide support for students"
- "Promot[ing] a trauma-sensitive framework for policies, procedures and behaviors to entire staff"
- "Creat[ing] connected communities and positive school climates"
- "Implement[ing] effective academic and behavioral practices, such as positive behavioral interventions and supports and social and emotional learning"
- "Promot[ing] safe, stable and nurturing relationships"
  (American School Counselor Association, 2016)

More information or resources for this intervention:

- School Counseling Small Group Curriculum for First Generation College-going Students – Counselor Clique: www.teacherspayteachers.com/Product/First-Generation-High-School-Counseling-Small-Group-4221880?aref=rywsugap
- School Counseling Small Group Curriculum for Stress Management – Counselor Clique www.teacherspayteachers.com/Product/Stress-Management-High-School-Counseling-Small-Group-4664833
- School Counseling Small Group Curriculum for Middle School Transition – Pathway 2 Success www.teacherspayteachers.com/Product/Middle-School-Transition-Kit-2375348

Counseling Small Groups for Support

Students experiencing grief, divorce, parental deployment, parental incarceration, foster care, or other difficult life circumstances can all benefit from group support at

196 The TSC Model

school. When students know that there are other students experiencing the same challenges as them, it can enhance feelings of belonging and school connection (Centers for Disease Control and Prevention, 2009). In addition to connection, groups can also teach specific skills to help these students cope with challenges. These topics are all very sensitive. Parent/guardian permission must be given for students to participate in this type of group counseling. Great efforts should be made to keep confidentiality within the group to ensure the emotional and physical safety of the students (American School Counselor Association, 2016a).

Support groups can also be positive experiences for students who have a common identity with other students. Students who identify as a part of the LGBT community, Gifted and Talented, or with a diagnosis such as Autism, ADHD, or a health concern could be supported through confidential and parent-permitted group counseling.

This intervention meets the ASCA recommendations for trauma-sensitivity by:

- "Focus[ing] on resilience and strengths so that trauma does not predict individual failure"
- "Creat[ing] connected communities and positive school climates"
- "Promot[ing] safe, stable and nurturing relationships"
    (American School Counselor Association, 2016)

More information or resources for this intervention:

- Bolstering School Based Support by Comprehensively Addressing the Needs of an Invisible Minority: Implications for Professional School Counselors, By Jennifer R. Curry and B. Grant Hayes http://jsc.montana. edu/articles/v7n7.pdf
- Professional School Counselors Address Grief and Loss: A Creative Group Counseling Intervention, By Reshelle C. Marino, Mark D. Thornton, and Tyler Lange – American Cousneling Association VISTAS www. counseling.org/docs/default-source/vistas/article_66965a22f16116603ab-cacff0000bee5e7.pdf?sfvrsn=4
- Get Your Group On! Facilitating Psychoeducational Groups in Schools – ASCA Webinar www.schoolcounselor.org/asca/media/asca/Webinars/ GetYourGroupOnHandouts.pdf

Mentoring Programs

School-based mentoring programs, both adult-to-student and peer-to-peer, are highly successful at improving students' feelings of connectedness to school (National Mentoring Resource Center, 2018).

Benefits of mentoring include:

- Positive benefits for both mentors and mentees in cross-aged peer mentoring.
- Mentees have increases in positive attitudes toward school, adults at the school, and themselves after successful mentorship programs.

Creating Connectedness   197

- Large, positive effects on mentees with a committed, consistent mentor. Mentors who were affirmed, motivated, and committed to their mentees had the most success.
- Potential improvements in students' academic achievement, attendance, and attitudes toward school.

(National Mentoring Resource Center, 2018, 2019)

School counselors and school leadership are essential to the development and maintenance of a school-based mentorship program. As a Tier 2 intervention, students can be selected to participate based on a wide variety of criteria. Mentorship should be focused on building positive relationships to meet goals related to these criteria.

For example, students at risk for chronic absenteeism could participate in a mentorship program to encourage school attendance. Whether or not the mentor ever discusses attendance, attendance may improve due to the student's desire to attend in order to meet with the mentor. Close relationships with a mentor are more important to the overall effectiveness of the relationship than mentors' specific focus on discussing the goals with the mentee (National Mentoring Resource Center, 2019).

This intervention meets the ASCA recommendations for trauma-sensitivity by:

- "Focus[ing] on resilience and strengths so that trauma does not predict individual failure"
- "Creat[ing] connected communities and positive school climates"
- "Promot[ing] safe, stable and nurturing relationships"
- "Collaborat[ing] with community resources to provide support for student"

(American School Counselor Association, 2016)

More information or resources for this intervention:

- *Tier 2 Mentoring* – PBIS World www.pbisworld.com/tier-2/mentoring/
- *Cross-Age Peer Mentorship Programs in Schools*, By Michael Garringer & Patti MacRae – UCLA Mentoring Resource Center http://smhp.psych. ucla.edu/pdfdocs/mentoring.pdf
- *How to Design a School-Based Mentoring Program* – Minnesota Programs of Study www.mnprogramsofstudy.org/iseek/mnpos/pdf/MnPOS-SchoolMentoring.pdf
- ABCs of School Based Mentoring – The Hamilton Fish Institute on School and Community Violence & The National Mentoring Center at Northwest Regional Educational Laboratory https://educationnorthwest. org/sites/default/files/abcs-of-mentoring.pdf
- *School-Based Mentoring Programs: Using Volunteers to Improve the Academic Outcomes of Underserved Students*, By Amanda Bayer, Jean Grossman, and David L. DuBois – MDRC www.mdrc.org/publication/school-based-mentoring-programs
- *School-based Mentoring* – National Mentoring Resource Center https:// nationalmentoringresourcecenter.org/index.php/component/k2/item/182-school-based-mentoring.html

198   The TSC Model

- *Peer Mentoring* – National Mentoring Resource Center https:// nationalmentoringresourcecenter.org/index.php/30-topic-areas/152-peer-mentoring.html

Restorative Conferences

RPs refer to a school-wide policy to build trust and community, and repair harm when it was caused. A Tier 2 level intervention within the RP initiative is a restorative conference. This is like a conflict mediation with a few slight differences. A restorative conference allows both parties involved (both the person responsible and the person impacted) to be part of the solution making process. Restorative conferences are facilitated by a counselor or leader trained in RP who understands that the decision-making power must lie within the two parties involved and not within the leader. Restorative conferences lead to restorative agreements that must be followed up to ensure their implementation and to build community trust (Wachtel, 2016).

These conferences can be very time-consuming, taking between 30 min to 2 hours depending on the severity of the situation and how many people are involved. They are not disciplinary, but instead seek to build empathy and understanding between the two opposing parties. The end goal of a restorative conference is to create a plan to prevent the same harm in the future. Restorative conferences are not punitive and rely on natural consequences and social pressure to correct the behavior of others as opposed to doling out arbitrary discipline measures such as lunch detention or Saturday school (Wachtel, 2016).

This intervention meets the ASCA recommendations for trauma-sensitivity by:

- "Promot[ing] a trauma-sensitive framework for policies, procedures and behaviors to entire staff"
- "Creat[ing] connected communities and positive school climates"
- "Implement[ing] effective academic and behavioral practices, such as positive behavioral interventions and supports and social and emotional learning"
- "Promot[ing] safe, stable and nurturing relationships"
- "Avoid[ing] practices that may re-traumatize students"

(American School Counselor Association, 2016)

More information or resources for this intervention:

- *Restorative Conference Script* – San Diego Unified School District www.sandi.net/staff/sites/default/files_link/staff/docs/restorative-practices/toolkit/conferencing/Conference-Script.pdf

School Counseling Tier 3 Interventions

The following section contains examples of Tier 3 interventions that are both trauma-sensitive and within the scope of a professional school counselor role. These interventions support the development of school

Creating Connectedness 199

connectedness and perceptions of positive school climate. Interventions included in this section are:

- Crisis Counseling
- Home Visits
- Individual Student Planning
- Referrals for Community Resources

Crisis Counseling

School counselors are often the school's first responders in the case of student crisis. Suicidal ideation, self-injury, risk-taking behaviors, and child abuse are often disclosed to school counselors or other trusted adults at school. School counselors are brought into these situations to quickly triage the case and make professional recommendations based on the risk or severity of the situation.

School counselors should view their role in these crises as parent informers and resource providers, not as risk assessors. According to the ASCA Ethical Standards, in cases of suicidal ideation, counselors have two non-negotiable roles:

1 To inform parents of the suicidal statements or actions of their child, and
2 to provide parents with mental health resources in the community so that parents can pursue more thorough evaluation and support for the mental health of their child (American School Counselor Association, 2016a).

When school counselors do use a suicidal risk screening tool (e.g. Columbia Suicide Severity Rating Scale), they must do so only to help themselves in determining a best course of action. If risk screening results are shared with parents, the focus should be on the severity of ANY suicidal ideation, not the risk-level determined by the rating scale. The results of these screeners should never be used to minimize the severity of the student's suicidality to parents or other stakeholders (American School Counselor Association, 2016b).

School counselors have a unique position that includes student-educator confidentiality to a level not found elsewhere in schools. Due to the feelings of emotional safety when working with a school counselor, crisis disclosures to school counselors are common. However, at no time should a school counselor promise to keep reports of potential harm confidential. Whether from an adult to a student, self-harm of a student or a threat of a student to harm another person, these disclosures must be taken seriously. A breach of confidentiality in these cases is both ethical and legal.

School connectedness is supported through the quick, appropriate, ethical, and thorough response of school counselors to crisis situations.

This intervention meets the ASCA recommendations for trauma-sensitivity by:

- "Recogniz[ing] the signs of trauma in students"
- "Focus[ing] on resilience and strengths so that trauma does not predict individual failure"

200   *The TSC Model*

- "Avoid[ing] practices that may re-traumatize students"
- "Provid[ing] community resource information to students and families dealing with trauma"
- "Educat[ing] staff on the effects of trauma and how to refer students to the school counselor"
- "Collaborat[ing] with community resources to provide support for students"

(American School Counselor Association, 2016)

More information or resources for this intervention:

- *Suicide Contracts, Assessments and Parental/Guardian Notification: Err on the Side of Caution,* By Carolyn Stone – ASCA School Counselor blog www.schoolcounselor.org/magazine/blogs/november-december-2013/ suicide-contracts,-assessments-and-parental-guardi
- *School Counselor Questioned by Student's Parents After Child Abuse Report,* By Carolyn Stone – ASCA School Counselor blog www. schoolcounselor.org/magazine/blogs/march-april-2016/school-counselor-questioned-by-student-s-parents-a

(American School Counselor Association, 2016)

Home Visits

Home visits build school connectedness among students and families when they are used for positive relationship building and not as a punitive or "gotcha" tactic. Home visits allow schools to bring needed resources to families who may not be able to come to school for conferences or workshops due to work hours or a lack of transportation. They also allow for teachers, counselors, and administrators to learn about their students and families on a more personal level by experiencing their neighborhood environment, living conditions, hobbies, interests, and family dynamics. An educator's job at a home visit is to listen and seek to understand the family and their unique situation. It is not to bring bad news, implicate the parent for misbehavior of their child, or to judge the student's home life.

School counselors participate in home visits as a partner to provide social-emotional or community resources to families. No one should ever attend a home visit alone. By ensuring that parents receive adequate notification of home visits, and that home visits are conducted in the family's native language, counselors can break down barriers between home and school, enhancing school connectedness instead of detracting from it.

This intervention meets the ASCA recommendations for trauma-sensitivity by:

- "Avoid[ing] practices that may re-traumatize students"
- "Creat[ing] connected communities and positive school climates"

- "Provid[ing] community resource information to students and families dealing with trauma"
- "Collaborat[ing] with community resources to provide support for students"
  (American School Counselor Association, 2016)

More information or resources for this intervention:

- *Home Visits* – Teaching Tolerance www.tolerance.org/magazine/fall-2017/home-visits

Individual Student Planning

Individual student planning involves preparing students for post-secondary success through curriculum and interventions based on personal interests and strengths. The bulk of individual student planning can be done through classroom lessons or assemblies. Universal (Tier 1) strategies such as annual 8th-grade classroom presentations about high school course selection are a part of the individual student planning process, but may not be enough support for all students. For students who receive special education services, have barriers to learning such as homelessness, or have a non-English native language, individual or family meetings may be necessary to fully develop an appropriate student plan.

Some students may be selected for more intensive student planning meetings based on disengagement during the Tier 1 strategies or lack of follow-up, such as not turning in paperwork, or not signing up for parent portals such as PowerSchool or Naviance. Holding individual meetings for every student is a very time-consuming strategy. It is therefore considered a Tier 3 intervention – only needed 1–5% of all students. The student who needs this individualized intervention may need more than one individual meeting in order to have a well-rounded plan. Meetings could include parents, teachers, resource specialists, or administrators depending on the nature of the meetings.

School counseling techniques used in individual student planning may include possible selves theory, RIASEC, and other career counseling assessments, and strengths-based assessments to help students' develop a forward-thinking plan for themselves.

This intervention meets the ASCA recommendations for trauma-sensitivity by:

- "Recogniz[ing] the signs of trauma in students"
- "Focus[ing] on resilience and strengths so that trauma does not predict individual failure"
- "Promot[ing] safe, stable and nurturing relationships"
- "Provid[ing] community resource information to students and families dealing with trauma"
- "Collaborat[ing] with community resources to provide support for students"
  (American School Counselor Association, 2016)

202   *The TSC Model*

More information or resources for this intervention:

- *Possible Selves* – Excellence in School Counseling http://excellencein-schoolcounseling.com/develop-a-cba/define-student-excellence-overview/motivation-overview-3/possible-selves/
- *Career Counseling* – California Department of Education www.cde.ca.gov/ls/cg/cc/careercounsel.asp
- My Next Move: www.mynextmove.org/

Referrals for Community Resources

At the Tier 3 level, many interventions, including mental health therapy, housing assistance, legal advice, or medical treatment, are beyond the professional scope of the school counselor. It is the responsibility of the school counselor to provide appropriate resources for the student and family to access these services within the community. Coordinating a current, updated resource list and making timely referrals guarantee that families can access the services they need without getting lost in the process.

Referrals for community assistance are a Tier 3 program because they are generally only needed for a small percentage of students. They also take substantial time to coordinate effectively. School counselors should make personal contact with both the student and their family prior to a referral. Contact should also be made with the agency receiving the referral. After a few days, follow-up contact should be made to make sure that the referral was processed, and the family is receiving support. Without adequate follow-up, the referral process easily breaks down, leaving families feeling disconnected from the help they need instead of supported by the school.

This intervention meets the ASCA recommendations for trauma-sensitivity by:

- "Recogniz[ing] the signs of trauma in students"
- "Provid[ing] community resource information to students and families dealing with trauma"
- "Collaborat[ing] with community resources to provide support for students"
  (American School Counselor Association, 2016)

More information or resources for this intervention:

- *School Counselor Referral Process Guide* – Missouri Department of Elementary and Secondary Education https://dese.mo.gov/sites/default/files/guid-respon-serv-referral-process-guide.pdf
- *Position Statement: The School Counselor and Student Mental Health* – ASCA   www.schoolcounselor.org/asca/media/asca/PositionStatements/PS_StudentMentalHealth.pdf

Creating Connectedness   203

- *Bridging Students to the Community*, By Jacqueline Zeller – New Jersey School Counseling Association News www.schoolcounselor.org/newsletters/october-2017/bridging-students-to-the-community?st=NJ

References

American School Counselor Association. (2016a). *ASCA Ethical Standards for School Counselors*. Retrieved from American School Counselor Association: www.schoolcounselor.org/asca/media/asca/Ethics/EthicalStandards2016.pdf

American School Counselor Association. (2016b, August). *The School Counselor and Trauma-Informed Practice*. Retrieved from American School Counselor Association: www.schoolcounselor.org/asca/media/asca/PositionStatements/PS_TraumaInformed.pdf

American School Counselor Association. (2018). *School Counselor and Equity for All Students*. Retrieved from American School Counselor Association: www.schoolcounselor.org/asca/media/asca/PositionStatements/PS_Equity.pdf

Attendance Works. (2016). *Key Research: Why Attendance Matters for Achievement and How Interventions Can Help*. Retrieved from Attendance Works: https://awareness.attendanceworks.org/wp-content/uploads/Research2016.pdf

Centers for Disease Control and Prevention. (2009). *School Connectedness: Strategies for Increasing Protective Factors among Youth*. Atlanta, GA: U.S. Department of Health and Human Services.

National Mentoring Resource Center. (2018). *Peer Mentoring*. Retrieved from National Mentoring Resource Center: https://nationalmentoringresourcecenter.org/index.php/30-topic-areas/152-peer-mentoring.html

National Mentoring Resource Center. (2019). *School-Based Mentoring*. Retrieved from National Mentoring Research Center: https://nationalmentoringresourcecenter.org/index.php/component/k2/item/182-school-based-mentoring.html

San Francisco Unified School District. (2019). *Restorative Dialogue Overview*. Retrieved from Restorative Practices in SFUSD: Curriculum and Supporting Documents: www.healthiersf.org/RestorativePractices/Resources/documents/Repairing%20Relationships%20and%20Restoring%20Community/Restorative%20Dialogue/Restorative%20Dialogue-%20overview.doc

Shaw, J. (2018, June). *Trimming Truancy*. Retrieved from Harvard Magazine: https://harvardmagazine.com/2018/05/truancy-letter

U.S. Department of Health and Human Services. (2019, May 30). *What is Bullying?* Retrieved from StopBullying.gov: www.stopbullying.gov/bullying/what-is-bullying

Van Eck, K., Johnson, S., Bettencourt, A., & Lindstrom Johnson, S. (2016). How School Climate Related to Chronic Absence: A Multi-Level Latent Profile Analysis. *Journal of School Psychology, 61*, 89–102. https://doi.org/10.1016/j.jsp.2016.10.001

Wachtel, T. (2016). *Defining Restorative*. Retrieved from International Institute for Restorative Practices: www.iirp.edu/images/pdf/Defining-Restorative_Nov-2016.pdf

12 Conclusion
Next Steps for Counselor Leaders

The path is clear, and you are ready. You have a trauma-sensitive vision, a plan, and the will to accomplish it. Your toolkit is full of ACEs research, school-wide frameworks for change, and school counseling interventions to support affected students. You know the path toward trauma-sensitivity, and you are eager to begin the journey. One thing stands in your way: The first step.

Moving from information gathering to implementation can feel daunting. Questions and doubts cloud the once clear vision. Logistics and competing priorities slow down the fast-moving plan. It is easy to get discouraged. As counselor leaders, these challenges are hurdles to jump over, not walls to stop us. Our students deserve better than zero-tolerance and unsafe schools. They need caring communities. They need a voice. They need a chance to thrive.

Using the information in this book, you can change your practice, change your school culture, and change your district policies. This chapter includes your first steps. Take your time. Gather a team. Celebrate small wins. Share what you learn. Soon, you will build the trauma-sensitive movement you desired.

Changing Your School Culture

Collaborate. No One Can Do This Work Alone

Creating system-wide change is impossible on your own. By its very definition, a system involves "a set of things working together as parts of a mechanism or an interconnecting network" (Oxford University Press, 2019). After getting the green-light from school administration to explore trauma-sensitivity school-wide, school counselors bring together their collaborative network.

Since trauma-sensitive practices span all facets of the school environment, a collaborative network includes administrators, school counselors, psychologists, education specialists (e.g. SPED teachers, speech and language pathologist, school occupational therapist, intervention/resource teachers), general education teachers, secretaries, paraeducators, parents, community mental health partners, coaches, after-school care providers, community experts

Conclusion 205

for specific student populations (e.g. refugee resource center, military family liaison, etc.), and others (National Child Traumatic Stress Network, Schools Committee, 2017). The purpose of this trauma-sensitivity taskforce is to develop and execute sustainable, collective efforts on the journey toward fully implemented trauma-sensitivity in the school. These efforts will:

1   *Develop and Sustain Trauma-Sensitive Policies and Practices*: This taskforce uses the Flexible Framework model from Chapter 6 to determine the school's culture, staff perceptions about trauma, gaps in trauma-sensitivity, and currently unsupportive policies and practices. The task force then organizes these findings according to basic school functions (e.g. Instructional practices, classroom management initiatives, discipline methods, family communication policies, etc.). Ultimately, the task force creates an action plan to establish school-wide, trauma-sensitive practices (National Child Traumatic Stress Network, Schools Committee, 2017).

2   *Provide Clear and Consistent Messages Among All Groups*: The trauma-sensitive task force creates community-wide messaging about the school's trauma-sensitive priorities. The taskforce creates talking points for all school events and communication. Families, students, and all community members who interact with the school should understand the trauma-sensitive philosophy and adhere to its basic tenets when interacting with students. These messages are transparent about the implementation progress and the ongoing effectiveness of trauma-sensitive policies, practices, and procedures (National Child Traumatic Stress Network, Schools Committee, 2017).

3   *Map Resources and Coordinate Services*: Schools and community/government agencies collaborate to ensure that students connect to their school communities. Based on universal screenings and needs assessments, the trauma-sensitive task force generates a list of necessary services and interventions. Many of these interventions are listed in Chapters 9–11 of this book. The school counselor and other school leaders on the taskforce use the MTMDSS model (Chapter 8), or other Tiered-Intervention model to organize trauma-sensitive, school-based services, universal practices, and intensive community resources. Then, educators can deliver the services to students equitably and with fidelity to the evidence-based models they came from (National Child Traumatic Stress Network, Schools Committee, 2017).

4   *Determine Student Eligibility for Tiered Interventions*: The trauma-sensitive taskforce collaborates with other multi-disciplinary teams in the school, including RTI and SST teams. These teams use universal screenings and progress-monitoring data to determine student eligibility for Tier 2 and Tier 3 services. The screenings and data are for academic, social-emotional, or behavioral needs. Teams facilitate student placement into trauma-sensitive interventions, "monitor progress and effectiveness of interventions, and collectively collaborate to make adjustments to the

206   *The TSC Model*

student's intervention plan" (National Child Traumatic Stress Network, Schools Committee, 2017, p. 12).

5   *Consult and Provide Trauma-Sensitive Coaching to Other School Staff and Community Members*: Trauma-sensitive systems include consultation services for school staff who need help with a uniquely challenging situation or need to talk-through possible interventions for a student. Availability of personalized coaching and opportunities for consultation decreases the potential impact of compassion fatigue, also known as secondary trauma (National Child Traumatic Stress Network, Schools Committee, 2017).

Addressing Barriers to Adoption of the Trauma-Sensitive Lens

Not everyone buys in to the trauma-sensitive approach right away. Consult Chapter 6 for more recommendations about how to address specific staff concerns like:

- "the tendency to see trauma as a home problem rather than a school problem";
- "misplacing blame on students or parents (whether intentionally or unintentionally)";
- "the personal impact on staff of dealing with these issues, including feelings of helplessness and being overwhelmed";
- "balancing individual student needs with the needs of the class as a whole"; and
- "lack of skills and resources for handling trauma"

(Cole, O'Brien, Gadd, Wallace, & Gregory, 2005, p. 49)

The trauma-sensitive taskforce must identify, acknowledge, and address these staff concerns in the beginning of the change process. When this step is missed, disinterest turns into frustration. Frustration becomes resentment and possibly refusal as teachers are pushed to take on new responsibilities they are not ready to accept. The taskforce uses teacher and staff feedback to develop appropriate trainings and manage the rollout of new initiatives, providing necessary support for more difficult steps.

When developing trauma trainings for school staff, consider the following training topics to incorporate staff feedback and boost staff efficacy regarding their role in the trauma-sensitive shift.

- *You Matter to a Child*: Boost staff morale by sharing the significance of their role, the importance of school connectedness, and how to make a difference simply by caring for a student (Cole et al., 2005).
- *The Teacher is not a Therapist – When to Ask for Help*: Give staff the opportunity to clarify the differences between a trauma-sensitive educator and a trauma therapist or trauma-sensitive school counselor. Compassion

Conclusion   207

fatigue is reduced when teachers understand their own roles and are supported by other mental health experts when the needs of their students are too great to handle alone (Cole et al., 2005).

- *Beyond Instructional Expertise*: Build on teacher competencies by adding new trauma-sensitive information to areas of identified success. For example, many teachers are eloquent communicators, brilliant planners and organizers, and naturally empathetic. By adding new small skills to these existing abilities, trauma-sensitivity will not seem like as big of a change (Cole et al., 2005).

Advocate for More Mental Health Services for Staff and Students

Trauma-sensitivity is an emotionally challenging work. As a part of the journey toward trauma-sensitivity, school counselor leaders advocate for additional mental health services for both students and staff. This systematic shift in philosophy can only stand on a foundation of adequate and appropriate staffing.

If a school of 1,500 only has one counselor and a part-time psychologist, the trauma-sensitive system can't be fully realized. Tier 2 and Tier 3 interventions need staff to lead them. Universal practices need staff to support them. ASCA recommends a student-to-school counselor ratio of 250:1 and the National Association of School Psychologists recommends a student-to-school psychologist ratio of 700–1,000:1 (American School Counselor Association, 2019; National Association of School Psychologists, 2017).

Additional school counselors, school psychologists, instructional coaches, social workers, and other support staff are necessary to provide Tier 2 and Tier 3 services, support Tier 1 providers through coaching and collaboration, and provide consultation opportunities to discuss challenging cases. Consultation time allows staff to reflect upon their own emotions and the impact of the trauma-sensitive work on their well-being (Cole et al., 2005).

School counselor leaders use facts and suggestions from this book to advocate for additional mental health funding and staffing at their school sites if they do not meet the recommended ratios. Data-driven initiatives like TSC clearly demonstrate the effectiveness of trauma-sensitive programs and the need for more support. If your ratio isn't 250:1, don't give up hope. You can still be a trauma-sensitive school counselor in your own practice. Your leadership and interventions will inspire others to change as well.

Celebrate Small Victories and Progress

The process toward trauma-sensitivity is a long and winding path. As a school counselor leader, take time to celebrate small victories with your team. After the completion of an initial trauma training, or the development of your first universal SEL screening, or when student responded positively to self-regulation lessons – share the celebrations with each other. Noticing progress

208   *The TSC Model*

and acknowledging small changes encourage the team. Keep fighting the good fight. Continue the hard and necessary work toward trauma-sensitivity by acknowledging the wins.

Changing Your Own Practices

Try on Trauma-Sensitivity Yourself

As a separate path toward trauma-sensitivity, school counselors take individualized steps to become trauma-sensitive. If your school is developing a trauma-sensitive model, then your individualized development bolsters the efforts of the whole school. Your own professional development deepens the feasibility of the systemic shift toward trauma-sensitivity. If your school – despite your best efforts – is still not interested in a school-wide model, or you lack adequate staffing to support it, you can still make a difference for students by becoming a trauma-sensitive counselor on your own.

After reading this book, you are well on your way toward trauma-sensitivity. Chapter 5 listed additional trainings and interventions to deepen your knowledge of ACEs and boost confidence in implementing new strategies. Using the MTMDSS model in Chapter 8, you can reorganize your own comprehensive counseling program to align with the TSC model of trauma-sensitive school counseling. Then, use Chapters 9 through 11 to add missing interventions and strategies to your counseling program. This ensures that the program is comprehensive and trauma-sensitive. Using an organizational method such as MTMDSS helps your administrator better understand your role as a counselor. This understanding is especially helpful as you advocate to decrease non-counseling duties in order to achieve trauma-sensitivity.

This concern about lack of school/system support is a common one I receive. As I am writing this book, my own schools are not fully trauma-sensitive. This process is long and involves many stakeholders. To give ourselves some common school counseling guidance – "The only person you can control is yourself." Think about the changes you can make to your own practice. Change your communication. Change your interventions. Change your style of counseling. Gather some like-minded and supportive colleagues. Work together and share ideas. There are a multitude of solutions you can employ even as the only counselor on campus or as the only trauma-sensitive educator in your building.

Get Involved Outside Your Walls

Support yourself professionally by connecting with like-minded school counselors through professional organizations or social media. Many school counselors are the only counselors in their building, and possibly even in their district. We all need a supportive ear, a sounding board, and creative new ideas. By networking with other school counselors, we can share resources, consult about difficult situations, and encourage each other in our work.

Check out the American School Counselor Association (www. schoolcounselor.org), your state chapter of ASCA (www.schoolcounselor.org/ school-counselors-members/about-asca-(1)/state-associations) for conferences, webinars, workshops, and other valuable professional development. Attending conferences is a great way to learn the most up-to-date and practical information for school counselors. Join the ACEs Connection Network online (www. acesconnection.com) for daily research highlights about ACEs. Or follow the many trauma-sensitive school counselors sharing their work on Facebook, Instagram, Teachers Pay Teachers, and other social media sites. For some suggestions of other counselors to follow, check out my own school counseling Instagram feed (@CounselingWithImpact) or Facebook page (www.facebook. com/counselingwithimpact/).

Sow Seeds. You May Never See the Outcomes

I hope that your path is clear. I hope you begin your journey toward trauma-sensitivity with all the determination and gumption you need to achieve it. When you are in the middle of the journey, and the end is not in sight, remember that we are in this together. Reach out for help. Ask questions. Step back and reflect. Care for yourself. When you get a small win, take pride in it. When you get a big win, share it!

The path will not always be straight on this journey, but trauma-sensitive work is life changing for you and for your students. Your good work does not go unnoticed. Though you may never see the outcomes of your empathetic listening, creative interventions, advocacy, and planning, know that you are making a difference. You are sowing seeds toward a better future for all children.

References

American School Counselor Association. (2019, May 7). *ASCA Releases Updated Student-to-School-Counselor Ratio Data*. Retrieved from American School Counselor Association: www.schoolcounselor.org/asca/media/asca/Press%20releases/ASCA-Student-to-SC-Ratios-Press-Release-5_2019.pdf

Cole, S., O'Brien, J., Gadd, M. R., Wallace, D., & Gregory, M. (2005). *Helping Traumatized Children Learn: Supportive School Environments for Children Traumatized by Family Violence*. Boston, MA: Massachusetts Advocates for Children and Harvard Law School, Trauma and Learning Policy Initiative.

National Association of School Psychologists. (2017). *Shortages in School Psychology: Challenges to Meeting the Growing Needs of U.S. Students and Schools*. Bethesda, MD: National Association of School Psychologists. Retrieved from National Association of School Psychologists.

National Child Traumatic Stress Network, Schools Committee. (2017). *Creating, Supporting, and Sustaining Trauma-Informed Schools: A System Framework*. Los Angeles, CA and Durham, NC: National Center for Child Traumatic Stress.

Oxford University Press. (2019). *Definition of System*. Retrieved from Lexico.com: www. lexico.com/en/definition/system

Appendix A
Finding your ACE Score

Adverse Childhood Experience (ACE) Questionnaire

While you were growing up, during your first 18 years of life:

1. **Did a parent or other adult in the household often …**

   Swear at you, insult you, put you down, or humiliate you?
   or
   Act in a way that made you afraid that you might be physically hurt?
   Yes   No   If yes enter 1 _____

2. **Did a parent or other adult in the household often …**

   Push, grab, slap, or throw something at you?
   or
   Ever hit you so hard that you had marks or were injured?
   Yes   No   If yes enter 1 _____

3. **Did an adult or person at least 5 years older than you ever…**

   Touch or fondle you or have you touch their body in a sexual way?
   or
   Try to or actually have oral, anal, or vaginal sex with you?
   Yes   No   If yes enter 1 _____

4. **Did you often feel that …**

   No one in your family loved you or thought you were important or special?
   or
   Your family didn't look out for each other, feel close to each other, or support each other?
   Yes   No   If yes enter 1 _____

5. **Did you often feel that …**

   You didn't have enough to eat, had to wear dirty clothes, and had no one to protect you?
   or

212   *Appendix A*

Your parents were too drunk or high to take care of you or take you to the doctor if you needed it?

Yes   No   If yes enter 1 _____

6. Were your parents ever separated or divorced?

Yes   No   If yes enter 1 _____

7. Was your mother or stepmother:

Often pushed, grabbed, slapped, or had something thrown at her?
or
Sometimes or often kicked, bitten, hit with a fist, or hit with something hard?
or
Ever repeatedly hit over at least a few minutes or threatened with a gun or knife?

Yes   No   If yes enter 1 _____

8. Did you live with anyone who was a problem drinker or alcoholic or who used street drugs?

Yes   No   If yes enter 1 _____

9. Was a household member depressed or mentally ill or did a household member attempt suicide?

Yes   No   If yes enter 1 _____

10. Did a household member go to prison?

Yes   No   If yes enter 1 _____

Now add up your "Yes" answers: ____ This is your ACE Score

Appendix B
PBIS Matrix Example

Celebrating Kind-Hearted Students at Carlton Hills
Carlton Hills Jaguars "ROAR"

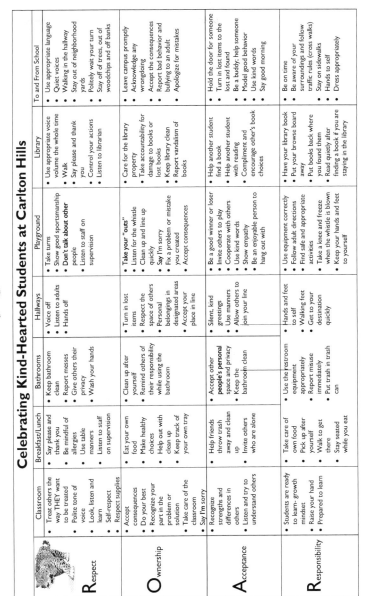

	Classroom	Breakfast/Lunch	Bathrooms	Hallways	Playground	Library	To and From School
Respect	• Treat others the way THEY want to be treated • Polite tone of voice • Look, listen and learn • Self-respect • Respect supplies	• Say please and thank you • Be mindful of allergies • Use table manners • Listen to staff on supervision	• Keep bathroom clean • Report messes • Give others their privacy • Wash your hands	• Voice off • Listen to adults • Hands off	• Take turns • Show good sportsmanship • **Don't talk about other people** • Listen to staff on supervision	• Use appropriate voice volume the whole time • Walk • Say please and thank you • Control your actions • Listen to librarian	• Use appropriate language • Quiet voices • Walking in the hallway • Stay out of neighborhood yards • Politely wait your turn • Stay off of trees, out of woodchips and off banks
Ownership	• Accept consequences • Do your best • Recognize your part in the problem or solution • Take care of the classroom • **Say I'm sorry**	• Eat your own food • Make healthy choices • Help out with clean up • Keep track of your own tray	• Clean up after yourself • Remind others of their responsibility while using the bathroom	• Turn in lost items • Respect the space of others • Personal belongings in designated areas • Accept your place in line	• **Take your "outs"** • Listen for the whistle • Clean up and line up quickly • **Say I'm sorry** • Fix a problem or mistake you created • Accept consequences	• Care for the library property • Take accountability for damage to books or lost books • Keep library clean • Report vandalism of books	• Leave campus promptly • Acknowledge any wrongdoing • Accept the consequences • Report bad behavior and bullying to an adult • Apologize for mistakes
Acceptance	• Recognize strengths and differences in others • Listen and try to understand others	• Help friends throw trash away and clean up • Invite others who are alone	• Accept other **people's personal space and privacy** • Keep the bathroom clean	• Silent, kind greetings • Use manners • Allow others to join your line	• Be a good winner or loser • Invite others to play • Cooperate with others • Use kind words • Show empathy • Be an enjoyable person to hang out with	• Help another student find a book • Help another student with reading • Compliment and encourage other's book choices	• Hold the door for someone • Turn in lost items to the lost and found • Be a buddy; help someone • Model good behavior • Use kind words • Say good morning
Responsibility	• Students are ready to learn- growth mindset • Raise your hand • Prepared to learn	• Take care of own food • Pick up after yourself • Walk to get there • Stay seated while you eat	• Use the restroom appropriately • Report misuse immediately • Put trash in trash can	• Hands and feet to self • Walking feet • Get to your destination quickly	• Use equipment correctly • Follow adult directions • Find safe and appropriate activities • Take a knee and freeze when the whistle is blown • Keep your hands and feet to yourself	• Have your library book • Put your browse board away • Put books back where you found them • Read quietly after finding a book if you are staying in the library	• Be on time • Be aware of your surroundings and follow traffic rules (cross walks) • Stay on sidewalks • Hands to self • Dress appropriately

Appendix C

Trauma-Sensitive School Counseling Interventions

School counseling programs and responsibilities not specific to self-regulation or school connectedness

Tier 1	Tier 2	Tier 3
Administrator–counselor collaboration	Behavior contracts	Crisis interventions
Community education	Check-in check out	Referral to SPED
Equity and access to courses and services	Small group school counseling	Referral for community resources
School-wide awareness initiatives	Student study team meetings	Solution-focused brief therapy
Trauma training	Teacher workshops – opt in	

School counseling programs and responsibilities that help students self-regulate

Tier 1	Tier 2	Tier 3
Brain breaks, exercise and yoga	Cognitive behavioral therapy in school settings	Referral to behavior specialist
Calm down kits and spaces	CBITS	Section 504 protection for students with disabilities
Flexible environments	Coping skills training	Structured breaks and other intensive behavior support strategies
Mindfulness and meditation	Visual support strategies	
Modeling emotion Management and healthy communication	Superflex	
	Trauma-informed psychoeducation	
Positive behavior interventions and supports (PBIS)	The ZONES of regulation	
Social emotional learning (SEL)		
Sensory opportunities		

Appendix C 215

School counseling programs and responsibilities that build school connectedness

Tier 1	Tier 2	Tier 3
Attendance awareness	College application/	Crisis counseling
Award ceremonies	FAFSA support	Home visits
Bullying and discrimination	Counseling small groups	Individual student
Prevention	for friendship building	planning
College/career counseling	Counseling small groups	Referrals for Community
Community circles	for transition	Resources, Inc.
Ensure equity and access	Counseling small groups	Mental health
Extracurricular activities	for support	therapy
and clubs	Mentoring programs	
Modeling healthy	Restorative conferences	
relationships and		
connections		
Restorative questions and		
language		
Transition programs		

Appendix D
The ASCA Mindsets & Behaviors for Student Success

The ASCA Mindsets & Behaviors for Student Success:
K-12 College- and Career-Readiness Standards for Every Student

Each of the following standards can be applied to the academic, career and social/emotional domains.

Category 1: Mindset Standards
School counselors encourage the following mindsets for all students.

M 1. Belief in development of whole self, including a healthy balance of mental, social/emotional and physical well-being
M 2. Self-confidence in ability to succeed
M 3. Sense of belonging in the school environment
M 4. Understanding that postsecondary education and life-long learning are necessary for long-term career success
M 5. Belief in using abilities to their fullest to achieve high-quality results and outcomes
M 6. Positive attitude toward work and learning

Category 2: Behavior Standards
Students will demonstrate the following standards through classroom lessons, activities and/or individual/small-group counseling.

Learning Strategies		Self-Management Skills		Social Skills	
B-LS 1.	Demonstrate critical-thinking skills to make informed decisions	**B-SMS 1.**	Demonstrate ability to assume responsibility	**B-SS 1.**	Use effective oral and written communication skills and listening skills
B-LS 2.	Demonstrate creativity	**B-SMS 2.**	Demonstrate self-discipline and self-control	**B-SS 2.**	Create positive and supportive relationships with other students
B-LS 3.	Use time-management, organizational and study skills	**B-SMS 3.**	Demonstrate ability to work independently	**B-SS 3.**	Create relationships with adults that support success
B-LS 4.	Apply self-motivation and self-direction to learning	**B-SMS 4.**	Demonstrate ability to delay immediate gratification for long-term rewards	**B-SS 4.**	Demonstrate empathy
B-LS 5.	Apply media and technology skills	**B-SMS 5.**	Demonstrate perseverance to achieve long- and short-term goals	**B-SS 5.**	Demonstrate ethical decision-making and social responsibility
B-LS 6.	Set high standards of quality	**B-SMS 6.**	Demonstrate ability to overcome barriers to learning	**B-SS 6.**	Use effective collaboration and cooperation skills
B-LS 7.	Identify long- and short-term academic, career and social/emotional goals	**B-SMS 7.**	Demonstrate effective coping skills when faced with a problem	**B-SS 7.**	Use leadership and teamwork skills to work effectively in diverse teams
B-LS 8.	Actively engage in challenging coursework	**B-SMS 8.**	Demonstrate the ability to balance school, home and community activities	**B-SS 8.**	Demonstrate advocacy skills and ability to assert self, when necessary
B-LS 9.	Gather evidence and consider multiple perspectives to make informed decisions	**B-SMS 9.**	Demonstrate personal safety skills	**B-SS 9.**	Demonstrate social maturity and behaviors appropriate to the situation and environment
B-LS 10.	Participate in enrichment and extracurricular activities	**B-SMS 10.**	Demonstrate ability to manage transitions and ability to adapt to changing situations and responsibilities		

Index

Note: Italic page numbers refer to figures

academic and non-academic strategies 69
administrator-counselor collaboration 136–137
adverse childhood experience (ACE): ACE score 7–9, 8, 211–212; additional findings 10–11; vs. adult health-risk behavior 7, 9, 10; categories 8–9; childhood adversity 7; childhood trauma impact on student learning and child development 2; chronic disease 7; concentration and learning 41–42; dose-response relationship 9; Dr. Robert Anda 7; Dr. Vincent Felitti 7; disabilities 43; exposure level 7; implications on education 11–12; neurobiology (see neurobiology and learning); original study 7–9, 8; public health epidemic 2–3; real-life examples 3; research 10–11; school counseling strategies 2; stress domains 12–13; surface-level behaviors 1; symptoms 14–15, 33; themes 105 (see also Tiered Interventions, Student Self-Regulation, Creating Connectedness (TSC)); trauma-sensitivity 2; see also mental health
adverse childhood experience (ACE) score 7–9, 8, 211–212
Ainsworth, M.D. 33
amygdala: emotional regulation 23–24; and learning 25; over-responsiveness 23–25; supportive environment 23–24; survival mode 23
Anda, R. 7, 9, 10
anxiety 36–39, 37
ASCA National Model 112–113, 216
Atkins, M.S. 51

Attachment, Self-Regulation, and Competency (ARC) model: clinical model 106; competency 109–110; emotion management 107–108, 108; healthy attachment relationships 107; meaning making 106; regulation 108; resilience 106; school counselors 110–111; self-regulation skills 108–109; skill building 106; stress response 107–108, 108; tiered interventions 111, 111–113; trauma-sensitive strategies at home 110
attachment theory 33–36, 34
attendance awareness 182–183
attention deficit hyperactive disorder (ADHD) 40–42
award ceremonies 183–184
awareness events 140

Ballard, M.B. 169
Bayer, A. 197
behavior contracts 143–144
Behavior Intervention Plan (BIP) 176, 177
behavior specialist referral 176–177
Behavior Support Plan (BSP) 90, 176, 177
Biel, L. 167
breach of confidentiality 199
Buddies/Lunch Bunch 194
bullying and discrimination prevention 184–185

Calm Down Kits and Spaces 159–160
caring relationships 121–122
cerebellar vermis 30
Chappell, S. 184
Check-in/Check-out (CICO) 144–145
chronic absenteeism 126, 182, 197
Clifford, A. 187

218 *Index*

clubs 188–189
Cognitive Behavioral Intervention for Trauma in Schools (CBITS) 169–170
cognitive behavioral therapy (CBT) 168–169
collaboration with families 70–71
Collaborative for Academic, Social and Emotional Learning (CASEL) 79
collaborative leadership 65
collaborative network 204
college application/FAFSA support 193–194
college/career counseling 185–186
community circles 186–187
community education 137–138
community referral 152–153
community resources 202
Compassion Fatigue/ secondary trauma appropriate strategies 72, 73, 141; compassion fatigue 72; secondary trauma 72–73; stressors for turnover 71–72; teacher and school counselor turnover 71; see also secondary trauma
competency 109–110
comprehensive school counseling programs 51; school counseling programs 105, 214–215
concentration and learning 41–42
contextual memories 26
Cook, A. 194
Cook, C. 190
coping skills training 170–171
creating connectedness 119–120; attendance awareness 182–183; award ceremonies 183–184; bullying and discrimination prevention 184–185; college application/FAFSA support 193–194; college/career counseling 185–186; community circles 186–187; community resources referrals 202; counseling small groups for friendship building 194; counseling small groups for support 195–196; counseling small groups for transition 195; crisis counseling 199–200; equity and access 187–188; extracurricular activities and clubs 188–189; healthy relationships and connections 189–190; home visits 200–201; individual student planning 201–203; mentoring programs 196–198; restorative conferences 198; restorative questions and language 190–192; transition

programs 192–193; trauma-sensitive school counselor role 181
crisis counseling 199–200
crisis interventions 150–151
Crone, D.A. 144
Curry, J.R. 196

declarative memories 26
The Deepest Well (Harris, 2018) 10
depression 36–39, *37*
Deris, T. 161
disorganized attachment 119
Driscoll, L. 169
DuBois, D.L. 197
Dweck, C. 161, 162

Elder, T. 41
Elementary and Secondary Education Act 82–83
emotional alertness 175
emotion management 107–109, *108*, 164
episodic memories 26
equity and access to courses and services 138–139, 187–188
exercise 158–159
extracurricular activities and clubs 188–189

Fazio-Griffith, L.J. 169
Felitti, V. 7, 8, 10
fight-or-flight mode 23–25
Flexible Framework 65–66, 66
flexible seating 160–161
friendship skills group 194
frustration 206
Functional Behavior Analysis (FBA) 176

Grossman, J. 197
growth mindset 161–162
guided opportunities for helpful participation 124–125

Harris, N.B. 3, 9, 10, 42, 56
Hatch, T. 113–114, 116–117
Hawken, L.S. 144
Hayes, B.G. 196
health-risk behavior 7, 9, 10
healthy relationships and connections 189–190
hippocampus: and learning 26–27; memory 25–26; neuroplasticity 26; representational map 27
home visits 200–201

Horner, R.H. 144
hypothalamic-pituitary-adrenocortical (HPA) system 19
hypothalamus and ventral tegmental area (VTA) 30

Individualized Education Program (IEP) 152
individual student planning 201–203
Individuals with Disabilities Education Act (IDEA) 151, 152
informal community education 137
insecure resistant and avoidant attachment 33–36, 34
internal locus of control 28
intrusive memories 39

Keat II, D.B. 194

Lange, T. 196
language deficits 44
learning disabilities 44–45
locus coeruleus 30

Marino, R.C. 196
Matheson, E. 165
McDonald, J. 194
McLean, M. 45
memory 25–26
mental health: for abused children 33; anxiety and depression 36–39, 37; attachment theory 33–36, 34; attention deficit hyperactive disorder (ADHD) 40–42; comorbidity 33; diagnoses 33; post-traumatic stress disorder (PTSD) 39–40; pull-out mental health therapy 50; services for staff and students 207; SPED eligibility 43–45
mentoring programs 196–198
Metzgar, K.L. 194
Midgett, A. 185
mindfulness 162–163
minute meetings 190
Multi-tiered Multi-domain Model for Student Support (MTMDSS) 113–114, 114–116, 116–117; see also Hatch, T.
Multi-Tiered Systems of Support (MTSS) 77, 78, 78, 100, 100

National Bullying Prevention Month 140

National Child Traumatic Stress Network 14
National Education Association 48
Neag, R.P. 194
needs assessment 142
neurobiology and learning: amygdala 23–25; cerebellar vermis 30; hippocampus 25–27; hypothalamus and ventral tegmental area (VTA) 30; locus coeruleus 30; pre-frontal cortex 27–30; stress 17–19; stress hormones 19–22
neuroplasticity 26

O'Donnell, M. 45
Olsen, J. 165
Oswald, S. 160

Perry, B. 25
physical and emotional safety 125
policies and protocols 70
Positive Behavior Interventions and Supports (PBIS) 70, 77; Behavior Support Plans (BSP) 90; core values/behavioral expectations 87–89, 88; Examples of PBIS 87, 88; vs. RTI 87; self-regulation 164–165; functional behavior assessments (FBAs) 90; goal 86–87; individualized behavior interventions 90; intervention and reintegration 89–90; matrix example 87, 213; positive reinforcement 89; preventative behavioral interventions 86; staff capacity for leadership 87; Student Study Team/Student Success Team (SST) meeting 90; theory and practices 87; with trauma-sensitivity 90–92, 91; universal screening and progress monitoring 89
positive reinforcement 165
positive school climate 62
positive stress 17–18
post-traumatic stress disorder (PTSD) 39–40
pre-frontal cortex: empathy development and perspective taking 28–29; higher-order and critical thinking 27–28; internal locus of control 28; and learning 29–30; rational decision making 28
Premack, D. 171
Premack Principle 171–172
professional development 147–148, 208–209

220 *Index*

progress monitoring 85, 148–150
protection for students with disabilities 177–178
psychoeducation 174–175
public education 177

Raykovitz, D. 194
reactive counseling 150
Red Ribbon Week 140
referral: behavior specialist 176–177; Community Resources 152–153, 202; Special Education (SPED) 151–152
relationship coach 124
representational map 27
resilience: common themes and findings 130–131; components 130–132; definition 129; oppression 139; positive adaptive response 129–130; risk factor 131–132
resources and services 68–69
Response to Intervention (RTI) 77; academic achievement 82; components 83, 83; data-driven decisions 85; Elementary and Secondary Education Act 82–83; progress monitoring 85; tiered interventions system 84, 84–85; with trauma-sensitivity 86; universal screening 85
Restorative Practices (RPs) 67, 70, 77; academic outcomes 92; affective statements 95; community circles 95–96; continuum 94–96, 95; practices 94–95, 95; restorative circles 96; restorative conference 96–97; social discipline window 93–94, 94; restorative conferences 198; restorative questions and language 190–192; with trauma-sensitivity 97–98; zero-tolerance discipline 92–93
Rojas, E.D. 194

Santee School District 67–68, 105
school connectedness: academic achievement 128–129; assumptions, observe, and question 123–124; caring relationships 121–122; components 120; decreased behavior concerns and violence 127; guided opportunities for helpful participation 124–125; high expectations 123; high standards and learning supports 121; improved attendance 126–127; mental

health 127–128; outcomes 126–129; physical and emotional safety 125; relationship coach 124; teen wellness 126; unconditional positive regard (UPR) 122–123
school counseling interventions *see* tiered intervention system
school counseling programs 105, 214–215; *see also* comprehensive school counseling programs
school culture 204–206
school-wide awareness initiatives 140–141
schoolwide programs: evidence-based programs 78; MTSS 78, 78, 100, 100; Positive Behavior Interventions and Supports (PBIS) 86–92, 88, 91; Response to Intervention (RTI) 82–86, 83, 84; Restorative Practices (RP) 92–98; school counselor 98–100, 100; Social-Emotional Learning (SEL) 79–82, 81; trauma-sensitive vision 78
secondary trauma 72–73, 141
Section 504 of the Rehabilitation Act of 1973 177–178
secure attachment 33–36, 34
self-monitoring 143–144, 172
self-regulation 107–109, 108, 117–119; behavior specialist referral 176–177; brain breaks, exercise, and yoga 158–159; Calm Down Kits and Spaces 159–160; Cognitive Behavioral Intervention for Trauma in Schools (CBITS) 169–170; cognitive behavioral therapy (CBT) 168–169; coping skills training 170–171; emotion management and healthy communication 164; flexible seating 160–161; growth mindset 161–162; mindfulness and meditation 162–163; positive behavior interventions and supports (PBIS) 164–165; Section 504 Protection for Students with Disabilities 177–178; sensory opportunities 166–167; social emotional learning (SEL) 165–166; structured breaks and other intensive behavior support strategies 178–179; Superflex® 173–174; trauma-sensitive psychoeducation 174–175; trauma-sensitive school counselor role 157; visual support strategies 171–173; The ZONES of Regulation® 175–176

Index 221

sensory opportunities 166–167
small groups counseling 145–146; for friendship building 194; for support 195–196; for transition 195
small victories and progress 207–208
social discipline window 93–94, *94*
social-emotional interventions 50–51
Social-Emotional Learning (SEL) 50, 51, 77; Collaborative for Academic, Social and Emotional Learning (CASEL) 79; competencies 79–81, *81*; definition 79; relationship skills 81; responsible decision making 81; *Second Step* curriculum 82; self-awareness 80; self-management 80–81; self-regulation 165–166; social awareness 81; teach 79–80; with trauma-sensitivity 82
solution-focused brief therapy 154
spatial memories 26
Special Education (SPED): eligibility 43–45; referral 151–152
Steiner, R.J. 128
Stone, C. 200
Strange Situation Test 33
stress: biological stress 12–13; cognitive stress 13; emotional stress 13; initial stressor 12; positive stress 17–18; prosocial stress 14; social stress 13–14; tolerable stress 18; toxic stress 18–19; types *17*, 17–18
stress hormones: adrenaline 19, *20–21*; amygdala over-responsiveness 23–25; cortisol 19, *20–21*; dysregulated cortisol 21–22; fight-or-flight mode 23–25; hippocampus 25–27; hypothalamic-pituitary-adrenocortical (HPA) system 19; and learning 21–22, *22*; limbic system 22; neural pathways 19; stress cycle 19, *20–21*; sympathetic-adrenomedullary (SAM) system 19
structured breaks 178–179
Student Study Team (SST) meetings 146–147
suicidal ideation 38–39, 150–151, 199
Suicide Prevention Awareness Month 140
Superflex® 173–174; "5 Step Power Plan" 173
Suttie, J. 185
sympathetic-adrenomedullary (SAM) system 19

Taylor, C. 45
teacher turnover 71
teacher workshops 147–148
Terada, Y. 190
thinking brain *see* pre-frontal cortex
Thornton, M.D. 196
Tiered Interventions, Student Self-Regulation, Creating Connectedness (TSC) 2; ARC model 110–113, *111* (*see also* Attachment, Self-Regulation, and Competency (ARC) model); ASCA National Model 112–113, 216; creating connectedness 119–120; goal 105; interventions list 105, 214–215; Multi-tiered Multi-domain Model for Student Support (MTMDSS) 113–114, *114–116*, 116–117; needs 105; resilience 129–132; school connectedness (*see* school connectedness); school counselors 110–111; special education services 105; student self-regulation 117–119; and trauma-sensitivity 113–114, *114–116*, 116–117
tiered intervention system: administrator-counselor collaboration 136–137; ASCA National Model *111*, 111–113; behavior contracts 143–144; check-in/check-out (CICO) 144–145; community education 137–138; community resources referral 152–153; crisis interventions 150–151; equity and access to courses and services 138–139; levels 84, *84*; misconceptions 84–85; MTSS 78, *78*; Multi-tiered Multi-domain Model for Student Support (MTMDSS) 113–114, *114–116*, 116–117; PBIS 89–91, *91*; progress monitoring 148–150; school-wide awareness initiatives 140–141; small group school counseling 145–146; solution-focused brief therapy 154; Special Education (SPED) referral 151–152; Student Study Team (SST) meetings 146–147; teacher workshops 147–148; trauma-sensitive school counselor role 135; trauma training 141; universal screening 141–142; wrap-around plan 155; *see also* creating connectedness; self-regulation
tolerable stress 18
toxic stress 18–19

222 *Index*

transition programs 192–193

Trauma and Learning Policy Initiative (TLPI) 53, 62, 65, 67

trauma-sensitive school: academic and non-academic strategies 69; accountability and punitive disciple 63–64; characteristics 62, 62–63; collaboration with families 70–71; collaborative leadership 65; counselors 74–76; early adopter incentives 64; educational outcomes 61; Flexible Framework 65–66, 66; goal 62; leadership 67; meaningful support 71–73; policies and protocols 70; positive school climate 62; professional development 67–68; resource and service access 68–69; restorative practices (RP)/behavior contracts 67; Santee School District 67–68; school counselor role 74; school culture 63; shared values 62, 62–64; strategic planning teams 67; subconscious/espoused beliefs 64; Trauma and Learning Policy Initiative (TLPI) 65; trauma-sensitive educators 64–65

trauma-sensitive school counselor: ACEs and student behavior 51–52; comprehensive school counseling programs 51; mental health and education 48–50; parent workshops/staff development 49; pull-out mental health therapy services 50; resources for 55–56; as safe space for ACE students 54–55; social and emotional learning (SEL) 50, 51; social-emotional interventions 50–51; special education 52; as staff trainers 52–54; as student advocates 50–52; students with disabilities 51; trauma and learning 49; Trauma Learning and Policy Initiative (TLPI) 53

trauma-sensitive taskforce 206–207

trauma-sensitivity: barriers 206–207; connectedness (*see* creating connectedness); framework system 77; mental health services for staff and students 207; outcomes 209; practices 208–209; programs (*see* schoolwide programs); school (*see* trauma-sensitive school); school counselor 157; school counselor role 135; school culture 204–206; small victories and progress 207–208; student behaviors 77; student self-regulation (*see* self-regulation); themes (*see* Tiered Interventions, Student Self-Regulation, Creating Connectedness (TSC)); tiered interventions (*see* tiered intervention system)

trauma training 141

Trudeau, K. 160

unconditional positive regard (UPR) 122–123

universal screening 85, 86, 89, 141–142

U.S. Department of Education–Office of Safe and Healthy Students 48

van der Kolk, B. 40, 56

visual support strategies 171–173

White, S. 192

Winner, M.G. 173; "5 Step Power Plan" 173

Woerkom, M. van 187

Wolpow, R. 123

yoga 158–159

zero-tolerance discipline 92–93

Zimmerman, E. 161

The ZONES of Regulation® 175–176

Printed in the United States
By Bookmasters